100
SIDE HUSTLES

100 SIDE HUSTLES

UNEXPECTED IDEAS FOR MAKING EXTRA MONEY
WITHOUT QUITTING YOUR DAY JOB

CHRIS GUILLEBEAU

TEN SPEED PRESS

California | New York

Contents

I. Real People, Real Money 8

Earning real money on the side isn't a fantasy—it's real life. Consider how these people created income and security for themselves, often in surprising ways.

II. Ideas Are Everywhere 26

By mastering the skill of observation, you'll learn to spot opportunities wherever you go. That's what the people featured in this chapter did—and the results speak for themselves.

III. Use the Skills You Already Have 50

Don't go back to college; use what you know *now*. The people featured in this chapter's stories used a skill they already had to make extra money—sometimes a lot of it.

IV. Buy Low, Sell High 76

This business opportunity started approximately 150,000 years ago. It's evolved a bit since then, but the principles remain the same. These modern-day merchants find ways to buy goods at one price, and then sell them at a higher one.

V. Teach What You Know 98

Your knowledge is valuable: take what you've learned and share it with others.

VI. Bring People Together 120

Have a knack for producing events or experiences? Use the power of community to connect people while getting paid.

VII. Get Crafty, Get Paid 146

If you have a penchant for a paintbrush or a love of making pottery, you might be able to turn your creations into money—just like the people in these stories did.

VIII. Automate Your Income 168

"Earn money while you sleep" is the ultimate promise—and for these people, it's part of their daily routine. These stories illustrate how working smarter, not just harder, can help you create systems that will pay out over and over.

IX. See the World Without Going Broke 186

If you don't want to be confined to a desk, how about living in an RV or jetting out on a series of one-way plane tickets around the globe? For those looking for a room with a view, preferably one that someone else pays for, read on.

X. Eat, Drink, and Be Merry 200

Cookies, coffee, ice pops, and beer—these stories really take the cake.

XI. Do Good *and* Do Well 220

Don't choose between profit and philanthropy—do both. You can do good *while* doing well.

XII. There's an App for That 244

Social media and the "sharing economy" aren't just about being neighborly. There's money to be made! These stories feature affiliate marketing, mobile applications, and more.

XIII. Keep It in the Family 258

Some side hustlers start young, and some parents involve the whole family in their entrepreneurial adventures. These stories feature kids, families, or partnerships.

XIV. Start Your Own Factory 278

If you build it, will they come? Maybe, but first you have to build it. The people in these stories learned about sourcing, manufacturing, or both. Even complex projects (a boat in a backpack?) can be done part-time, without quitting your job.

XV. Ramp Up: Million-Dollar Side Hustles 302

Side hustles are great for earning extra cash—and sometimes they earn a *lot* of it. These stories represent people with hustles that produce high six figures or seven figures in annual income.

Introduction

Each morning at 6:01 a.m. eastern time, I publish a new episode of *Side Hustle School,* my daily podcast. Every story features someone who creates a moneymaking project without quitting their job. On average, forty thousand people download or stream it over the next seven days, and then many more listen later. Since I started the show on January 1, 2017, the stories have been downloaded more than twenty million times.

But why? Why do people keep listening week after week and month after month, even though the essential lessons of "starting a side business" don't change much from day to day? I've thought a lot about this question, and I've heard a lot of feedback from listeners.

As it turns out, people love the idea of making money without quitting their day jobs.

Earning extra money without having to give up the stability of an existing job is a powerful motivator. And more than anything else, we respond to stories.

For instance, Teresa Greenway (pages 13–15) didn't know much about the world of online education, and she wasn't particularly skilled with technology. She'd recently hit a rough patch in life, leaving an abusive relationship, raising a son with autism, and even going on food stamps to supplement her meager income as a motel housekeeper. Through it all, one of her favorite things to do was bake. And in particular, she loved to bake sourdough bread.

Everything changed when Teresa's daughter suggested she teach a course on baking bread. Instead of putting up flyers and renting space in her local community center, Teresa signed up with an online service that would allow her to sell the course to anyone online. Using cheap equipment, she filmed "Sourdough Bread Baking 101," and then released it to the world. That course produced $25,000 in net income for Teresa—a truly life-changing amount for her at the time. The next year, she created half a dozen other courses and made $85,000, more money than she'd ever made in her life. With the profits from her courses, Teresa was able to make a down payment on the first home she's ever owned.

Or consider Kyler Russell (pages 270–72), who started his side hustle with a little help from his mom, Brandi, when he was just eight years old. Kyler loved baseball, but he didn't love the uncomfortable athletic cup he had to wear.

Brandi and Kyler created a much better cup, one that was more comfortable but still provided the necessary protection. Then they learned how to make it in bulk and sell it to parents of other young athletes. The Comfy Cup is now manufactured in Hong Kong and then shipped by the case to Lenexa, Kansas, where the whole family is involved in mailing the finished product to customers.

It's not just a nice story—it's also a profitable one: the Comfy Cup is selling at a rate of *more than $10,000 a month*. They currently have a proposal in with Walmart, and are hoping to break six figures in annual profits soon.

These aren't "startup" stories of people risking it all, going around in search of investors to rescue them. They're stories of regular people with jobs, responsibilities, and busy lives, who start moneymaking projects in their limited time.

Most of the people featured in this book didn't even consider themselves entrepreneurs when they started out. Many *still* don't. They just wanted to make some extra money while holding on to the stability of the jobs they already had.

Some of these people might earn an extra $1,000 a month. Some go on to earn much more, sometimes even multiple six figures a year—and some of them have indeed gone on to quit their jobs. Whatever the outcome, most of us can relate to these inspiring stories precisely because they are about regular people doing things that almost anyone can do.

I wanted to gather some of my favorite stories from the show and present them to you in this visual compilation. Maybe they'll give you an idea for a side hustle of your own, or maybe you'll just enjoy seeing what other people have done.

Either way, I hope that you'll find these stories as inspiring and engaging as I do.

Yours in the hustle,

TERMS AND CONDITIONS
There are a lot of facts, figures, and anecdotes mentioned in this book. Financial details were supplied by the people featured in the story, but with so many different case studies in dozens of locations, I probably got something wrong—and by the time you read this, some of the info may have changed. In addition, some of the side hustles and websites featured here may no longer be active, or the people that run them may have switched to another focus of operations. This is normal. You don't have to do the same project forever, nor do you have to do it in the same way. *In other words: the details will change with time, but the principles are timeless.*

Real People, Real Money

Earning real money on the side isn't a fantasy—it's real life. Consider how these people created income and security for themselves, often in surprising ways.

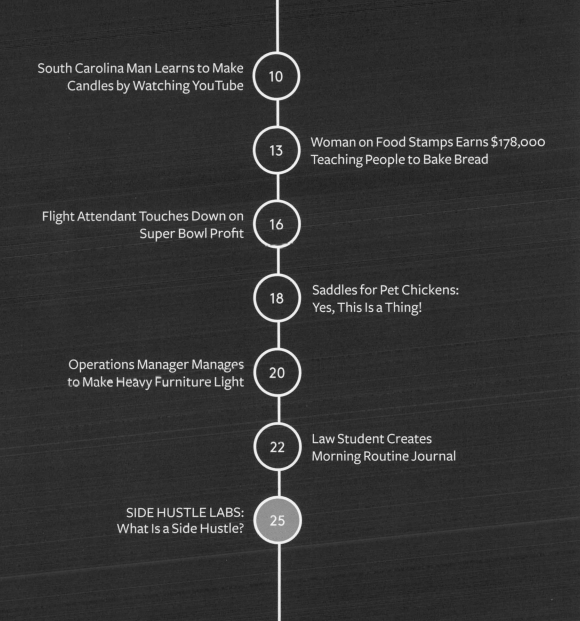

SOUTH CAROLINA MAN LEARNS TO MAKE CANDLES BY WATCHING YOUTUBE

After coming across handmade scented candles in a boutique shop, one man starts his own candle-making company.

NAME
MARC GASKINS

LOCATION
CHARLESTON, SOUTH CAROLINA

STARTUP COSTS
$200

INCOME
$43,000/YEAR

WEBSITE
MEETINGANDMARKET.COM

"I knew *nothing* about candles when I started, and don't have a creative bone in my body. The coolest part for me has been figuring out this process." —Marc

In historic Charleston, South Carolina, Marc Gaskins owns and operates a kitchen equipment business, which provides commercial equipment on wheels for wedding venues. The business is predictable, based largely on the spring and fall wedding seasons. Demand slows to a trickle during the cold winter months as well as the hot summer months.

This job was originally a side gig he did while he was bartending. When the bar he worked at burned to the ground, the kitchen equipment business became Marc's full-time job. (Another important reason to start a side hustle: You never know when you may have to rely on it.)

During the downtime in his new job, Marc began his new hustle: buying wholesale candles from a local company and selling them on Amazon.com. He'd place orders to the company, they'd ship the candles to Amazon, customers would order, and Amazon would ship the candles to the customer. The model is called Fulfillment by Amazon, and you'll read about it in a few other stories throughout the book.

That was a nice starter project. Soon, however, Marc realized he'd make more money if he manufactured and sold his own brand of candles. His aha moment was when he walked into an upscale men's store in Austin, Texas, and saw a nine-ounce candle selling for a whopping $85. On the flight home, he began to develop his own brand. He called it Meeting and Market.[*]

How do you learn to make candles if you've never done such a thing? Well, you do it just like the ancient Egyptians did: you log on to YouTube!

Marc took pages of notes while watching countless video tutorials from a company called Candle Science, which happens to be the largest purveyor of DIY candle supplies in the country. After his free education was

FUN FACT After his cousin posted a photo of some personalized candles that Marc had made for his wedding, Marc received a lot of interest from people who wanted to purchase them. Without really trying, he found a new niche to focus on.

[*] The name references the intersection of two streets in a historic market in Charleston.

complete, he went to a craft store, bought some supplies, and started messing around. He gave away more than two hundred candles to friends and family as part of the trial-and-error process, which contained more errors than works of art.

His initial candles were white wax in clear glass with a white label. The design felt very retro—and not in a good way. He wanted something more modern, so he started searching far and wide for glassware until he found an amber cube he really liked. With the new glassware and a redesigned label, sales took off.

The biggest issues Marc has dealt with have been with supplies: glassware shortages, label issues, a bad batch of wax, a bad batch of oil that didn't mix well with the wax, and so forth. He also worries about receiving large orders and not being able to meet people's needs due to glassware issues.

Marc's candles cost about $7.50 to make, and he sells them for $16 wholesale, $25 at markets, and $32 retail. Expenses include supplies, advertising, and the chunk of sales Amazon takes, so his net profit on Amazon is around 50 percent. In addition to selling on Amazon, he also sells at farmers' markets and in some retail stores, as well as on Etsy and through his website. Popular scents include lavender chamomile, red ginger saffron, and blackberry sage.

In his second year of business, sales were $43,000. His goal is to make at least $5,000/month in Amazon sales, in addition to his other channels. Other goals include increasing wholesale buyers through trade shows, and eventually to make Meeting and Market a national home goods brand—all while continuing his commercial equipment business during the wedding season.

He's burning the candle at both ends, but at least these candles pay him back in real money.

WOMAN ON FOOD STAMPS EARNS $178,000 TEACHING PEOPLE TO BAKE BREAD

Overcoming a difficult situation, this woman rises to the top with a series of online courses teaching the art of baking sourdough bread.

Teresa Greenway's love of baking began when one of her daughters decided to try to bake authentic sourdough bread. The daughter gave up after a month of trying, but not before making a passing comment that would change Teresa's life: "No one can make real sourdough bread, Mom . . . *not even you!*"

Teresa liked a good challenge, and there's nothing quite as motivating as someone saying you can't do something. She would go on to try her hand at baking sourdough over and over, proving the prophecy wrong and becoming an expert baker. Unknowingly, the work she put in paid off years later as she was able to monetize her expertise on a website that broadcasts online courses all over the world.

But she wasn't always a tech-savvy baking instructor. The year before her hobby became a serious source of cash, Teresa had just left an abusive relationship and had barely any income of her own. She had to juggle multiple part-time jobs, including one as a housekeeper at a motel. She was even surviving on food stamps for a while.

Teresa wasn't able to work full-time because she had to care for her adult son, who had a disability—all while her mother was suffering from a terminal illness. The situation was bleak until she attended a workshop that opened her mind to starting a business. She then took some courses on the online learning platform Udemy, which gave her all the information she needed.

The courses were diverse, ranging from YouTube channel management to photography and video editing. They cost $10 each at a discounted price, but for her at the time, it was real money. It was also an investment in herself.

She had the idea to create her own course, and she had just the topic in mind: *baking sourdough bread*. She knew there was a market for online courses—after all, she had just

NAME
TERESA GREENWAY

LOCATION
WESTPORT, WASHINGTON

STARTUP COSTS
MINIMAL

INCOME
$178,000 IN FIRST TWO YEARS

WEBSITE
NORTHWESTSOURDOUGH.COM

ACTION PLAN

1. Identify a specific skill that you'd like to pass on to others. Don't be too general: Teresa focused on *sourdough* bread, not just *baking,* and not even just *baking bread.*

2. Develop an outline of how you'd like your course to be structured. A basic model is to choose four to six "modules," each consisting of a series of outcomes and milestones.

3. Select an online platform to teach your course. Teresa chose Udemy, but there are many other options. Alternatively, if you're comfortable with technology and already have an existing audience, you may not *need* to use another platform. What you'll give up in discoverability, you'll gain in greater profit margins.

4. Prepare your lesson plans, practice your instruction, and start recording! There's no time like the present.

"At first, I filmed in my garage and was certain no one would want a course made in such an ugly place. Most people are used to seeing beautiful kitchens in baking shows. I *almost* gave up. Then, I decided to give it a try anyway." —Teresa

purchased a few of her own. Perhaps it would be possible to create her own course, and then get others to buy it.

In those early days, Teresa didn't have much in the way of fancy equipment. She had no professional camera or high-quality editing software. In fact, she didn't even have a real *kitchen*. She used a makeshift space in her garage, with poor lighting and a cracked, stained concrete floor that didn't exactly spell professionalism.

Nevertheless, she persisted. It took her four months to launch her own course, but she did it. The first month, she made a thousand dollars in revenue. By the end of the year, she had made more than $28,000. All from a course on baking bread!

And she wasn't done. Sometimes the best form of marketing for your project is to think about extensions, where you create the next logical solution for people who've purchased the first version. That's what Teresa did for her courses. She continued to create more Udemy courses over the next two years, eventually ending up with ten of them.

Did she branch out from baking? Nope . . . instead of going wide, Teresa went deep. Her next course was *also* about sourdough bread ("More Fun with Sourdough Bread Baking"). So were the next *five*:

- "Professional Sourdough Baked at Home"
- "Extreme Fermentation: Bake Modified-Gluten Sourdough Bread"
- "Make Your Own Sourdough Starter: Capture and Harness the Wild Yeast"
- "Discovering Sourdough Part II: Intermediate Sourdough"
- "Discovering Sourdough Part III: Advanced Sourdough"[*]

FUN FACT There are instructors with celebrity chef credentials on Udemy, but when you search "baking," you'll see all of Teresa's courses appear on the first page of results. Personality matters!

* Gamers will recognize this as the "hard mode" of bread baking. Attempt at your own risk!

The result of all this filming with flour? She made over $86,000 in year one, and an additional $90,000 in year two. Along the way, her profile grew as well. She now has a following of fifty thousand people spread like butter across her social media accounts, with another five thousand on her mailing list. It's a solid, sourdough foundation for expanding her hustle and growing it even further.

The extra income and financial stability from pursuing her side hustle has literally changed Teresa's life. In that first year of her first course, when she went from being on food stamps to earning $86,000, it was the most money she had ever made in a year. It allowed her to quit the part-time housekeeping job and put a down payment on the first home she'd ever owned.

Being able to combine her passion for helping others with baking has brought Teresa great joy and financial security. Her story proves that you can create a profitable side income from doing all sorts of things. Your idea doesn't need to be cutting edge or something no one has ever heard of before. You just need to stop loafing around!

CRITICAL FACTOR

When people think of online courses, they tend to think of topics that relate to technology. Teresa's megapopular bread-baking courses prove that even classic skills can be monetized with the right approach and voice.

FLIGHT ATTENDANT TOUCHES DOWN
ON SUPER BOWL PROFIT

A Dallas-based flight attendant capitalizes on the Super Bowl craze by providing rentals for the big game, putting homeowners in the end zone and earning herself a championship payout.

NAME
STEFFANIE RIVERS

LOCATION
DALLAS, TEXAS

STARTUP COSTS
$1,000

INCOME
$50,000/YEAR (FOR SEASONAL WORK!)

WEBSITE
TOUCHDOWNRENTALS.COM

Fifty-one-year-old flight attendant Steffanie Rivers designed and launched her side hustle while facing some unexpected turbulence in her life. In 2010, she was let go from the airline she worked for, and she wasn't sure what to do next.

But for as long as she can remember—in fact, as early as her Girl Scout days of selling cookies—Steffanie has been a hard worker. She's done door-to-door sales, moonlighted as an Uber driver, and even partnered with overseas physicians to market low-cost cosmetic surgery. So when faced with a stint of temporary unemployment, she asked herself, "What's next?"

She made it through the rest of that year working in car sales, and then signed up to work with a company that was renting out homes for the Super Bowl. That year, the game was held in Dallas, where Steffanie is based. She saw great potential for the business model. But she was also disappointed to see that the company treated both the homeowners and the salespeople poorly.

She decided she wanted to take the same idea but do it better on her own. And then she set about doing just that, launching her own business ahead of the following year's Super Bowl.

Since Steffanie is a big Dallas Cowboys fan, the business was an easy fit. She understands and shares the excitement around the game. And she knows the event is the perfect opportunity to make money, since tens of thousands of people, willing to throw lots of money around, pour into the host city.

She also knew that each year the host city, stadium, and team owners all make money, but not necessarily the taxpayers. Furthermore, she learned

FUN FACT As a flight attendant, Steffanie uses her day job to advance her side business. She stops over in cities planning to host the Super Bowl, canvasses them for the most upscale neighborhoods and houses, and then pitches homeowners on renting out their homes for the big game.

that the Super Bowl often blocks off up to 75 percent of the host city's hotel rooms for companies and affiliates, leaving few options for regular fans looking to see their team play.

Her new company, Touchdown Rentals, provides solutions to both sides of this equation. She gets homeowners paid and helps sports fans live a "baller" lifestyle for the weekend. The approach is simple: Ahead of the Super Bowl, Steffanie reaches out to high-end homeowners. Then she posts properties online of those willing to rent, connects her clients looking for rentals, and takes a commission for negotiating the deal.

Although she has to compete with the likes of Airbnb, Steffanie says she's stayed ahead of the game by creating all-inclusive packages for the renters. They get the house, a concierge to help with entertainment, maid service, and even private party planning. Each year since starting, she's rented at least sixty properties, from condos to five-bedroom estates, all priced at $1,000 to $3,000 per day.

With the business now in its sixth year, Steffanie has landed a healthy profit, bringing in about $50,000 annually. Since the business is seasonal, this represents just a few months of work. On average, she typically works fifteen hours a week, almost all of it leading up to Super Bowl weekend.

The business has grown through a smart, low-cost approach to marketing. After randomly picking him up as a passenger while driving for Uber, she enlisted a celebrity spokesperson in NFL player Toben Opurum. And she started throwing house parties where homeowners invite their friends over for free food and drinks while Steffanie explains the benefits of renting out their homes.

Now Steffanie is working as a flight attendant again. She uses that job to her advantage. While flying around the country, she carries promotional material to pass on to airports, hotels, and other venues. And since she's passing through most major cities, she can easily stop over to research the different neighborhoods in upcoming Super Bowl destinations.

All this effort has been worthwhile. As a result, Steffanie has been able to purchase and renovate her own condo, and is now renting it out for additional passive income.

As for Touchdown Rentals, Steffanie hopes to improve brand recognition to eventually become the Airbnb of the Super Bowl. There are no penalties here . . . this hustle is safely in the end zone.

"Tens of thousands of people attend the Super Bowl every year. They spend lots of money having a good time, all while renting cars and hotel rooms. Since they're in the habit of spending money anyway, why not jump in front of that wave and get paid?"
—Steffanie

CRITICAL FACTOR

When a large group of visitors arrives in a city for a major sporting event, they need somewhere to stay. Steffanie gets paid by connecting those visitors with homeowners interested in making some easy cash.

SADDLES FOR PET CHICKENS: YES, THIS IS A THING!

An Oregon woman creates an unusual product with almost $0 in manufacturing costs. Don't cry fowl just because you didn't think of it first.

NAME
JILL BONG

LOCATION
MEDFORD, OREGON

STARTUP COSTS
MINIMAL

INCOME
$900/MONTH

WEBSITE
CHICKENARMOR.COM

Have you ever had a beloved pet? Jill Bong from Oregon had one, but it wasn't a dog or cat . . . it was a chicken named Speck. Speck the chicken greatly enriched the lives of Jill and her family, until one sad day when Speck the chicken went on a long walk. Okay, let's just tell it like it is: Speck the chicken *passed away*, leaving the family in mourning.

The cause of death was a molting injury. Huh? Yes, this is a thing . . . just like the product that Jill eventually made. Many domestic chicken deaths are caused by such injuries, but they can usually be prevented with a special kind of "saddle" or "vest" that is worn by the chicken.

In memory of Speck, and to protect the lives of other chickens, Jill decided to develop a new form of chicken saddle. The existing chicken saddles on the market all had a fatal flaw: they had to be laundered on a regular basis. Because of the difficulty, most chicken owners don't use saddles, which means their hens are susceptible to the kinds of injuries that caused Speck to die. Jill's innovative design used vinyl material, meaning that the vests didn't need to be laundered. They could just be hosed down or wiped clean.[*]

After a year's worth of testing on her eighty-chicken flock, Jill's Chicken Armor debuted for sale wherever chicken saddles are sold . . . which means mostly on her website. The mission statement of Chicken Armor is to help chicken keepers save time and money with that special design that makes the saddles easy to use. In addition to the troubling laundry requirement, other saddles had to be hand-sewn, which takes a lot of time. The Chicken Armor advancements allowed Jill to price her product lower than all the other saddles on the market.

FUN FACT   As strange as it sounds, chicken saddles (also known as chicken "vests") have been around for a while. When Jill went to patent her version, she discovered that someone had patented a different kind—way back in 1910!

[*] Another benefit: No more expensive chicken vest dry-cleaning bills!

Operating costs are also very low. All Jill pays for is the cheap vinyl material, and then the packing and shipping charges when someone places an order.

Most people who keep chickens don't keep just one. They tend to have a whole flock, or at least half a dozen. A single chicken saddle costs just $2.50, and Jill sells a pack of one hundred for $75. By selling in bulk, Chicken Armor brings in a profit of between $500 and $3,000 each month, depending on the season or if they've had major media exposure. Since launching the hustle, Jill has shipped saddles to proud chicken owners in all fifty states and to four continents. She's been featured in numerous media outlets including the Associated Press, the *New York Times*, and *ABC News* . . . and, of course, *Side Hustle School*.

No doubt there will be a rush on chicken saddles once this book is out in the world—Jill, I hope you've stocked up—and for everyone out there who needs to saddle up their chickens, now you know where to go.

Or if you're ready to fly the coop yourself, maybe you need a project of your own.

"We're happy to keep Chicken Armor small, but are open to licensing deals. In the meantime, I'll continue to write and publish books on self-sufficiency." —Jill

 CRITICAL FACTOR

Other chicken saddles had serious flaws. Jill was truly "first to market" with a new design, helping chicken keepers (and the chickens too) across the country and beyond.

OPERATIONS MANAGER MANAGES TO MAKE HEAVY FURNITURE LIGHT

A Maine university employee uses her logistical savvy to deliver IKEA enthusiasts their goods at greatly reduced prices.

NAME
PEG DONOVAN

LOCATION
PORTLAND, MAINE

STARTUP COSTS
$6,000

INCOME
$2,000/MONTH

WEBSITE
SVENDELIVERS.COM

Peg Donovan has worked in operations for the University of New England for more than fifteen years. Over the years, she's mastered the tasks of budgeting, forecasting, and solving all sorts of problems.

For example, when the faculty offices needed new furniture, Peg was placed in charge of selecting, ordering, and supervising the arrival and setup of hundreds of items. That kind of logistical savvy—and a sharp eye to see how to fit things in tight spots—served her well when she assembled her side hustle: delivering IKEA goods to customers in Maine and New Hampshire at a substantial discount to them, with a profit to her.

The joys and perils of assembling IKEA furniture has furnished plenty of joke fodder for late-night comedians, but the company remains beloved for its inexpensive, durable goods. Assembling the goods, however, which are often packaged in large, heavy boxes, is enough of a challenge. When the store is hours away, the weight of the burden doubles.

Peg knew this from experience. Her own trek to get to IKEA's Portland, Maine, location took almost five hours round-trip. But delivery charges could drive an IKEA customer crazy too. Their most popular item, a Billy bookcase that retails for $70, costs *three times* that to have it delivered to Maine. For a lot of New Englanders, it's like building a bookcase out of credit cards.

The delivery idea came to Peg in a flash. While wrapping up a meeting at the university, she mentioned she was going to IKEA the next day. When people quickly asked if she could

ACTION PLAN

1. Identify a store, product, or service that isn't easily available in your area or to people in your circle.

2. Test the waters by asking around, "Does anyone want me to pick something up from _____?"

3. If there's enough interest, announce a service that will deliver the desired items direct to customers' doors.

4. Set up an online process where people can select the items they want and schedule delivery.

5. Buy, lease, rent, or borrow a vehicle large enough to contain a substantial supply of items.

6. Hit the road and grab a lingonberry muffin for sustenance!

FUN FACT On one busy delivery day, the truck broke down as Peg was leaving to pick up a full load of orders. She got a ride back to her house and ended up leading a caravan of three small cars to IKEA, where she managed to stuff all the orders in and on top of the cars.

pick something up for them, she saw the angle right away. She figured she could drive to the store, charge a 25 percent delivery fee to save people money, and make something for herself on the side. She just needed a name for the project. With an homage to the retailer's Nordic roots in mind, she called it Sven Delivers. Experience in operations management has extended benefits. Peg signed up with Squarespace to design and publish her delivery business website. Then she started posting on Facebook, targeting young families and moms. She also got free exposure when a local newsletter featured her business.

The biggest expense she had was buying a used van for just under $6,000. Once she had a larger vehicle, customers started arriving like a horde of hungry shoppers lined up for cinnamon rolls. Some of them didn't have a car big enough for furniture boxes, others just didn't want to drive the long hours, and *nobody* wanted to pay those inflated shipping fees.

"Who doesn't love IKEA products? We even deliver their cinnamon buns, chocolate, coffee, and frozen Swedish meatballs."—Peg

Even so, Peg says she almost fainted when Sven got its first order for one of those $70 bookcases. Even with her business experience, the fact that someone would pay her through PayPal and trust her new service to come through shocked her.

Since starting up, Sven Delivers has gone from earning several hundred dollars a month to nearly $2,000 a month. She's tripled her once-monthly jaunts to IKEA to three, and will now assemble the goods for an extra fee. Her customers don't even need their own screwdrivers!

Of course, happy customers only come through great service. Peg is focused on the customer experience: she texts, emails, sends out invoices, and confirms delivery times. The Sven Delivers site has plenty of testimonials from pleased people, spells out delivery options and timing, and provides several ways to get in touch.

Continuing to work full-time at the university, Peg spends about an hour processing orders and answering delivery questions each weeknight, plus a chunk of hours on the weekends for the actual trips. The success of the business has given her the confidence to explore other ideas—so much so that she has two other side hustles in progress. Neither of them requires screwdrivers, but it's clear she already has all the tools she needs.

CRITICAL FACTOR

IKEA furniture is loved, or at least *purchased*, by millions of people around the world. And if you don't live near a store, delivery can be expensive. Peg used her background in logistics to bring bookcases and standing desks to people in her area, earning a steady profit from customers happy to pay for a more affordable delivery option.

LAW STUDENT CREATES MORNING ROUTINE JOURNAL

A law student and two friends create a side hustle helping others hack their habits for more productive mornings.

NAME
ARI BANAYAN

LOCATION
LOS ANGELES, CALIFORNIA

STARTUP COSTS
$10,500

INCOME
$80,000/YEAR

WEBSITE
HABITNEST.COM

Habits have always played a huge role in Ari Banayan's life. He wakes up early, meditates, and exercises. While he was in his second year of law school, two friends approached him about creating an app to help people develop healthy lifestyle habits. They went to dinner that night to run through ideas, and then met a few times over the next month to start fleshing out ideas about an app they wanted to call Every Damn Day.

They started by each putting $3,500 into the company. They spent that money on an email newsletter service, a Shopify store, a social media scheduling program, and other applications. Next, they created a free accountability-partner email chain called Partners in Grind, where they'd match up people with similar habits so they could hold each other accountable.

To do this, they created a landing page with a form where people could sign up, select a habit they wanted to work on (exercise, meditation, eating healthy, or waking up early), and share their geographic location. Users would then receive a series of emails with specific content related to the habits they signed up for, and they'd connect with other users interested in the same habit.

Ari and his friends marketed the service however they could. They used Instagram and did a question-and-answer session on Quora. They reached out to self-help websites, offering to guest blog—and in the posts, Ari would mention Partners in Grind. They also purchased "social media shoutouts," where influencers would mention the service to their large groups of followers.

As a result of the marketing and media coverage, they had hundreds of signups within a few hours. Partners in Grind died out, however, when they learned through user interviews that email wasn't the right way to connect people for something like this. People wanted to be matched with others for accountability, but found that email was a difficult way to connect, and it was hard for partners to stay consistent.

This wasn't the business they would stick with. Still, Partners in Grind helped Ari and his partners get their name out, build an email list of

FUN FACT If you end up doing something other than what you planned or trained for, you're not alone. Ari left the legal field to work on the Habit Nest, even after completing law school and a master's program in tax law.

six thousand people, and test out the concept of matching people for accountability.

For their second attempt, they decided to create *Morning Sidekick*, a journal to help people wake up earlier and build a morning routine, which was the habit that the majority of their users were interested in developing. Ari wrote the introduction and put together some content, one of his friends organized it into sections and added more content, and the other friend worked on the design.

They launched a Kickstarter campaign and promoted it to the email list they'd built. They also reached out to YouTube channels and podcasts related to habits that they'd mentioned in the journal. Meanwhile, Ari continued his strategy of writing guest posts on popular blogs, which now linked back to the Kickstarter page, and answered online questions related to morning routines, productivity, and habits.

Morning Sidekick made just under $20,000 on the Kickstarter campaign. After the campaign ended, they launched an Indiegogo campaign, using a refreshed version of their Kickstarter content. Indiegogo promoted the campaign to its large mailing list, which brought them more sales. They also got the word out through journalists, talking to anyone who would listen. (Notice a theme here? These guys hustled!)

Two strategies helped most of all. They offered a free PDF of the first week of the *Morning Sidekick Journal* to get people signed up for their newsletter, and they created step-by-step action guides for their articles— fillable PDFs you can get after giving them an email address. Then they'd market the journal to the people on the email list, with the goal of achieving consistent sales over time.

So far they've sold almost four thousand units of the *Morning Sidekick Journal*, which cost $33.99 on their website and a bit less on Amazon.com and various flash sale sites. They manufacture the journals in China, store them in a warehouse in Los Angeles, and then ship them to buyers as they're ordered.

Halfway through this process, Ari had moved to New York to begin a master's program in tax law, all while continuing to work with his partners remotely. He moved back to Los Angeles when he finished his program, and went to work on Habit Nest full-time. Through sales from the growing website and newsletter, the three founders are able to consistently make $6,500 in net profit a month on the journal. They've now set their sights on more goals: an app and an additional series of journals.

CRITICAL FACTOR

Ari and his friends wanted to help people be more productive, but their first attempt—an email accountability matching service—didn't pan out. They regrouped and asked themselves what else they could try that still fit with the goal. From that brainstorming session, the *Morning Sidekick Journal* came to life.

What Is a Side Hustle?

You may have heard the phrase "side hustle" before picking up this book, and maybe you even have one yourself. But what is it, exactly?

Since "side hustle" can mean a lot of different things, let's get specific on how we use it here.

A SIDE HUSTLE IS NOT

- A second job or other form of employment that you go to after your 9 to 5 (or whatever your main gig is)

- Something that drains your energy without providing a substantial reward

- A hobby or something you just do for fun, without any goal of making money

A SIDE HUSTLE IS

- Something you have control over (you're the one making the decisions)

- An asset you build for yourself so that you have more options (even if you love your job)

- A different kind of work than what you do for your day job

In other words, a side hustle should be both profitable *and* fun.

For more, visit SideHustleSchool.com/basics.

Ideas Are Everywhere

By mastering the skill of observation, you'll learn to spot opportunities wherever you go. That's what the people featured in this chapter did—and the results speak for themselves.

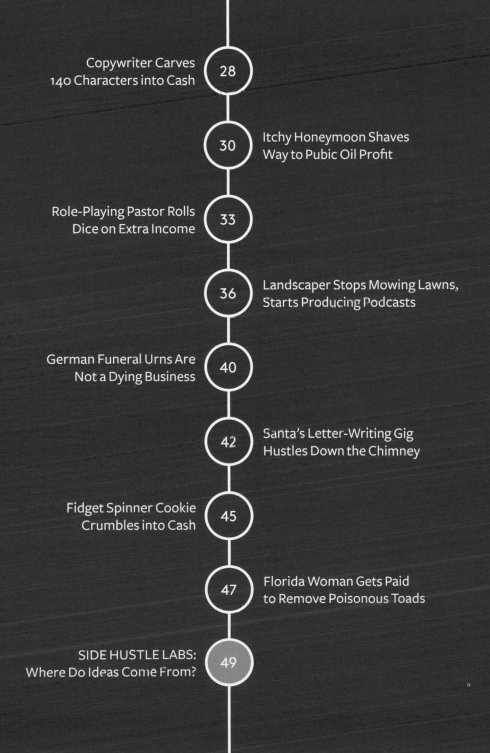

COPYWRITER CARVES
140 CHARACTERS INTO CASH

A creative director and copywriter makes an April fool's joke that turns into a long-term income stream.

NAME
BRIAN THOMPSON

LOCATION
AUSTIN, TEXAS

STARTUP COSTS
$15,000

INCOME
$50,000/YEAR FOR SEVERAL YEARS

WEBSITE
LASERSMAKEITAWESOME.COM

Ever since high school, Brian Thompson aspired to be an entrepreneur. He had no shortage of ideas, and he dutifully wrote them down in a growing stack of notebooks. Sometimes he'd even buy a domain name, but then he'd lose interest and move on to something else.

After he'd settled down and began raising a family, something clicked and he began to take more action on those ideas. He created a line of Valentine's Day cards for people who hate Valentine's Day. A Kickstarter for "passive aggressive notepads" was successful in meeting its crowdfunding goal. These projects were small, but encouraging. As he continued to experiment in the off-hours from his day job in advertising, he grew bolder and began looking back at those notebooks he'd filled up years earlier.

His greatest success to date started as a joke. On April 1, 2014, Brian launched a site offering to turn digital "tweets" (posts to Twitter) into physical works of art. He hoped that people would share the site, but he didn't think that much else would come from it. Would anyone really value their 140-character message enough to shell out real money for it to be engraved on a plaque?

It turns out that they did. The site was picked up by several popular design blogs, and people started placing orders—some as gifts for friends or office mates, and others for themselves. Without much publicity, all of a sudden he was making several hundred dollars a week. Even better, the orders didn't stop after the initial buzz died down. It helped that the finished pieces were essentially a marketing campaign: most people

CRITICAL FACTOR

It was just a crazy idea . . . but Brian wondered, *What if someone would actually pay for this?* By installing an order button on a website he'd first made as a joke, he got back his answer in cash.

FUN FACT   It never fails: at every corporate event Brian does, someone has too many drinks and asks him to make custom engravings for someone else, sometimes with disastrous consequences. At one party, a guy requested a coaster with his girlfriend's name . . . but misspelled it. Brian tried his best to cover for the guy, telling the girlfriend that he was the one responsible for the typo.

> "Instead of letting fear stop me, I realized that even if I failed, I wouldn't lose the house and put my family on the street. So instead of always wondering 'what if,' I went for it." —Brian

displayed them on their desk or in another prominent location, and people who walked by would take notice and ask, "What's that?!"

Interestingly, around this time Twitter itself got involved by sending him what he calls the world's nicest cease-and-desist letter. They didn't tell him to stop the project, they just asked him to modify the name. So he changed his site from PermanentRetweet.com to Permanent140.com, and carried on with the engraving.*

A few months later, he got another letter from Twitter. This time, however, they were asking him to work at one of their events.

Up until this point, Brian had been using a third-party service to do his engravings. After agreeing to work at the event, however, he made a big decision: to invest in his own laser engraving machine.

After the site had been up for a while, Brian realized that the one-off sales were nice, but the real potential for this hustle came from doing larger orders for brands and events like weddings and bar mitzvahs. He created a new site called LasersMakeItAwesome.com to offer custom laser engraving for these events. To his surprise, wooden nickels and tokens have been his best seller. Businesses love handing out something small but personalized, and it's great word of mouth for his side hustle as well.

More than four years later, Brian is still operating the project part-time. His income has dropped off quite a bit from the $50,000 a year it was making in the beginning, but he still makes at least five figures from it. For Brian, the best part about this April Fool's Day project has been the flexibility it has given him to freelance and be more selective about the projects he takes on. Gaining freedom from financial pressure is no joke!

* Astute readers will note that Twitter now allows 280 characters instead of the original 140. Brian jokes that he hasn't doubled his prices in response.

ITCHY HONEYMOON SHAVES WAY
TO PUBIC OIL PROFIT

Two friends embrace the reality of pubic area discomfort and build a haircare oil product from scratch, turning it into a moneymaking business despite the skepticism of literally every person they talked to.

NAME
**DAVID GAYLORD
AND TIM BURNS**

LOCATION
OTTAWA, CANADA

STARTUP COSTS
$750

INCOME
**JUST UNDER $100,000
IN YEAR TWO**

WEBSITE
BUSHBALM.COM

David Gaylord was on a trip with a good friend when the side hustle of this story came to life. His friend, Tim, had recently returned from his honeymoon. He was excited about a personal discovery and *just had* to share it with David. The discovery was an intimate one: he had been using beard oil in his pubic region—*and it was working wonders.*

Now, before you cringe, consider the benefits of beard oil on a man's face:

- It reduces irritation and redness after shaving.
- It soothes sensitive or dry skin.
- It reduces the risk of ingrown hairs.
- It makes him smell nice.

The discomforts that beard oil can remedy don't just apply to faces—they exist in the pubic area as well. The thing is, nobody talks about these issues (except on *Side Hustle School*, of course), because they have to do with a more private area of the body.

After dispelling the weird feelings that came with hearing about Tim's new hygiene habit, David caught on to the opportunity. They'd been looking for a side hustle—could this be it?

The fact that *no one* was talking about such a thing meant that there was effectively zero competition, at least not yet. And to be among the first in the pubic oil space, they had no time to beat around the bush.

David and Tim returned to Ottawa. In their spare time, they began researching ingredients, nutrition, and essential oils. They discovered that the basic beard oils worked okay, but they refined the recipes to be even more suited for the pubic region. They also wanted their product to be relevant for both men and women.

They continually worked up better recipes, but with each step that took them closer to a sellable product, the more hesitant they became. For some reason, their families and friends didn't understand why they were

CRITICAL FACTOR
No one else was willing to go down on this market.

pursuing such an odd idea. "You're going to sell what?" was a typical response. Despite the lack of support, they kept at it. They couldn't let the pubic profit potential go!

David eventually rounded up some other friends who were willing to take the product for a spin. He invited them over to have a "testing party," where they narrowed down their recipe options through feedback.*

After having a chance to actually try it, families and friends were on board. This was further confirmation to David and Tim that they could convert skeptics into customers, if they could get samples into their hands.

With a product ready to sell, it was time to figure out manufacturing. Each partner threw in $250, which covered the bill for their Shopify store, packaging, and one hundred bottles' worth of precious pubic oil.

Finally, from the strange passion of two men with little outside support, Bush Balm officially launched.

FUN FACT The owners of Bush Balm hand-package and ship every single order, and even include a hand-written thank-you note in the package.

* Despite my otherwise rigorous investigation for *Side Hustle School* stories, I decided not to ask about how they acquired this feedback.

Things started off slowly: a sale here, a sale there. They didn't invest a single dollar into advertising, relying only on word of mouth. Luckily, two popular blogs responded to David's cold emails. Bush Balm saw a major boost in sales from the press, and before long, the hundred bottles were sold out. And to everyone's surprise, the orders kept rolling in. They clearly displayed a wait time of over a month on their online store, but customers continued to order.

It was clear that they had something special. The two friends were tapping into a severely underserved niche, all because of their willingness to "go there." The Bush Balm team reinvested all the income back into the business, purchasing five hundred bottles of oil for their next order. With the extra money, they also began experimenting with ads to drive traffic and sales more consistently.

Through feedback, David realized that the $25 price tag was too high for many people who were skeptical of the new oil category. They needed a less expensive way to get product into their hands.

The solution was to introduce a sampler package: three scents, 2 milliliters each, for just $10. Included in this sampler was a discount on the next purchase. Despite actually losing a couple dollars on each sampler package, Bush Balm has found that it's been an effective way to acquire customers who return a few weeks later for larger orders.

Bush Balm has stepped out of the experiment phase. The two friends are now spending more money on better ads, reaching out to spas and other retail partners, and eagerly awaiting the arrival of their brand-new packaging.

What started as an odd yet exciting side hustle has nearly grown into a six-figure business in under two years. As it turns out, there was treasure hidden in the bush all along.

ROLE-PLAYING PASTOR
ROLLS DICE ON EXTRA INCOME

This Presbyterian minister was about to burn out. After a series of low-level projects, he learned how to save time, sell products, and turn his role-playing passion into profit.

For David Derus, his full-time job as a Presbyterian minister is a labor of love—but it's never been quite enough to pay the bills. In order to help him continue to serve his local parish, he's spent his adult life fitting in odd jobs around his church duties. Among other things, he's tried dog-walking, handiwork, and house-sitting. Although some of these gigs were good for a while, they never provided him with the consistent support he needed. They were also a huge drain on his time and energy.

On the verge of burnout, David decided he wanted a side hustle where he didn't have to exchange his time for money.

When he talked about this problem with a member of his church, the parishioner recommended that David check out a podcast called *Side Hustle School*. He said it was filled with stories of people who'd achieved the same goals he had, and it just might help him find a profitable idea.

When David got home that evening, he downloaded an episode and was instantly hooked. After just a few episodes, he figured out what he needed to do: instead of selling his time, he was going to sell a product.

For the next several weeks, David took a close look at his life and interests. He didn't want to sell a product he knew nothing about, like some people were doing. He wanted to sell something that mattered to him.

Ever since he was a young boy, he'd been interested in role-playing games like *Dungeons and Dragons*. It was a way for a self-described awkward teenager to meet like-minded people, and he'd been playing ever since. He also figured it might be a good place to start in his hunt for a way to make money without walking dogs or repairing dishwashers.

David paid a visit to his local gaming group and got to talking with a friend who was showing off his new custom dice. He told his friend he had "dice

NAME
DAVID DERUS

LOCATION
LOS ANGELES, CALIFORNIA

STARTUP COSTS
$3,000

INCOME
$9,000/MONTH

WEBSITE
DICEENVY.COM

ACTION PLAN
1. Identify a product and a clear market (in this case, custom dice for role-playing gamers).
2. Design the dice with the help of a friend.
3. Research manufacturers on Alibaba or similar networks.
4. Place an initial order while building a website.
5. Sell the dice and plan to expand!

envy" and was instantly struck with both an idea and a name for his new venture. With low startup costs and a market he understood, dice seemed like a simple product to sell.

Getting straight to work, David put together some simple sketches of what he thought would make a good-looking set of dice. He sent them to a designer friend, who turned them into an Adobe file that could be sent to a potential manufacturer.

Finding a manufacturer was less of a scientific process and more of a Hail Mary. He headed over to Alibaba.com, found someone who made dice, put in an order, and hoped he wasn't about to get ripped off by someone on the other side of the world. The supplier put him at ease when he delivered the dice ahead of schedule.

With his product ready, David took Dice Envy online, setting up a site through Squarespace. He found platforms to sell his product on Facebook, eBay, and through his own website, allowing him to reach lots of new people organically.

The total startup costs for David came in at around $3,000. This included his initial investment in the dice, creation of the website, legal fees, and advertising the initial release of his first set. While this was slightly more money than he intended to spend, the investment has more than paid for itself. In its first year, Dice Envy was bringing in around $2,800 per month. Sales then spiked, hitting a pair of lucky sixes and rising to $9,000 per month in year two.

Because of the visual aspect of the product, these custom dice have been easy to market through social media. Instagram and Pinterest help catch people's attention with the dice and refer them back to David's website, and his posts on Facebook send people directly to a check-out page where they can purchase the dice.

He's also tried his hand at advertising, but with less success. With his initial launch of the product, he left an advertisement running for one week too long, and ended up spending more on the ad than the entire launch had made.

FUN FACT David relied heavily on Fiverr.com for the branding of his site. It allowed him to find cheap and quick-responding designers who created artwork for his new website.

Deliveries can also be a stressful part of the business, especially since his shipments arrive from the other side of the world. Knowing when and how much to order is still an art form that David is trying to master.

Despite the challenges, David loves his new project and is looking for ways to expand. He's now implementing a subscription system for people to get new dice every month, as well as selling in person at gaming conventions.

With his wedding on the horizon, David is using the extra cash to help pay for the ceremony. He's also able to do his pastoral work without constantly stressing about money.

"Don't try and reinvent the wheel. Ideas do not need to be revolutionary to be profitable." —David

LANDSCAPER STOPS MOWING LAWNS, STARTS PRODUCING PODCASTS

A Canadian landscaper lands on the side hustle trifecta: passion, skill, and opportunity. He eventually uses his new income to quit his job and travel to ten countries.

NAME
JEREMY ENNS

LOCATION
VANCOUVER, CANADA

STARTUP COSTS
$0

INCOME
$40,000 IN YEAR ONE

WEBSITE
COUNTERWEIGHTCREATIVE.COM

Back in early 2016, Jeremy Enns was working at a landscaping job in Vancouver, British Columbia—a job he knew he didn't want to do forever. The search for a side hustle had a natural starting point: Jeremy had gone to school for audio engineering and production, and he loved podcasts. While mowing lawns and trimming hedges, he listened to episodes nonstop, sometimes up to fifty hours a week at double speed.

As he started thinking about doing podcast editing and production, he realized that there was a significant audience for these services. He had hit the side hustle trifecta: *passion*, *skill*, and *opportunity*.

His first step was to reach out to some friends who had their own podcast. He wanted to learn more about their workflow and understand how they found their editor. One of those friends put him in touch with another guy who worked as a freelancer for a podcast production company. After connecting with him, Jeremy started doing some freelance editing of his own for the same company.

While he was seeing who else he could connect with in his network, he was also actively trying to land his first client. He combed through the listings on Apple Podcasts to identify one hundred shows that were big enough that they might be able to hire an editor, but not so established that they would already have one. Then he sent one hundred individual emails, hoping for a 5 to 10 percent conversion rate.

Unfortunately, he only received a single response that led to a paying client. The good news was that the cold email campaign wasn't his only marketing idea. At the same time, he was also applying for audio production gigs on Upwork.com, a network of opportunities for freelancers. Within a week, he had landed another client, and the validation gave him a boost.

ACTION PLAN

1. Put together a simple pricing structure that answers any questions your potential client might have. Make it clear so they understand exactly what they're getting and how much it costs.

2. Get experience however you can, even if it means volunteering your services for free. You shouldn't work for free for long, but sometimes it can help get you in the door.

3. A service business runs on referrals. Jeremy was far more successful in gaining business from happy customers than he was in cold-pitching every podcast he could find. Ask each customer if they can help you find more clients.

"This job started out as a side hustle, until one day I realized I was making just as much working twenty hours a week as I was at my full-time job as a landscaper working forty hours a week." —Jeremy

Over the next three months, Jeremy continued to learn and experiment. His initial website had focused on helping indie musicians who wanted to record albums. Since he wanted to produce podcasts, he needed to adjust the copy and pricing options. With minor changes and no additional marketing, Jeremy continued to get new clients via word of mouth and Upwork.

At the ninety-day point, he hired a graphic designer to make an infographic for his site. That was literally the first expense he incurred, since he hadn't spent a single dollar until then. He also signed up for a few low-cost tools to help him organize and manage some administrative processes. In all these efforts, he tried to keep things as cheap and as simple as possible.

As he approached the half-year mark in his new role, Jeremy started thinking about turning podcast production into his full-time work. He made a deal with himself: once he'd saved enough money for three months' expenses, he'd quit his job. He figured if it didn't work out, the landscaping job (or another one) would still be there for him to fall back on. Therefore, on August 15, 2016, he gave notice to his employer.

The best part of this story is that Jeremy had money coming in from multiple clients, and hadn't actually totaled up all of the income he was making. A couple of weeks after he gave his notice, he finally did the math and realized that he had made more money that month on his side hustle than with his day job. That was the moment he knew he had made the right decision. Within a couple of months of quitting his day job, he was bringing in an average of $4,000 per month, more than enough for him at that point in his life.

Since going full-time, he's turned all his energy to his podcast production hustle. He wrote an e-book on podcasting gear. He got serious about email marketing. And about a year and a half after starting up, he brought on a couple of freelancers of his own to help with all the work.

Not only has this transition paid off financially, it's had other major benefits. After launching, Jeremy spent ten of the next nineteen months traveling across four continents and thirteen countries. He has less free time since he's now managing his own company and freelancers, but the freedom he's gained and the ability to pick his own direction in life more than makes up for the lost hours.

He also has a new podcast of his own, focused on another of his favorite topics: *ice cream*. Yep, that's right. Jeremy's goal for the new show, *Rain City Scoop*, is for it to become the go-to source for all things ice cream. It's unclear if this one has the same financial potential as his podcast editing gig—but he certainly has the passion and the skill.

CRITICAL FACTOR

Jeremy's skill in audio production, combined with his love for podcasts, led to a freelance-turned-full-time role where he earned as much money as his day job, while working half the time.

GERMAN FUNERAL URNS
ARE NOT A DYING BUSINESS

Two friends learn to manufacture funeral urns that double as personalized works of art.

NAME
DANIEL MACK AND MARCO BILLMAIER

LOCATION
HEIDELBERG, GERMANY

STARTUP COSTS
€5,000 (ABOUT $5,800)

INCOME
$5,000/MONTH

WEBSITE
MEMENTI-URNS.COM

Daniel Mack works as a product development manager for a large building material company in an English town that borders Wales. His side hustle is selling handcrafted funeral urns to private customers and funeral directors. He does this with his friend Marco Billmaier, who's based in a small town close to Heidelberg, Germany.

Marco works for a company producing industrial cameras, and was into street art, painting, and tattoos. One day, he passed by a funeral director's storefront and had an unusual idea. A big set of funeral urns was on display, but they had almost no variance in their design. If you wanted to honor your loved one with something colorful or creative, there was simply no option. Marco thought that this was a business he and Daniel could go into, providing a genuine alternative. At first, Daniel thought his friend was crazy, but he agreed to give it a try.

How does one go about making funeral urns? Daniel and Marco started by sourcing raw materials from a funeral director, and they built a single webpage using the platform Wix. The page didn't have any way to purchase, just a request form and phone number for people to call and ask questions.

After doing some research on search engine keywords, they spent about $200 marketing the page using Google AdWords to see if there was any interest. The process was slow since they both had day jobs and were in separate countries, but six months later, they felt it was promising, so they decided to proceed.

They compiled a list of funeral directors who bought urns for their customers on a regular basis. Their simple webpage slowly grew into an online shop with photos and a portfolio. And over time, they built Mementi Urns into a real business.

The two friends now sell several kinds of urns: wooden, ceramic, marble, and biodegradable. The urns come in a wide selection of colors and beautiful designs, including butterflies, angels, bicycles, lighthouses, and religious symbols. They've had as many as two hundred different designs

CRITICAL FACTOR

A creative idea meets a renewing market, and one with essentially no competition. The biggest challenge was winning over a traditional industry that was typically opposed to change.

available at one time, and more than six hundred urns available to ship as soon as an order has been placed.

They also sell sets that allow customers to paint on the urns themselves. And after they'd been going for a while, they started to offer the option to purchase customized urns. In short, whatever you can imagine in a funeral urn, they've probably got an option for it.

Since they live in different areas, Daniel and Marco call each other weekly to discuss issues, as well as communicate via email and WhatsApp throughout the week. They outsource website programming, writing, flyer and brochure creation, packaging, shipping, and preparation.

Mementi Urns has now been around for nearly three years, selling an average of forty urns a month, and bringing in an average income of $5,000 a month. They hope to eventually expand to the rest of Europe, and they're now working with a freelancer on an ad campaign targeting funeral directors.

With an intention to help people honor their loved ones after death, this business is full of life.

FUN FACT Once they got their first customer, Daniel and Marco celebrated with beers. They then created a list of rewards they'd get for each other if they met specific milestones— sales figures, website visits, and various financial achievements. Although they reinvest much of the income back into the project, this allows them a series of small celebrations for each goal they accomplish.

"We were always looking for opportunities. [Marco] was always the creative, artsy person, and I was more the numbers and IT guy. We complement each other perfectly." – Daniel

SANTA'S LETTER-WRITING GIG
HUSTLES DOWN THE CHIMNEY

An inspired elf starts a monthlong, part-time project writing personalized letters from Santa Claus.

NAME
BRY LARREA

LOCATION
WASHINGTON, DC

STARTUP COSTS
$150 OR LESS

INCOME
$5,000/YEAR (SEASONAL)

WEBSITE
LETTERS-FROM-SANTA.ORG

Santa Claus might sit around and get fat most of the year, but come December, this jolly old man becomes overwhelmed. He gets so much mail that it's hard to keep up! Even in our hyperconnected world, a lot of people prefer to communicate with Santa in the old-fashioned social network known as *letter writing*. And recently, he's found some seasonal help from a creative thinker.

Right out of college, Bry spent all of her savings on a four-month backpacking trip. Upon her return, she got a part-time job as a waitress in Yakima, Washington, while her boyfriend at the time worked on a political campaign. With a lot of time on her hands, she knew she needed to make more money, but she was also just *bored*. A side gig would help in lots of ways . . . but what would it be?

Bry sat down and asked herself what she was good at. She knew she was a strong writer, but she didn't have time to write a book. She had previously tried her hand at writing resumes, and that didn't work well. Maybe there was another option.

She's not completely sure how the idea showed up, but one day she started advertising a service that promised "handwritten letters from Santa." She posted on Craigslist, Facebook and Tumblr, but got no response at first. She then included a few pictures of the ones she had drafted, but they looked corny and low quality. She learned quickly that parents wouldn't pay for something they could easily do themselves.

FUN FACT Bry's sales increased when she added a note saying that parents could approve the letters before they were sent. This was comforting to potential letter buyers, since they didn't want to be on the hook for something that "Santa" had promised without their knowledge.

"I get hundreds of emails from parents each year with pictures of their children, beaming with their letters from Santa and baggies of reindeer food. It's fulfilling to know that the work you have complete ownership of means something to people." —Bry

So she sat down once again, discouraged but determined, and mapped out how she could improve the letters. She focused first on personalization. She would learn key things about a child from a list of questions and customize the letter, making sure they knew Santa was watching and that he was proud of them. She also upped her game with better printing and design.

But here's the winning element: Bry started to advertise that these deluxe letters *had an option that included reindeer food*. What parent who loved Christmas didn't want to watch their child leave out magic reindeer food on Christmas Eve?*

This turned out to be the Santa letter jackpot.

She advertised her letters as the most personalized option on the market, with attention to detail and reindeer food to boot. And it worked. All of a sudden she was making more sales than she could handle.

The first year she sold around three hundred letters at $9.95 each or a deluxe package at $11.95. The letters cost her about $1.50 each to write and package, so she made around $4,000.

The second year she sold about four hundred and raised the prices slightly (to $11.95 and $13.95, respectively). However, she outsourced the writing of the letters to a virtual assistant she found online, so her profit margin was slightly less. This time, they cost about $3 to write and package.

The third year, something interesting happened. After first thinking she wouldn't do it again—because even with outsourcing to elves, it was a lot of work—she finally decided to go for it, but started late and did very little marketing. However, here's the surprise: she raised her prices to

ACTION PLAN

1. Identify an opportunity to create "surprise and delight" for parents and children. It needn't be seasonal like this story—what if the letters came from the tooth fairy, and arrived a few days after a child lost a tooth?

2. Consider the needs and concerns of parents—your actual customers, since they're the ones spending the money—and make sure they have a way to provide input or at least review the letters prior to sending.

3. Create a personalized touch ("reindeer food") that helps you stand out *and* provides the opportunity for an upsell.

4. Market your service using free or low-cost methods. Who do you know that can help spread the word?

* Since you're learning her secrets: the reindeer food is discounted bird seed from her local pet store, with a little glitter mixed in.

CRITICAL FACTOR

With a low price, sending your child a letter from Santa (or perhaps his helper) is an easy impulse purchase—and the reindeer food makes for an ideal upsell.

$19.95 and $26.95, so in doing less work, she actually made a lot more money. That year, she sold 250 letters and made just under $6,000.

Naturally, this is a seasonal hustle—you can't sell Santa letters in July. She typically begins the process around November 15th and letters are sent by December 10th. For something she does once a year, it's a great payoff. She also regularly receives replies in the form of letters from kids thanking Santa for their personalized message.

Let this be a reminder: you'd better watch out, you'd better not pout . . . and you'd better get to work.

FIDGET SPINNER COOKIE
CRUMBLES INTO CASH

A viral sensation inspires a TV producer to create an edible fidget spinner cookie.

Based in Dallas, Texas, Jessica Grose is the executive producer of a popular YouTube channel. For the past ten years, she's worked on TV shows including *Oprah*, *Ricki Lake*, the *Rosie O'Donnell Show*, and *TMZ*. Her side hustle is unrelated to the entertainment business, or at least it's not *directly* related—Jessica bakes delicious, custom cookies with unique designs.

When it started, she took cookie orders from friends and family, accepting cash or checks for around $3 a cookie. She'd make cookies in the shape of dump trucks for a kid's birthday party or in the shape of pink feet for a baby shower. At some point, Jessica made a Facebook page and set up accounts with PayPal and Venmo to receive payment. With this simple setup, she had a steady stream of customers, enough to keep her busy baking and delivering her creations after work and on the weekends.

She kept things simple for years, taking her side hustle with her to multiple jobs and different states. She was having fun and making some extra money, with no plans to strike it rich.

But then at the end of May 2017, Jessica made a *fidget spinner cookie* . . . and it went viral. The trail of cookie crumbs got picked up by publications nationwide, and was featured on the Food Network. In the weeks that followed, she gained thousands of social media followers and made hundreds of sales. It led to some long nights of baking in order to fulfill all her orders, but she wasn't complaining.

While her fidget spinner cookie story was still going around the world, the CEO of T-Mobile tweeted about it. So Jessica—proactive hustler that she is—reached out to the public relations representative at the company

NAME
JESSICA GROSE

LOCATION
DALLAS, TEXAS

STARTUP COSTS
MINIMAL

INCOME
$2,000/MONTH

WEBSITE
INSTAGRAM.COM/CLEARLYCOOKIES

"If you want to sell a food product, start with your family and friends first. They'll be your biggest cheerleaders. Expand out to different networks from there."
—Jessica

FUN FACT Jessica has made many cookies for many happy customers over the years, but sometimes it's the mistakes that stick out. One time, a customer ordered *chevron* cookies for a party. Not knowing that "chevron" was a type of pattern, Jessica proceeded to make cookies in the shape of the Chevron Corporation's logo. She then dropped them off in person to a very confused client.

and offered to make some T-Mobile branded cookies and spinners. They happily accepted and the CEO gave her another shoutout, posting photos all over social media. One phone call and one batch of cookies led to some priceless marketing for Jessica.

Her average cookie now sells for $5, sometimes more and sometimes less, depending on the amount of time required to design and decorate the specific cookie. And since her customer base is now nationwide instead of just her own zip code, she's had to learn to ship cookies in such a way that they don't break.

All the attention has translated to an average of $2,000 a month in new sales.

Following a trend is not normally a good business strategy. Once in a while, though, being in the right place at the right time—and with the right idea—can pay off. Don't let the cookie crumble!

FLORIDA WOMAN GETS PAID
TO REMOVE POISONOUS TOADS

A high school science teacher earns an extra $3,000 a month removing an invasive species of toads throughout Florida.

If something "ribbits" in your neighborhood, who you gonna call? *Toad busters*! Or, more specifically, you'll call Jeannine Tilford, the owner of a most unusual side business in South Florida.

After spotting a dangerous shift in her local environment, this high school science teacher decided to take matters into her own hands, earning an extra $2,000 to $3,000 a month along the way. A herpetologist by trade, Jeannine had noticed the diversity of the local reptiles—animals she loved to collect and study—had begun to dwindle, and the rate of dogs dying from eating poisonous toads was on the rise. This destruction was all thanks to one particular species, the nefarious Bufo toad.

FUN FACT Researchers from the University of Queensland in Australia have found that cane toad poison kills off prostate cancer cells while sparing healthy cells. The team has received a grant from a Chinese institute to further the research.

NAME
JEANNINE TILFORD

LOCATION
PALM BEACH GARDENS, FLORIDA

STARTUP COSTS
$2,100

INCOME
$30,000/YEAR

WEBSITE
BUFOBUSTERS.COM

> "The best part has been making a positive change by allowing our native species to thrive. Also, our customers are ecstatic that they can take their dogs out at night without worrying that one will be poisoned by a Bufo toad." —Jeannine

The system of getting rid of these toads with pesticides was effective, but expensive and damaging to nearby flora and fauna. There was no way to get rid of the toads without making the rest of the area sterile. Unless, well . . . unless someone went out each night *to collect the toads and remove them one by one.*

That's where Jeannine found her calling—or at least a highly unusual side gig. She felt that if *she* could be the one to go out and collect the toads, it would be the perfect part-time evening job to boost her modest teacher's salary. So that's what she did.

Initial startup costs for Toad Busters came in at around $2,100. Among other expenses, Jeannine needed a license to remove the toads ($100) and some sort of pest control insurance ($800 a year).

Unlike the crew from Ghostbusters, however, she didn't have to invest an untested, unlicensed, nuclear accelerator to carry on her back. Instead, she spent the rest of the money on a high-visibility jacket, as well as gloves, headlamps, toad carriers, and advertising for the side of her vehicle.

Needless to say, the job comes with a lot of perils. It's highly active work and requires climbing into areas where there are plenty of mosquitoes, spiders, venomous snakes, and alligators—and that's even without the poltergeists coming after you. Each toad has to be picked up by hand. One night, Jeannine retrieved a record-setting 138 reptiles near a pond at a country club in South Florida. (Unfortunately, she doesn't get paid per toad.)

From time to time, Jeannine also finds herself explaining to the police why she's walking around someone else's property late at night with a flashlight and a big stick.

CRITICAL FACTOR

No one wants poisonous toads in their yards, but who wants to deal with the problem? This woman, apparently.

Toad removal requires strict regulations to be followed, but disposing of these excess frogs pays well. When we last spoke, Toad Busters was bringing in at least $3,000 a month, with Jeannine working just a few nights each month. Looking forward, Jeannine would like to expand into new areas and regions of Florida. She's also putting together a pitch for a TV series called *What's in My Yard?*, which she hopes will help educate people about the native and invasive species in their backyards.

For every problem, there's a ribbiting solution.

Where Do Ideas Come From?

One of the most valuable skills you can learn is the art of generating viable business ideas. Once you acquire this skill, you'll have no trouble identifying potential profit centers. In fact, this is the easy part—you'll spend far more time on making your ideas come to life.

Ideas can come from ...

- Observation: paying attention to the world around you, perhaps noticing something that could be improved

- Problem solving: making lists of problems and brainstorming solutions in the form of products and services

- Asking questions: looking for the reasons, stated or subtle, for why people spend money (and deciphering what else they might buy)

- Experimentation: just trying out whatever comes to mind

As you read through this book, notice which stories you identify with the most. Then, see if you can think of *another way* those people could make money. Before you know it, you'll be on track to generating all the ideas you could ever need.

For more, visit SideHustleSchool.com/ideas.

Use the Skills
You Already Have

Don't go back to college; use what you know *now.* The people featured in this chapter's stories used a skill they already had to make extra money—sometimes a lot of it.

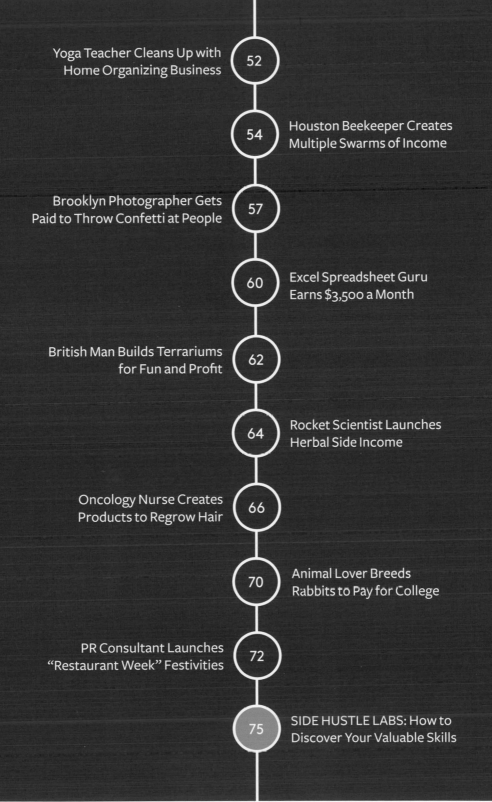

Yoga Teacher Cleans Up with Home Organizing Business — 52

Houston Beekeeper Creates Multiple Swarms of Income — 54

Brooklyn Photographer Gets Paid to Throw Confetti at People — 57

Excel Spreadsheet Guru Earns $3,500 a Month — 60

British Man Builds Terrariums for Fun and Profit — 62

Rocket Scientist Launches Herbal Side Income — 64

Oncology Nurse Creates Products to Regrow Hair — 66

Animal Lover Breeds Rabbits to Pay for College — 70

PR Consultant Launches "Restaurant Week" Festivities — 72

SIDE HUSTLE LABS: How to Discover Your Valuable Skills — 75

YOGA TEACHER CLEANS UP WITH
HOME ORGANIZING BUSINESS

This Seattleite found a new passion in helping people declutter their homes—but little did she know it would make $4,000 a month and touch the lives of hundreds of refugees.

NAME
LISA HOLTBY

LOCATION
SEATTLE, WASHINGTON

STARTUP COSTS
$2,200

INCOME
$4,000/MONTH

WEBSITE
LISAHOLTBY.COM

Lisa Holtby has built an entire career around side hustles. Since 1993, she's been teaching yoga, writing books, running seminars, and hosting weekend health retreats, all while being an active mom. But toward the end of 2016, she decided it was time for a change.

She'd always had a penchant for helping people organize their spaces, and doing it never felt like work. As Lisa herself says, "It's how I play." So after attending a Seattle taping of Gretchen Rubin and Elizabeth Craft's *Happier* podcast, she went home and felt like she was born to be a home organizer.

BEFORE

AFTER

While getting set up, Lisa also began to volunteer as an English as a Second Language teaching assistant at her local Refugee Women's Association. After meeting some amazing and courageous people, she felt the need to help these women and their families transition into America. That's when her two passions collided to form the perfect side hustle.

Lisa would offer decluttering services to her clients, and donate the unwanted items to the refugees who needed them. She would essentially become a modern-day Robin Hood—only without stealing from anyone. It would be as fulfilling as it would be enjoyable, and Lisa got straight to work.

She began her home organizing business with a $2,200 investment from her savings account. Two designers helped her create a website and show her how to modify and optimize it for search engines for $1,400, and $300 went into the site itself, which she hosts through WordPress, using the StudioPress Genesis Framework. The remaining costs were liability insurance, business cards, and a signature red bucket that she takes to every client's home.

Lisa began promoting her services through the network of people she'd built through her previous side hustles. She was met with an enthusiastic response. They loved the idea of improving their own well-being and donating stuff they weren't using to people who would benefit from it. The concept itself helps Lisa create a lot of word-of-mouth marketing.

Lisa offers every potential client a free one-hour consultation to talk through her process. After that, her services are priced at $65 per hour, with a three-hour minimum. She's able to charge a good hourly rate partly because of a unique system that she's developed that she calls SPACE. It stands for Sort, Pare Down, Assign, Contain, and Establish. The system is designed to coach clients through the process of decluttering.

During the first year of the project, Lisa earned an average of $3,000 per month, which increased to $4,000 a month a bit later. A quick glance at her testimonial-filled website shows why: in short, her clients love what she does and speak highly of her work. One of Lisa's clients, an attorney, had her organize most of her 4,000 square foot home and all of her daily working processes. This made her feel lighter and more focused, which she credits largely to Lisa's work.

While her clients gain clarity, the resettled refugees gain items and essentials that they couldn't otherwise afford. For example, an Iraqi family split up and fled their homes after refusing to join ISIS. Somehow, they found safe passage to America, were granted refugee status, and were reunited to build a new life. Expecting a child in the coming months, they came to Lisa for help finding a crib and some baby clothes.

Using donations from her side hustle, she put together a box that included a portable bassinet, baby blankets, diapers, almost-new infant and toddler clothes, picture books, baby toys, and a leather diaper bag. Because of her new work, she's able to make a donation like this almost every weekend.

If you're thinking of doing something similar, Lisa says that research and preparation are vital. Going into someone's home to help them declutter is a deeply personal experience and should be handled with care. It's also important to get written reviews from clients that you've worked with that can be shared on your own website, as well as third-party sites like Yelp, Google, and Nextdoor. This can be a big driver of web traffic, and it helps to back up your services with social proof—a powerful factor in converting someone to a customer.

Lisa hopes to find volunteers to help her distribute the donations door-to-door to reach more families and better manage her own workload. In her words, "This is the work I was born to do."

FUN FACT Lisa has taught over four thousand yoga classes in her life, and has worked with everyone from cancer sufferers to veterans with PTSD.

CRITICAL FACTOR

The pain of a messy, cluttered house is real for everyone, but Lisa's financial success can be traced to her decision to focus on wealthy homeowners. In addition to having larger spaces to organize, they're also more easily able to spend money on services like hers.

HOUSTON BEEKEEPER CREATES
MULTIPLE SWARMS OF INCOME

After multiple career moves, this Texas woman found her dream job as a beekeeper and cheesemonger. What's all the buzz about? Keep reading . . .

NAME
NICOLE BUERGERS

LOCATION
HOUSTON, TEXAS

STARTUP COSTS
**$5,000 FROM SAVINGS, $13,500
RAISED THROUGH INDIEGOGO**

INCOME
$7,000/MONTH

WEBSITE
BEE2BEEHONEY.COM

The landscape of Houston, Texas, America's fourth largest city, is known for Beyoncé, NASA's Johnson Space Center, and an impressive number of monster truck rallies—but until recently, it was *not* known as a thriving hub for bees. In fact, there was no beekeeping service anywhere in the city, and this was a crisis.

Why is this fact so buzzworthy? Well, honeybees play an important role in the environment. Among other contributions, our food supply is dependent on the pollination they provide. Even small towns typically have at least one apiarist collective, but the Texas metropolis was a beekeeping laggard.

With this service, a beekeeper is essentially a property manager of bees. Similar to a landscaper or swimming pool service, the beekeeper visits the beehives regularly, removing honey for sale while inspecting the bees to make sure their hive is humming along.

That's where Nicole Buergers, our Queen Bee, enters the story. Nicole discovered beekeeping while working as a search engine optimization (SEO) specialist and a cheesemonger. Through her job as a cheesemonger, Nicole had seen customers turn up their nose at honey varietals that just weren't local enough. She also knew

FUN FACT One time, about thirty of Nicole's bees snuck out of a hive that was resting at her feet and swarmed up her overalls to her midsection. The only solution was for her to slowly disrobe, being careful not to disturb the bees as she gave them an escape route. This all happened while she was facing a busy street, in front of a new client. Fortunately, the client was able to grab a towel to shield her from public viewing—and the bees got out without a single sting.

ACTION PLAN

1. Identify an unusual (yet important) need that's currently underserved in your local area.
2. Learn how to meet that need—in this case, beekeeping.
3. Tell your story! Use crowdfunding to raise funds and recruit supporters.
4. Hunt for landowners who will allow you to install beehives on their property.
5. Collect the honey each month, sell it to wholesalers, and deposit your sweet profits.

"Most beekeepers only maintain a hive once or twice a month, but I do it every day. By teaching others, my skill set has greatly increased." —Nicole

local beekeepers that were giving their honey away because they didn't know how to market it.

She started an Indiegogo crowdfunding campaign called Bee2Bee Honey Collective, with the mission to provide a healthy, sustainable habitat for honeybees while promoting urban beekeeping.

This isn't just a mission or an unusual hobby: it brings in a lot of sweet cash, especially during the high season. I asked Nicole to "show me the honey" and tell me more about how it worked, and she said, "Mind your own beeswax."[*]

So I had to dig into the hives myself.

Her income varies depending on season and number of clients. Clients pay a set fee of $600 for a new hive and starter set of bees. They also pay a monthly fee for Nicole to visit and care for the bees. During the visit, Nicole withdraws the honey, which she splits with the client (taking 35 percent for herself). She then resells the honey to local retailers, distributors, and customers in her own "Honey of the Month" club. In other words, she's created multiple swarms of income.

At the time we last spoke, she managed more than seventy hives. From all the different ways this busy bee gets paid, she earns more than $7,000 a month.

All of that income takes the sting out of the startup costs. Nicole withdrew $5,000 from her retirement fund to get going, and her Indiegogo campaign raised an additional $13,500.

She's quick to point out that her work is not all about eating cheese and honey—though that would be awesome—but she also has to do accounting, scheduling, and manage the real risk of being stung by those ungrateful bees she's trying to serve. Still, she loves being able to go outside each day to do something for the environment, while raising interest in protecting the local honeybee population.

Because one side hustle is not enough for people like Nicole, she's also busy with several other projects. She rents out a room in her apartment on Airbnb, she's helping a professor friend launch a tabletop game, and she does events for a local cheese shop.

If you're bumbling about, searching for your side hustle hive, let this story serve as inspiration.

CRITICAL FACTOR

Bzzzzzz! Beekeeping services are good for local areas, and Houston didn't have a well-coordinated one until Nicole traded part of her retirement fund for an apiary.

BROOKLYN PHOTOGRAPHER GETS PAID TO THROW CONFETTI AT PEOPLE

A former graphic designer turns a ninety-day personal challenge into a growing photography brand.

A graphic designer by day, Jelena Aleksich specializes in creating presentations for startups and other companies. But for the past two years, she's devoted much of her spare time to the Confetti Project—a photography series that profiles its subjects doused in confetti, all while asking the question, "What do you celebrate?"

From as far back as she's been working, Jelena has had a side hustle. Her first job out of college was being a startup's first hire as lead graphic designer and project manager. After roughly a year, she began freelancing and continued that on the side until she found herself longing for something new.

The Confetti Project began as a three-month challenge to find new opportunities. Jelena tackled her own limiting beliefs about whether or not she could truly become a full-time photographer, publish a book, or even see something through from start to finish. Since she started, she's now profiled over two hundred people, and has seen it transition from a passion project into a moneymaking brand with multiple revenue streams.

How do you get inspired to launch such a project? It all began when Jelena began immersing herself in lifelong, creative hobbies. Then, a series of random events happened. After getting glitter-bombed at a party, and taking home some confetti in her pocket after a concert, Jelena found herself fishing around in the pocket of her leather jacket on a particularly sad day. She pulled out the confetti and immediately dove back into the nostalgia and emotions that the confetti held.

Following a bit of quick research, she decided to do fifty photo shoots with her fellow Brooklyn creative entrepreneurs, design a book, and make it a best seller. Although she didn't meet all of her ambitious goals in the initial three-month deadline she set, she laid the groundwork for a successful side hustle. Once she completed the shoots with her friends, Jelena introduced

NAME
JELENA ALEKSICH

LOCATION
BROOKLYN, NEW YORK

STARTUP COSTS
MINIMAL

INCOME
$15,000 IN THE FIRST QUARTER OF 2018

WEBSITE
THECONFETTIPROJECT.COM

"There are no rights or wrongs on the side hustle path; you just have to take action. The Confetti Project didn't make money at first, but now it's a growing brand." —Jelena

her first revenue stream: paid photo shoots featuring confetti. These shoots started at $200 and are now $350 per session, bringing in $1,000 to $4,000 per month after expenses like studio rental (and confetti!) are covered. The income fluctuates so much because demand varies month to month.

On the surface, Jelena isn't doing anything groundbreaking: she's taking photos, telling stories, and throwing confetti. But when it's put together in her unique way, that's where the magic happens. The two hours she gets to spend with each subject is where she's most in her element.

Next, she plans to completely transform the Confetti Project into a brand with more individual shoots and charity campaigns, and to finish the coffee-table book she started in her initial three-month challenge.

FUN FACT   Confetti was first used in Paris in the early 1800s. The word *confetti* comes from an Italian confection with the same name, and it was originally a small sweet traditionally thrown during carnivals.

CRITICAL FACTOR

Jelena had a fun idea and expressed it with passion. Since the project is so visual, getting a few initial shoots done with her friends helped with recruiting paid participants.

EXCEL SPREADSHEET GURU
EARNS $3,500 A MONTH

An IBM employee in India creates a series of Microsoft Excel tutorials, earning hundreds of dollars per sale and thousands of dollars each month.

NAME
SUMIT BANSAL

LOCATION
NEW DELHI, INDIA

STARTUP COSTS
$200

INCOME
$3,500/MONTH

WEBSITE
TRUMPEXCEL.COM

For over three years, Sumit Bansal worked as a marketing manager at IBM in New Delhi, India. His work in data analysis and client presentations required him to use a lot of Excel spreadsheets and PowerPoint. Naturally, he got really good at it.

Sumit started a blog—which is now his full-time job—because he wanted to share answers to questions his colleagues were asking him about spreadsheets. When he got a positive response from those colleagues and a few friends, it gave him more confidence that his blog was useful.

Then he began to write tutorials and create videos every week. He signed up for Google AdSense, where he would get paid when website visitors clicked on ads. This wasn't an immediate gold rush: his first few months, he earned only a few dollars a month.

Traffic grew and the payouts increased, but not by much. It wasn't until a year and a half after starting the blog that he found a real way to make money: by creating online courses. Within an hour of sending the email announcing his first course, he got five sales. The course title was as basic as they came: he called it "Excel Course." Yet as basic as it was, it was clear that he was on to something.

Those first few sales affirmed his faith in the blog he'd worked on all this time. He celebrated by taking friends to dinner, he bought himself a few books, and then he got back to work.

That was four years ago.

FUN FACT   A few years after Sumit started his blog, some of his readers asked him to change the name because they thought it sounded political. He even had a few people offer to buy the site soon after the 2016 US election, but he decided to keep it.

ACTION PLAN

1. Identify a tool or resource that your colleagues spend a lot of time using—preferably one that can be tedious or difficult.
2. Learn shortcuts, tips, and strategies for improving workflow or saving time.
3. Write down what you've learned in a logical, orderly manner. Focus on what's essential and don't try to pack in *everything*.
4. Decide on a format to share your ideas: online course, blog, product, video series, or something else.
5. Package the lessons and offer them for sale.

Sumit now has three courses for sale: that basic Excel course (which sells for $127), an Excel Dashboard Course ($297), and a Visual Basics for Application course (also $297). The courses don't all sell every day, but more often than not, at some point during the day he'll get a notification that either $127 or $297 has arrived in his bank account.

Not only that, he often gets positive feedback on how the courses are helping people do better work. He recently read an email from one of his students who mentioned how he used the techniques shown in the course to create a dashboard. That employee received a standing ovation in a department meeting. Another student emailed him to say that the course helped her move from contract employment to a full-time job.

One of the reasons why Sumit's courses work so well is because he's intentional about what goes in them and what doesn't. Many similar training programs don't cover all the necessary topics, or they end up overwhelming the student. Sumit took a lot of time to make sure his are structured in a way where he includes the essentials without adding anything unnecessary.

From revenue of around $4,000 each month, he now makes about $3,500 in net income—a large amount of money in India. He has $700 in monthly expenses, including rent at his coworking space, some important subscriptions, and his email marketing tool.

Next, Sumit is focusing on creating two new online courses. He's also been able to start a different project with a friend, using earnings from his blog to get it started. Check your formulas: the spreadsheet hustle is thriving.

"People often share how my work is making a difference in their life, and I keep these emails saved in a separate folder. I feel blessed to be in a position where I can work with freedom, passion, and commitment, and see the real difference it makes in people's lives."
—Sumit

BRITISH MAN BUILDS TERRARIUMS
FOR FUN AND PROFIT

An avid plant collector makes the most of temporary unemployment by launching an online terrarium store from England.

NAME
ADAM SHAFI

LOCATION
LONDON, ENGLAND

STARTUP COSTS
£500 (ABOUT $642)

INCOME
£600/MONTH (ABOUT $800)

WEBSITE
GEODESIUM.CO.UK

CRITICAL FACTOR

Adam's love for plants and skill at craftsmanship complement each other well. By selling online, he can extend his local reach beyond the United Kingdom and serve customers worldwide.

Twenty-five-year-old Adam Shafi has always loved plants. Born and raised in the concrete jungle of London, he sought out all things green wherever he could. When he was a child, he was fixated on cacti, and usually had several with their arms raised in salute around the house. As a teenager, he moved on to carnivorous plants, collecting Venus flytraps and displaying them on his windowsill. Then in his twenties, he migrated toward the more peaceful tomato plant, at one time cultivating twelve different varieties. His house is now filled with one hundred of those tomato plants, in addition to bonsai trees and other treasures.

In the teenage years, while researching how to tend his plants, Adam had come across terrariums: geometric-shaped mini-greenhouses that people use to display their plants and decorate their homes. They're fairly popular now, but back then, they were much lesser known. They looked more like reptile tanks or clear plastic pots. But they achieved the same goal: improved humidity for growing the plants.

Fast-forward to three years ago: Adam had just graduated with a master's degree, but was initially unable to find work because of a turndown in his industry. In the downtime in between applying for jobs, he was also looking for a terrarium to hold his plants.

He had seen so-called geodesic domes online and in shops. Researching further, Adam learned that you could make your own glass dome using precut glass triangles and silicon filler. It is called the "Tiffany glass technique," and it uses copper foil to create three-dimensional stained glass shapes. Adam's interest was piqued, and—with extra time on his hands—he decided to attempt making one.

After about a month of toying with different approaches, he succeeded. His friends were so impressed by his creation that they encouraged him to sell the terrariums online. He tried his luck by posting one on Etsy, and after a few weeks, much to Adam's surprise, "a nice lady from across the ocean in the United States sent a message and put in an order." It was a transcontinental match made in heaven, or at least an exchange of PayPal

funds. Adam wrapped the finished product in layers of bubble wrap, and sent off his first sale.

He celebrated with a pint at the pub and a trip to the nearest stained glass shop to buy some new tools. He was already set up on Etsy, where his first customer—and soon many others—found him. He now invested about £500 ($642) for materials and tools, and created a website using Shopify.

Adam offers customers something a bit different from the mass-produced offerings by providing terrariums that are soldered rather than metal plated. He uses lead-free solder, and is constantly changing his methods and materials to perfect the finishing on his containers. To reflect this attention to detail, his handmade products cost slightly more than those that are mass produced, typically ranging from £35 ($45) for small ones to £90 ($115) for large ones.

After that brief time of unemployment, Adam was able to find work and now has a 9-to-5 job as a marketing assistant. He enjoys his job, and he has continued to work on Geodesium in his spare time. So far, he's sold over one hundred terrariums, averaging about £600 ($830) in monthly income. Though he uses Facebook and Instagram to feature his products, most of the current traffic comes from Etsy.

He's also making some changes. With each terrarium taking between three and four hours to complete, the project can be time- and labor-intensive. With an eye on the future, he's expanded to sell kits for filling terrariums, which include soil, gravel, activated charcoal, and moss. The kits have since become his bestselling items on Etsy—and they take far less time to make than the terrariums themselves.

A future goal is to expand to craft markets throughout London. Let's see what sprouts next . . .

FUN FACT Geodesium's priciest terrarium was made up of eighty different triangles of glass and cost £135 ($174).

ROCKET SCIENTIST LAUNCHES
HERBAL SIDE INCOME

Herbal medicine isn't rocket science, but this NASA scientist discovers a side hustle when she turns to nontraditional remedies to treat her immune diseases.

NAME
LISA AKERS

LOCATION
DENVER, COLORADO

STARTUP COSTS
$5,000

INCOME
$1,200/MONTH

WEBSITE
LISAAKERS.COM

By day, Lisa Akers is a real-life rocket scientist. She frequently travels from her home in Colorado to build spaceships, most commonly at the Kennedy Space Center in Florida. Her side hustle is more grounded: she promotes the message of herbalism, working with private clients suffering from autoimmune diseases and other chronic conditions.

The project stemmed from Lisa's own personal health struggles. As a result of the long hours, high stress, and "not so nontoxic" chemicals (as she calls them) used in spaceship building, she found herself with some systemic health issues that doctors couldn't figure out. She spent the better part of a year going to various experts, specialists, and even some nontraditional practitioners to try to find a solution—but it wasn't until she found an herbalist that she was able to figure out what was happening and work to improve her health.

While she was healing her body, Lisa decided to learn more about herbal medicine. She worked to get her master herbalist certification, and eventually completed postgraduate education in nutrition. As a busy scientist, Lisa was happy to be able to complete many of her certifications through distance learning. She'd download the lessons on her phone and do coursework while waiting for appointments, traveling, or during her lunch breaks.

At first, Lisa hoped that herbalism would become her main gig. She hired coaches, found mentors, and took classes, all in hopes of following an herbal dream. But she was making those decisions while recovering from serious illnesses of her own, so she wasn't in a great frame of mind to see how she could change her workflow at her day job to feel better. After starting down this frustrating path, she realized she could both keep her day job and have an herbal business. This is the *Side Hustle School* way!

Lisa's first offering was a group program, and it completely sold out. She soon realized, however, that group programs are difficult for health practitioners to manage. Keeping confidential health information private was difficult in a group situation. It was challenging to tailor the content

CRITICAL FACTOR

Lisa's personal story and "double life" as a rocket scientist gave her authority as she transitioned to the world of wellness.

to meet the participants' needs while protecting each person's privacy.

She now prefers one-on-one consults, where she can speak more directly and customize suggestions for individuals. The cost is $450 for an initial appointment package, and $250 for follow-ups.

Lisa works with clients in six areas: nutrition, sleep, movement, environment, stress, and joy. This approach helps them build a foundation of good health before working to restore their energy and specific nutrients in their bodies as well as to build resilience. For example, in one of her programs, she'll do a personalized review of lab blood tests and give her clients detailed insight into their results. This is much more informative and empowering than the call from your doctor where all you hear is "Your lab work is fine."

When working with clients, Lisa makes sure to tell them to see their physician if there's a situation outside of her ability to manage. She's not a doctor, so she can't diagnose or prescribe treatments. She sees herself as an educator, offering information and insight to help people find a healthier lifestyle, based on her own experiences with plants, food, and supplements. Lisa also has access to a larger herbalist community where people share their tough cases and get insight from one another.

To promote her programs and consultations, Lisa does talks and web classes, reaching out to people interested in learning more holistic approaches to their health situation. She also goes to groups where people who have autoimmune diseases gather, both in person and online, to participate and build relationships. When appropriate, she'll let them know what she does and opens the door to future conversations.

It cost her about $5,000 in educational expenses to get certified. She's now bringing in a minimum of $1,200 a month, with a goal of increasing it. Her work in building spaceships ebbs and flows—sometimes she's busy with assembly and testing, and other times she's not. She schedules appointments when she's got time and mental capacity, and starts a waiting list when necessary in order to avoid overcommitting.

While she's helping spaceships take flight, she's also helping people get well and building an asset for herself.

"Being able to work with people and see their health change radically with a few recommended changes is very inspiring. It's also a bit scary because of the self-doubt that people like me seem to face so often, but seeing that change happen is the best part of my day." —Lisa

FUN FACT Lisa is a winner of the Silver Snoopy award, which is given by NASA astronauts in recognition of significant contributions to crew safety and mission success.

ONCOLOGY NURSE CREATES PRODUCTS TO REGROW HAIR

After kicking cancer to the curb, a Texas oncology nurse discovers the power of essential oils for hair regrowth.

NAME
TANIEKA RANDALL

LOCATION
HOUSTON, TEXAS

STARTUP COSTS
$1,500

INCOME
$45,000/YEAR

WEBSITE
TEESHAIRSECRET.COM

Tanieka Randall's story is all about growth—growth she's experienced in her personal life, in her professional career, and even with her hair. Tanieka, or Tee, as she's more commonly known, started a side hustle selling natural hair products that promote healthy hair while also stimulating follicle growth.

Tee brings professional and personal experience to this venture. She works as an oncology nurse, often pulling twelve-hour night shifts from 7 p.m. to 7 a.m. A self-described "healthy hair junkie," she had begun experimenting with making her own products after being less than thrilled with everything else on the market. Those products were full of lots of questionable chemicals like parabens, sulfates, formaldehyde, and artificial colors. Not only that, the results were unimpressive.

She wanted more natural products for her hair, and she also enjoyed putting these products together. Her experimenting was put on hold, however, when a bone marrow test revealed that Tee had leukemia. She was a fighter, and pulled through the treatments cancer free—but five rounds of strenuous chemotherapy left her completely bald. Dismayed but victorious, she began to research the best ways to naturally regrow her hair.

"I'm simply amazed at all the people from all over the world that I've been able to meet through this business. Having a positive impact on their lives has been both humbling and inspiring." —Tee

That's when she discovered the world of essential oils. Much more so than artificial ingredients, the right recipe of essential oils made an immediate difference in her hair's regrowth. She tried a series of combinations before settling on her own unique recipe.

Naturally, Tee shared her newfound knowledge with her friends and family so they could benefit from all her research. As her hair regrew, people kept asking what her secret was—how did she get it to grow back so thick and healthy after chemo?

One day, it dawned on her that she was creating products that others may actually want to purchase themselves. Better yet, her target audience was right there on Facebook. On a whim, she decided to take the plunge and began accepting orders.

The response she received was overwhelmingly positive, and she knew that she'd be outgrowing her impromptu Facebook sales page before long. With this in mind, Tee went online to do what she does best—researching—so that she could put this positive momentum to work. She set up an LLC (limited liability company), and the next month she attended an event as an official vendor.

That event was a local women's networking group. As she describes it, "I made a few hundred dollars at that first event. While that's nothing to some people, to me it was a lot." More than just making some money, she saw that there was a real market for her products.

Tee took that first few hundred dollars in revenue and put it right back into her business. In total, she spent $1,500 to get going. Around $800 went to buying ingredients and supplies directly related to creating her products. Another couple hundred went to registering her business, and the rest went toward flyers and business cards. She also set up a website so that she could officially take orders on her own instead of just through Facebook.

The investments paid off. In her first year in operation, Tee cleared more than $20,000. Aside from spending a few thousand dollars on additional ingredients to prototype potential new products, she had very few expenses.

One thing she *did* invest in, however, was business coaching. She spent $3,000 to get some help learning how to run her own shop. While it's the single largest thing she's purchased in relation to her business, she said it was worth every cent.

From that business coaching, she learned to focus on what her customers were asking for, which led to introducing some new products as well as bundling existing products into sets.

Tee also learned more about connecting with potential customers. When she picked a name, she had grabbed accounts on most major social

FUN FACT One day, Tee was tired and didn't notice that instead of putting water in the microwave and a mix of wax and oil on the stove, she did it backward. When she lifted up the hot container, it melted and everything spilled all over the stove and herself. She says this is the kind of lesson you only have to learn once.

networks, and then set about establishing a presence on many of them. Tee also joined networking and entrepreneurial groups in her area.

Through all these efforts, she cleared $80,000 in sales in her second year. In her third year, she wasn't able to focus on the business as much, but still cleared $45,000.

Tee is continuing to grow her presence on social media, and is now working on being more targeted. She says that until recently she was a bit all over the place, trying to be everywhere at once. Now she's narrowed her focus so that she can be consistent in a way that combines promoting her products, teaching, and sharing more about her own journey.

She eventually hopes to turn this work into her full-time income. She's already put much of her profits toward payment on a house for her children to grow up in. There's no splitting hairs: as someone who moved from apartment to apartment growing up, this was a tremendous accomplishment.

ANIMAL LOVER BREEDS RABBITS
TO PAY FOR COLLEGE

An enterprising teen learns to breed rabbits, pocketing an extra $500 per month and eventually paying her way through college.

NAME
LEAH LYNCH

LOCATION
WILMINGTON, OHIO

STARTUP COSTS
$300

INCOME
$8,400/YEAR

WEBSITE
LEAH-LYNCH.COM

When Leah Lynch was sixteen years old, she was juggling a retail job around her high school studies. Like so many teenage jobs, the work was boring. Making minimum wage was better than nothing, but this was hardly her dream job. Still, what else could a teenager do?

One day while researching alternatives, she stumbled across a peculiar breed of rabbits called French Lops. As Leah discovered, they weren't just bred for pets, they were bred for shows too. *These are some talented rabbits*, she thought, and she decided to try her hand at breeding them. She'd been an animal lover her whole life, so it seemed logical enough.

Looking at local listings, she found a breeder in her part of Ohio. Then, armed with money she'd saved from her retail job, Leah *hopped* in her car and bought the best rabbits she could find. If she was going to do this right, she had to start with the best "partners."

FUN FACT   Did you know there are an estimated 6.1 million pet rabbits in the USA alone? Even celebrities like Clint Eastwood, Sienna Miller, and Michael Jordan have all owned rabbits.

Her new trio of rabbits—one male, two females—cost a few hundred dollars.

Luckily, there was no need to register as a breeder or apply for a license, so she could begin building up her rabbitry straight away.* She did this while working around two other jobs and eventually her college studies, learning along the way about what it took to breed these rabbits safely and to a show-quality standard, then selling them for a profit to responsible buyers.

To build up the business, she attended local shows and spoke with other breeders, companies, and attendees to make them aware of her rabbitry. And she used the Craigslist pages of the three largest nearby towns and cities to share the rabbits she had for sale. Sure enough, they began to fly off the shelves . . . or perhaps out of their cages.

Here's some math: for a show-quality rabbit, you can expect to sell (or buy) one for anywhere between $35 at the lower end and $200 at the higher end. In other words, the better your litter, the more money you stand to make.

When Leah started, there was a joke in her family that these rabbits would pay for her college tuition. Little did they know that joke would become reality. She graduated debt free, while also making a few thousand dollars each school year in spending money.

Leaping forward, Leah has stayed with her rabbitry alongside her new job as a test proctor at a local community college. And just like her rabbits, she's multiplied into new income streams. Her website, Busy Gals Homestead, teaches people how they, too, can raise rabbits to generate a side income. Although her site was around through college—it was originally titled Leah's Lovely Lops—it really took life when she added a blog and began to charge for coaching, as well as offering herbs and natural remedies for rabbits.

She's also invested more time and effort into learning how to market her products to people all over the country, leading her to make an additional $500 a month on top of the rabbit riches.

Leah is a rare breed of person . . . taking advantage of every hopportunity that comes her way.

"Think ahead about all the potential issues that could come up, and decide how you will respond to that situation before it happens. This will help you when you are dealing with a difficult customer, or when you have to make the call on what actions to take if something unexpected happens." —Leah

* There's no license required, but the rabbits do appreciate some romantic music being played in the background. I recommend John Legend or the "Evenings by the Fireplace" playlist on Spotify.

 CRITICAL FACTOR

When Leah decided to breed rabbits, she took the time to talk to everyone she could find who knew something about the industry. She then got the word out about her new rabbitry through those same people, in addition to posting free ads on Craigslist.

PR CONSULTANT LAUNCHES "RESTAURANT WEEK" FESTIVITIES

A California publicist earns an extra $20,000 a year producing an annual "Restaurant Week" that brings together chefs and new diners.

NAME
ELIZABETH BORSTING

LOCATION
LONG BEACH, CALIFORNIA

STARTUP COSTS
LESS THAN $100

INCOME
$20,000/YEAR

WEBSITE
DINEOUTLONGBEACH.COM

Elizabeth Borsting wears many hats. Based in Long Beach, California, she's a public relations consultant representing hotels, restaurants, and destination venues. She's also a travel writer with nine books to her name, as well as numerous articles for the *Los Angeles Times*, *National Geographic Traveler*, and other publications.

A few years ago, she took on yet another role: producing the city's annual Restaurant Week. For one week each February, restaurants produce, at a discount, special value-oriented menus reflecting their culinary style.

Lunch menus are available for $10, $15, and $20 per person, while three-course dinners are offered at $20, $30, $40, and $50 per person. The idea is to introduce diners to new restaurants, allowing them to sample from a range of featured items without breaking the bank.

It's called Dine Out Long Beach, and it didn't exist until Elizabeth made it happen.[*] Plenty of other cities have similar events, but for some reason no one had ever done it in Long Beach before.

The event was ideal for her—it taps into her natural strengths, experience, and the connections that she's built while handling PR for many restaurants in her day job. The fact that she enjoys good food doesn't hurt either.

Funding comes largely through sponsorship. Elizabeth is constantly networking, so most of her sponsors continue to be part of the event year after year. Startup costs were minimal, and the annual profit is around $20,000.

[*] She began the project with a cofounder, who later stepped away.

"Be prepared to be the salesperson, marketer, trainer, problem solver, and your own cheerleader. Once you make a public announcement, there's no turning back." —Elizabeth

Since she runs her own PR firm, Elizabeth's workday involves touching base with different clients, some of whom happen to be restaurant owners. Elizabeth promotes the event through a large billboard (which includes sponsor logos) at a very busy intersection. She estimates that it garners around 450,000 impressions. Additionally, the event is featured

on morning shows in Los Angeles, as well as on LA's number one radio station. This press coverage benefits the restaurants and helps to bring diners in.

Managed properly, Restaurant Week can be a win-win for everyone. Diners love trying new places at a fixed price, restaurants love getting new customers that they hope will return after the promotion is over, and the person who runs the operation gets paid. *Bon appétit!*

FUN FACT Long Beach is home to the only restaurant in the United States that serves Chianina beef, an Italian breed of cattle. The restaurant, Chianina Steakhouse, also breeds and raises its own herd.

How to Discover Your Valuable Skills

"Don't follow your passion, follow your skill." This recommendation can take you far, or at least get you on the right path to side hustle success.

So how do you know what your valuable skills are? I firmly believe that everyone's an expert at something. Whenever I meet someone who says they have no marketable skills, a three-minute conversation usually proves them wrong.

To get started, make a list of things you know how to do. What did you learn in school, college, or university? What have you learned in the workforce? What comes naturally to you that other people seem to struggle with?

All these answers will point to valuable skills. You may also want to ask your friends and coworkers. Sometimes the people who know us may have ideas or insights that we haven't considered ourselves.

Next, you need to think about how to apply those skills in a different way than you would in a traditional career. That's what many people in this book have done—but it all starts with a valuable skill.

For more, visit SideHustleSchool.com/skills.

IV

Buy Low, Sell High

This business opportunity started approximately 150,000 years ago. It's evolved a bit since then, but the principles remain the same. These modern-day merchants find ways to buy goods at one price, and then sell them at a higher one.

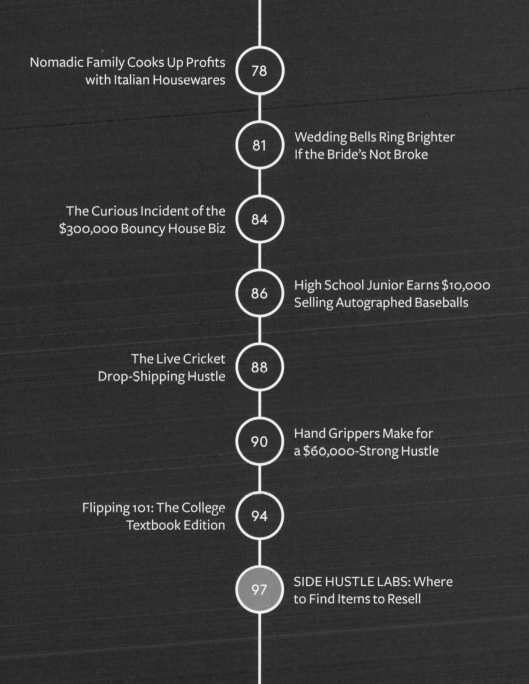

NOMADIC FAMILY COOKS UP PROFITS
WITH ITALIAN HOUSEWARES

After finding the frying pan of their dreams on a yearlong trip abroad, this family starts an importing business that allows them to keep seeing the world.

NAME
NATHAN AND KATHRIN SPACCARELLI

LOCATION
PORTLAND, OREGON (AND ITALY!)

STARTUP COSTS
$3,500

INCOME
MULTIPLE SIX FIGURES

WEBSITE
DATERRACUCINA.COM

Nathan and Kathrin Spaccarelli decided they wanted a different life for themselves and their children. After selling most of what they owned and taking a yearlong sabbatical from work, they'd returned from traveling with a completely different purpose.

While they were proud of the coffee business they operated and everything else they'd built back in Oregon, nothing compared to the rich experiences of exploring the world as a family. They wanted to be able to bring together their love of entrepreneurship and travel into an income-earning project that worked for the whole family. Or, in this case, something that put the whole family to work.

Nathan and Kathrin promised their two young sons that much of the profit from this new venture, and their work within it, would go into the family travel fund and give them more opportunities to explore the world.

Since they were determined to create something that would allow them to be location independent, they focused on reselling—but not in a way

that required them to spend hours standing in line at the post office. Through a podcast, Nathan had discovered the Fulfillment by Amazon program, where Amazon stores goods for you and ships them out whenever orders come in.* It sounded like the perfect fit.

They were just missing one thing: a product!

Like the savvy side hustlers that they are, they decided to capitalize on the skills and knowledge they already had. Over the twenty years they had been running their coffee distribution company, Kathrin and Nathan had learned a lot about water filtration systems. It occurred to them that they should do something useful with this knowledge.

It didn't make much sense for them to sell coffee filters, since companies like theirs were more likely to make their bulk filter purchases straight from the source. So, instead, they started to look into filters that anyone could purchase on their own.

One or two sales a day led to dozens of sales a day as they got better at managing their listings and bidding for "clicks" in search results. These filters served as an easy way for them to try their hand at something new, but they weren't the long-term solution. After the success of their first few months, they discovered a product that inspired them to shift focus from water filters to a different item that would allow them to build their own brand.

On their round-the-world trip, they'd picked up a healthy, nonstick ceramic pan at a market in Italy and brought it back with them to America. Nathan loves to cook, and even with months of use, the pan held up well.

The US market was saturated with Teflon pans that contain a chemical that raises health and environmental concerns. The ceramic-coated, nonstick Italian pan they'd acquired was not only a much healthier alternative to Teflon and other nonstick cookware, it could also easily transition from stovetop to oven. Finally, ceramics bake at half the temperatures required for conventional materials, so they use less energy.

They tracked down the manufacturer and customized the pans to accommodate a few design elements Nathan requested, including features like a longer, heat-resistant silicone handle and a high-heat aluminum

"At first we were only selling one or two a day, but a month later, we were getting sales notifications all the time. We finally had to turn them off because there were so many emails." —Kathrin

FUN FACT Think selling cookware is just a flash in the pan? Well, it's actually a $15 billion business and growing every year. It doesn't look like it'll be sizzling out any time soon.

* Amazon doesn't do this to be nice; they get paid a significant portion of the sales. The arrangement still works well for a lot of businesses because Amazon has such a large customer base.

base. Since this was their first order, they went with the minimum amount that they could, but it still ended up being fifteen hundred units. The initial investment caused them some hesitation at first, but despite the risk, Nathan and Kathrin were confident in the product.

They launched their cooking line under the name DaTerra Cucina—literally translated as "from the ground kitchen" due to the all-natural, volcanic minerals used to create the nonstick coating on their pans. The new product line was a hit, with early customers writing rave reviews, and the pans flying to the top of Amazon's kitchen and housewares search results.

During the first year, they had to carefully consider when to place their wholesale orders. There were times when it felt like they were drowning in stock and were going to be stuck with these nonstick items forever, and times when they'd have so few items their customers would be waiting longer than they'd prefer. Finding a balance proved tricky, and it's still an art that they're trying to perfect.

Still, they'd managed to make over $200,000 in sales by the end of their first year in business. Much of that money was reinvested into the business, but they were still able to add $40,000 into their family travel fund.

After the first quarter of year two, they'd already cleared $85,000 in sales, putting them on track for an even more profitable year than their last. This has allowed them to invest in more stock and grow their business by adding three more pan sizes.

With so many water filters and nonstick pans in the market, you may wonder how the Spaccarellis were able to create such a profitable project. Nathan says that the only secret is being fanatical about what you sell: "It's easy to throw a few products up on Amazon and make a little money, but to be truly successful and stand out, you need to present a quality experience."

That high standard is what Nathan and Kathrin strive to reach with all of their products. The rave reviews on all of their products show that their customers feel the same way.[*]

Whether this new business will ever come to replace their coffee distribution company remains to be seen. Either way, they'll be heading out again to see the world. Going forward, the Spaccarelli family plans to create their own e-commerce website as well as expand their income streams beyond Amazon and diversify their business . . . all while traveling together as a family.

* Two of their favorite reviews from thrilled customers: "My other pots and pans are jealous" and "Imagine replacing the jalopy in your driveway with a Maserati. It's like that."

WEDDING BELLS RING BRIGHTER
IF THE BRIDE'S NOT BROKE

A New York professional eases some of the painful prices for wedding goods by renting high-end accessories for brides.

Many childhood pursuits are lost to the past, but some take hold, transformed into an adult version of bygone ventures. Brittany Finkle couldn't foresee that planning the weddings of her three older sisters, starting when she was just twelve years old, could lead to owning an online boutique renting luxury bridal accessories—but that's exactly what ended up happening.

Her path continued to unfold in college, where she got a degree in fiber science while also designing wedding gowns as a part-time job. The pressure of a last-minute request to design one sister's gown sent them both out to shop for a reasonably priced one, and that's where she was inspired.

But first, she was offended.

Wedding dress prices were expensive enough, but Brittany expected that. What she was shocked at was the prices for the accessories, like veils and headpieces. With the dresses blowing out a bride's budget, accessory costs could send them into sticker-shock stupor. And they don't need to own all those accessories. After all, they're only used once.

Enter the idea: Why not supply brides with high-quality accessories that they could inexpensively rent and return? The idea led Brittany to her side hustle, Happily Ever Borrowed. She knew fabrics and quality, and she knew business dealings from her full-time job as a buyer for luxury brands. She used that savvy to work directly with bridal accessory designers, selecting from the new designs for the season from the twice-yearly Bridal Fashion Week in New York.

She had to say "I do" to some startup costs, including about $20,000 on inventory, legal and marketing fees, and a website. But the investment

NAME
BRITTANY FINKLE

LOCATION
NEW YORK, NEW YORK

STARTUP COSTS
$20,000

INCOME
$80,000/YEAR

WEBSITE
HAPPILYEVERBORROWED.COM

FUN FACT When Brittany got married, she borrowed all of her accessories from her own business. She was then able to experience the business from the perspective of a customer, putting it to the ultimate test.

"I think many people who are planning their wedding are shocked at the high costs of everything for a celebration that only lasts a moment in time. We're here to help with that!" —Brittany

paid off: the company has been doubling its sales year after year. She's now rented to over five hundred brides, and is well on track to earning six figures a year.

The Happily Ever Borrowed website lets brides-to-be check accessories by product, designer, or style, and the range of goods runs from veils to headpieces to jewelry. Oh, and don't forget tiaras, for that royal look every bride needs.

Prices are generally 20 percent of the retail price to purchase the item, and any minor spills and damages are covered. Rentals include a prepaid label to ship the package back after the magic is complete.

The company even has a "send before you spend" option for brides who want to try on up to three different pieces, at a flat price of $50 for a two-day rental, which includes a $25 off coupon on any selected wedding rentals, just for trying the service. Apparently, even accessories need rehearsals!

A few of those five hundred brides have had unusual requests, such as wanting to rent pieces for as long as a month—but that's discouraged, since prices would then start to approach retail.

The business isn't all champagne and toasts, however. Having to rely on the postal service can be harrowing, because the occasional lost package can heavily impact the bride's peace of mind. Brittany has worked hard to master precise lead times for all shipments.

Wedding ceremonies last only a moment in time, but they can create memories for a lifetime. Happily Ever Borrowed specializes in making those memories happen—sometimes with a crystal-tiara flourish.

CRITICAL FACTOR

Sure, a bride might keep her wedding dress forever—but does she really need to own the tiara, the veil, and whatever other accessories she wants to wear? Brittany created a rental market for expensive items that could easily be "recycled" by many brides.

THE CURIOUS INCIDENT OF THE
$300,000 BOUNCY HOUSE BIZ

A Texas man puts a bounce in his step by finding a uniquely profitable niche. This imaginative project earned multiple six figures in its first year.

NAME
RENE DELGADO

LOCATION
CEDAR PARK, TEXAS

STARTUP COSTS
$1,000

INCOME
MULTIPLE SIX FIGURES/YEAR

WEBSITE
BOUNCEHOUSESTORE.COM

Imagine someone comes to you with this pitch: "Hey, I've got a great business idea. It's an underserved market, a product that people enjoy, and a high profit margin. We could make a lot of money here."

You think, *Awesome, is this an app? I've heard that apps do well.*

And your friend says, "No, here's the secret—and don't tell anyone, because I don't want someone to steal my idea. Here's how we're going to get rich: *bouncy castles*. Also known as *bounce houses*."

Seems unlikely, right?

Well, one guy in Cedar Park, Texas, decided to follow his bouncy passion to the bank in the world of playhouse rentals. How in the world did he do it? Just like this.

During the day, Rene Delgado works in operations and supply chain management for a large consumer electronics company. In the evenings, he sells bounce houses to residential and commercial customers. Again, you read that right. *Bounce houses*.

Rene didn't decide to sell bounce houses because he has a lifelong obsession with them. He decided to sell bounce houses after some careful analysis. That research began when he set out to consider his side hustle options. He had a long list of ideas: using Fulfillment by Amazon, becoming a day trader, and flipping houses were all on the list.

But it was another idea that stood out most of all: drop-shipping high-ticket items. With drop shipping, he wouldn't have to carry any inventory (the manufacturers or distributors would handle storage and shipping), and it didn't really matter what he sold. If he found a way to profit on the difference in price (from what he paid for something to what he sold it for elsewhere), he'd be set.

He liked the low barrier to entry to this business. He also liked the fact that success wasn't dependent on factors outside his control, as was the case with some of the other options he'd considered.

CRITICAL FACTOR

After making a list of one hundred possible items for his first drop-ship effort, he ended up with something that met all the right criteria: a high price point with low competition.

Still, it didn't matter what he sold as long as he could profit from it—but what would that be?

Rene made a list of over one hundred possible options. It included everything from toy tractors to birdseed. He then narrowed the list, based on several important criteria: the average price per item was over $400, there were more than five manufacturers or suppliers, the product was hard to find in a retail store, *and* the level of competition for the item was low. Based on these criteria, he ended up with those bounce houses.

He built a website and spent a few hundred dollars creating an LLC. Once he had the legal framework in place, as well as his spiffy new domain (BounceHouseStore.com), he began calling around to establish relationships with as many bounce house manufacturers as he could. When he was approved to sell their products, he uploaded the images and descriptions to his site, and then moved on to the next manufacturer.

Rene launched in December and saw few sales until the following April. Was he wrong to choose this market? Not really—he was just early. It turns out that the bounce house business is a seasonal one. Once April arrived, sales picked up, and then hit a peak in June. How much money are we talking about? *A lot of money*.

Before the year ended, Rene had taken in *more than $300,000 in sales*. That's right, $300,000!

His tremendous success inspired him to delve further into the world of drop shipping. As bounce house demand declined when the winter approached again, he decided to start *another* business. This one was also seasonal: an indoor golf outlet. The indoor golf season is the opposite of the outdoor bounce house season, so the two projects work well together.

Remember, Rene wasn't particularly passionate about either of these markets. The choice came down to reasoned analysis. He works in supply chain management by day, so he was good at operations. He didn't care what kind of product he'd sell, he just wanted to be successful selling it.

In short, he followed his bounce to the bank.

FUN FACT Rene's first sale came while traveling for work. He had just installed the Shopify app on his phone so he could monitor his stats. In the middle of a meeting, a loud "cha-ching" sound suddenly chimed from his pocket. He casually pulled out his phone to take a look . . . and saw that he had earned a commission of several hundred dollars.

> "There are many moving pieces when it comes to starting and running a drop-ship business. Selecting a niche is absolutely crucial and can make or break your success. Do your research before starting!" —Rene

HIGH SCHOOL JUNIOR EARNS $10,000 SELLING AUTOGRAPHED BASEBALLS

A Maryland high school student parlays his love of baseball into a lucrative sports memorabilia business.

NAME
TIM HAREN

LOCATION
BALTIMORE, MARYLAND

STARTUP COSTS
MINIMAL

INCOME
$10,000 IN THE FIRST NINETY DAYS

WEBSITE
**INSTAGRAM.COM/
BALTIMOREGRAPHS**

In an era of endlessly available entertainment, the fan base of major-league baseball has diminished. Still, there's a sizable coast-to-coast contingent of enthusiasts who stake out their favorite teams, players, and spots in the stadiums where they long to catch a foul ball.

Most of those fans go home without nabbing a ball, but Tim Haren gives them a chance to get on base: he's happy to sell them a brand-new major-league ball, one signed by their favorite player.

When we first met Tim, he'd only recently finished his junior year of high school, but he already had some serious business savvy. He'd realized that he could cheaply collect autographs and goods from star prospects in the minor leagues, and then sell them at a premium when that player made it in the majors.

A lifelong baseball fan and current college student at the University of Maryland, Tim had been gathering autographs for more than a decade, usually keeping the balls and other items he obtained for his personal collection. But a couple of years ago, he transformed what was an expensive hobby into a self-sustaining side business. He started going to nearby Camden Yards (the practice park of the Baltimore Orioles) as often as possible to build up his collection.

Baltimoregraphs, his memorabilia side hustle, came from this new hobby. He buys major-league-issue balls in bulk for around $12 each, gets them signed at games, and then sells them and other baseball items on eBay. He also sells on a Facebook site called Autographs 101, as well as directly through Instagram. In addition to getting balls signed himself, he buys the signed balls of top prospects on the cheap from other, less savvy collectors, and later rakes in the cash when the players make good in the majors.

"I started off keeping everything I got, but it was an expensive hobby. I realized that these players I was watching as prospects were turning into the games' next stars. Then I switched to buying the young-star prospects for cheap and selling them when they came to the majors." —Tim

FUN FACT Every ball for use in major-league baseball is rubbed in a unique, "very fine" mud found only in a secret location near Palmyra, New Jersey.

Tim regards what he does as akin to a player's stock market. In essence, he's betting on a player's potential, and many of those players' "share prices" have gone over the fences.

In his first few months of business, he made $20,000 in sales. After subtracting his costs for goods and shipping, he was left with $10,000 in profit. A grand-slam home run!

Tim was pleasantly surprised that people would buy his wares, and even more pleased that he could go to games with his dad, get to watch players he'd staked a claim on perform, and expand his collection. And let's not forget: he was also making real money.

Tim advises deep research for anyone interested in playing in the memorabilia big leagues. Get to know the players while they are in the minors, and make sure they play for a big-market team, like the Yankees or the Red Sox. He suggests you buy only in small numbers at first. Then, lower your risk by investing in a variety of players, rather than putting a lot of money behind any one prospect.

He's now working on the next phase of his venture: signing a player to an exclusive memorabilia deal. Even for a prospect, that can cost between $5,000 to $50,000, and has to be done through the player's agent once a big-league team drafts him. With an exclusive deal, players only do autograph signings with the contract holder. They do several signings a year, with up to two thousand signed items each session.

This plan involves more risk, since most prospects never make it to the majors—but it seems that Tim knows what he's doing. Don't bat against him.

CRITICAL FACTOR

Tim's knowledge of baseball allows him to place bets on players who are rising through the minor leagues in hopes of playing in big stadiums. He also sought out other forums where he could buy signed items for less than their market value.

THE LIVE CRICKET
DROP-SHIPPING HUSTLE

A Pennsylvania man sells live crickets to reptile owners, all without ever handling any inventory.

NAME
JEFF NEAL

LOCATION
LANCASTER, PENNSYLVANIA

STARTUP COSTS
$100

INCOME
$700/MONTH

WEBSITE
THECRITTERDEPOT.COM

Jeff Neal works as a project manager for an industrial painting contractor. He sets up estimates for manufacturing facilities, and if the company makes the sale, he sees the project through to completion to make sure all goes well.

He's also a serial hustler. When we were first looking for stories for the podcast, he sent in several. Among other things, Jeff searches for side gigs on Craigslist, and in his first attempt made more than $500. He also has a coupon site, which is interesting and could make for a story of its own. But what interested us the most was a side note he made in the survey form: "By the way, I also sell live crickets to reptile owners. I've been doing this for more than six months and it's going really well."

Needless to say, that caught our attention.

It's probably safe to say that selling live crickets isn't something that most people would ever want to do. But wait! Before we continue, here's a key point: *Jeff does not receive or handle any inventory*. He doesn't have an ice chest full of crickets or a drawer in his refrigerator that he pulls from whenever he receives an order. In fact, he never sees the crickets at all—he's simply a *reseller* for a cricket farm. He takes orders and makes a profit on the markup, but an actual cricket farm does all the shipping.

How did this unusual endeavor come to be?

Jeff knew from his extensive hustling experience, as well as some previous work he'd done for an e-commerce website, to look for a niche that has low competition. Crickets easily fulfill that criteria . . . there just aren't tons of people out there reselling live insects, at least until this book is published and there's a mad rush to compete.

The greater problem was finding the right drop shipper—where a company, usually the original source but sometimes another distributor, will handle the actual shipments. Jeff learned that there were several cricket farms in the United States that offered drop shipping. But because they use FedEx and other private carriers, their shipping rates were so high that it made it very difficult to maintain a decent profit margin.

CRITICAL FACTOR

There's not a lot of competition in the live cricket business . . . or at least there hasn't been until now.

"Between some customer service and emailing my drop shipper, I put in about one to two hours per week and am still able to bring in at least $700 a month—and that's a slow month!" —Jeff

So after some digging, somewhere around page 10 of Google results, he found a small, family-owned business that looked a bit off the beaten path. He gave them a call, and they offered to handle fulfillment at a great price. They also shipped with the post office, which considerably lowered shipping costs.

Doing a trial run with this business was the one and only time he actually took possession of any crickets. It was good that he did, because he learned something important. He had them send a demo shipment, and it *looked* fine. He wondered if it was missing some instructions that he'd thought would be included, and that's when he learned an important lesson: the crickets would eat any paper that was in the box.

Fair enough. He decided to send the instructions in a confirmation email, after his customers placed their orders.

One recent month, he had over $1,200 in revenue on 28 percent profit margins. Unfortunately, the next month saw a big dip in sales, which ended up at $760. He thinks the reason was because many of the reptiles these crickets are fed to are going through reptile hibernation around that time of year.

Fortunately, his website began chirping with orders once the next month rolled around.

FUN FACT Jeff learned about drop shipping while working at an e-commerce site that also sold a living product. He used that experience as a benchmark when building his own creative project.

HAND GRIPPERS MAKE FOR
A $60,000-STRONG HUSTLE

These married fitness enthusiasts are pressing in on the grip-strength market, earning extra cash and peace of mind for their growing family.

NAME
MATT AND KRISTY CANNON

LOCATION
DAYTON, MINNESOTA

STARTUP COSTS
$5,000

INCOME
$65,000/YEAR

WEBSITE
CANNONPOWERWORKS.COM

Husband and wife duo Matt and Kristy Cannon are *literally crushing it* with their niche side hustle. The project consists entirely of selling grip-strength equipment, mostly in the form of hand grippers. These simple tools are used to increase hand strength and usually involve a torsion spring fitted with two handles.

Their muscular business, Cannon Powerworks, originally came about six years ago as a natural extension from the couple's shared passion for fitness.

Stay-at-home mom Kristy is a competitive power lifter. She's been training with heavy weights for over twenty years, and has competed in USA powerlifting meets. She can squat about 245 pounds, bench 150 pounds, and deadlift 300 pounds . . . and she's only getting stronger.

Her husband, Matt, a mortgage underwriter by day, is a competitive grip sport athlete. Yes, it's a real sport! Though grip sport isn't yet widely

known, its popularity is growing. Between 2010 and 2013, Matt competed regularly and held numerous world records in the 145-pound and 163-pound weight classes. He was the first athlete in a competition to close a hand gripper rated above his body weight—meaning that with one hand he crushed a gripper requiring more pounds of pressure than his entire weight.

He got his start in the sport in 2005, when he and Kristy attended a bodybuilding seminar. At the pool one night, a fellow attendee brought out his set of grip strengtheners. Matt gave them a try and was instantly hooked.

As a community began to organize around hand strength, the couple got more and more involved, and eventually spotted an opportunity. When they started, there was just one other company that sold different grip manufacturers' products under one roof, giving customers the chance to order a range with one low shipping fee. That company ended up closing its wholesale store, and Matt and Kristy figured they could fill this gap—and find a way to improve upon the concept.

Their improvement was that they would rate each hand gripper to determine its exact strength. Normally, each hand-gripper manufacturer has its own way of categorizing grippers into strengths. Cannon Powerworks offers a service where they test the grippers for what they call "pounds of pressure to close" so that the grippers can be compared in a reliable way. Customers could either send in their personal grippers to be rated and sent back, or they could buy new, rated grippers online.

When Matt and Kristy's website went live, the sales started rolling in right away. The couple was so stunned at how well things were going that they didn't even stop to celebrate—they just worked harder to fulfill the orders.

The first year, they made a consistent $3,000 per month in profit. By the second year, this had shot up to $5,000 a month. They've maintained that level ever since, and the couple now brings in about $60,000 each year selling their grippers.

FUN FACT   While relatively unknown, competitive grip sports are a growing market. The average healthy man can close a gripper rated at about 90 pounds of pressure, and it's uncommon for someone to close one rated over 120 pounds without specific training. Matt, on the other hand, has closed one rated at 164 pounds.

"Don't put yourself in a position where you'll be losing money before you figure out what you're doing. Frugality is how we had money to buy inventory to begin with." —Matt

Their online store offers sets of two, three, or six grippers—all from different trusted grip brands—that cost from $34 to $64. Their customers usually include rock climbers, powerlifters, CrossFit athletes, and strongman competitors. Most are repeat customers, and new customers usually arrive through word of mouth.

Startup costs were low, and anything they *could* do themselves, they did. They went with the least-expensive website template they could find, did no paid marketing, and bought as little inventory as possible, totaling about $5,000. To photograph products for the online store, Matt watched YouTube videos and learned to make a small light studio out of household supplies such as cardboard boxes, lamps, and paper.

In that first year, they reinvested much of their profits to buy inventory. From that initial outlay of $5,000, they now have more than $25,000 worth of goods on site and ready to ship at any given time.

Selling grippers has helped the Cannons pay off their mortgage and save for the future. They say the business has been a perfect way to feed their own interests while providing flexibility as they raise their three kids. And as it has plateaued in profits, they're now looking to flex their product line and marketing muscles.

Whatever comes next, Matt and Kristy have already proved their status as a power couple.

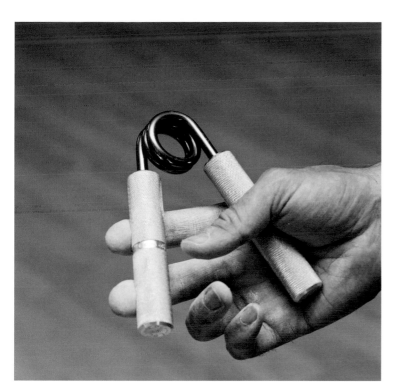

FLIPPING 101: THE COLLEGE TEXTBOOK EDITION

A college student with a family to support reads between the lines and turns a $20 startup into almost $70,000 within two years. This story will flip your lid!

NAME
MARCUS KUSI

LOCATION
CASTLETON, VERMONT

STARTUP COSTS
$20

INCOME
$68,000 IN TWO YEARS

Let's face it—college is downright expensive. And it's not just tuition that produces sticker shock: one of the biggest expenses is textbooks, which typically cost much more than any other books. It can be a real problem for cash-starved students.

The good news is, wherever there's a problem, there's a side hustle just waiting in the wings.

This brings us to Marcus Kusi, who found himself between a rock and a hard place. He was a full-time student at Castleton University in Vermont, heading toward a promising degree in computer information systems, but money was tight. Marcus had recently immigrated to the United States from Ghana in West Africa. When he wasn't cramming for exams, he was working part-time making furniture and providing IT assistance at the university. As if that wasn't enough to keep him busy, he was also a new father.

His wife, Ashley, stayed home with their daughter so that they didn't have to pay for child care, and Marcus was the primary breadwinner, despite also being a full-time student. There *had* to be a better way—and that's when he stumbled upon the wonderful world of reselling. He had read my book *The $100 Startup* and was motivated by stories of everyday people who used small amounts of money to start their own business.

Since he didn't have much money to spare, he took $5 every month for four months and set it aside for his startup costs. Then, with bills piling up, he put on his thinking cap. Unlike some of the people he'd read about in the case studies from my book, Marcus needed money *right away*.

"If you're going to be successful at reselling, you need to (a) make sure that what you're planning on selling is in high demand and (b) know the product like the back of your hand."
—Marcus

Not only was reselling low risk, it was something he could start immediately. The kind of reselling he was interested in was a simple "flip" business, where you buy something at one price and resell it for another—preferably a higher one. Now all he needed was something to flip.

FUN FACT As the textbook reselling project was nearing an end, Marcus was able to use some of the profits to start his next project: a blog, podcast, and set of resources about marriage for newlyweds. He runs this new side hustle together with his wife.

College book prices are a common pain point with university students, and Marcus believed that if you were going to resell something, it helped to find an item that a lot of people were looking for on a regular basis.

If artificial inflation continued to drive the price of textbooks sky high, cheap textbooks were never going to stop being in high demand. And who knows more about textbooks than a college student? It seemed like his best bet, and Marcus was eager to close the chapter on his financial woes.

He began his hunt where many resourceful college students find themselves when it comes time to buy books for class—eBay. With his $20 in startup capital, he purchased two books, relisted them for sale, and sold them right away for around $70. It seemed to be working, but was it sustainable?

Instead of pocketing that initial profit, he reinvested it in more books and created an Amazon seller account. In his experience, eBay was fine for occasional transactions, but your rate of return is mostly driven by the consumer. On Amazon, you can set your own price and have full control of profit margins. And since Marcus needed to get paid on a regular basis, he needed to expand.

Within his first year, Marcus pulled in $20,000. In year two, those profits climbed above $48,000—almost $70,000 in total! Over the course of those two years, he flipped more than five thousand college textbooks. And it all started with $20 saved in $5 increments across four months.

How did Marcus manage to score books so cheaply, and how did he know which books would sell?

First, he realized that many students *didn't actually know the value of their books*. They'd buy their books from the bookstore only to find that either the bookstore wasn't planning on selling them next term or that the bookstore would only buy them back for a small fraction of their selling price.

ACTION PLAN

1. A reselling project is all about buying something at one price, then selling it at a higher price.
2. Identify items that you might be able to resell. In this story, textbooks were perfect: it was a renewing market with lots of buyers and sellers, and Marcus was a student—therefore all too familiar with their high prices.
3. Begin experimenting by buying a few items at a time, listing them for resale, and paying attention to what works and what doesn't. (For best results, do more of what works.)
4. Increase your average selling price by providing impeccable service. This will generate positive reviews, which in turn creates trust from buyers.

What's a broke student to do with this excess of seemingly worthless books? Sell them on eBay! And that's where Marcus came in. He found that students are often desperate and motivated to get rid of their books, the sooner the better.

With that in mind, Marcus learned to reach out to sellers directly whenever he noticed a book he wanted to buy. He'd make a cash offer for immediate transfer. The impatience of youth often worked in his favor, and he'd use this technique early in the bidding when the bids were low, which made his offer look more desirable in comparison.

As for knowing which books would sell, it's not magic—it just involves keeping an eye on Amazon's sales ranking system.

When Marcus found something promising on eBay, he'd head straight to Amazon to see where that title landed on their ranking system. This was an easy way for him to determine whether it was in high demand and, therefore, if it was a worthwhile investment. With enough monitoring, he learned that if a book had a sales rank of 75,000 or lower, it was being purchased consistently. Those were the titles he'd then try to snap up and resell.

The side hustle proved to be a much needed lifeline for him and his family. It provided them with a way to pay their bills and save up an emergency fund. When the washer or heater broke, it didn't end up being the end of the world.

All things come to an end, even books, and the textbook flipping side hustle was no different. When Marcus graduated and started working as an IT business analyst, he stopped reselling textbooks and started thinking about a new project.

This chapter may have concluded, but the next is just beginning.

Where to Find Items to Resell

Reselling is probably the easiest side hustle to start. Even if you've never done it before, you can be up and running within a week.

Your basic goal as a reseller is simple: *buy low, sell high*. Or at least, sell at a price higher than you pay, and one that compensates you for your time and any other costs. So where do you find items to resell?

First, start with what you already own. Do you have comic books in the attic or old clothes in the back of the closet? Take an inventory, and then get paid for getting them out of your house.

Second, start thrifting. Go around to yard sales, garage sales, or flea markets. Bring your phone so you can discreetly look up average sales prices for anything you find. When you find a potential discrepancy (something you can buy for less than you think you can sell it for), snap it up.

Those actions will get you comfortable with the basics of selling online. To take it up a level like some of the people in this book have done, you'll need a more consistent source of products. It usually helps to specialize in something, and it's best if you specialize in something that isn't cheap—camera gear or luxury clothing, for example.

You may also want to look at a source like Alibaba. For more on that, see the Side Hustle Labs feature on page 301, or check out the notes at the site below.

For more, visit SideHustleSchool.com/resell.

Teach What You Know

Your knowledge is valuable: take what

you've learned and share it with others.

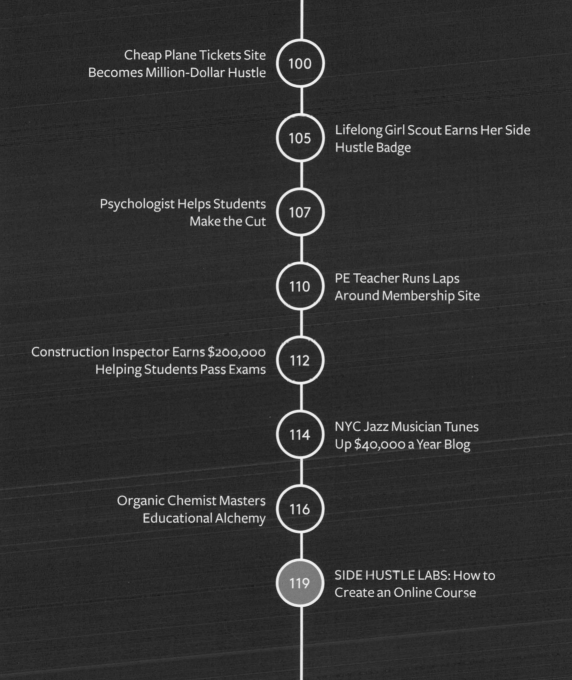

Cheap Plane Tickets Site
Becomes Million-Dollar Hustle

100

105

Lifelong Girl Scout Earns Her Side
Hustle Badge

Psychologist Helps Students
Make the Cut

107

110

PE Teacher Runs Laps
Around Membership Site

Construction Inspector Earns $200,000
Helping Students Pass Exams

112

114

NYC Jazz Musician Tunes
Up $40,000 a Year Blog

Organic Chemist Masters
Educational Alchemy

116

119

SIDE HUSTLE LABS: How to
Create an Online Course

CHEAP PLANE TICKETS SITE BECOMES MILLION-DOLLAR HUSTLE

A political analyst uses his travel skills to help travelers save money, attracting more than 275,000 email subscribers along the way.

NAME
SCOTT KEYES

LOCATION
PORTLAND, OREGON

STARTUP COSTS
$350

INCOME
SEVEN FIGURES/YEAR

WEBSITE
SCOTTSCHEAPFLIGHTS.COM

For many years, Scott Keyes worked as a political journalist in Washington, DC. He wrote about topics ranging from voting rights to homelessness, but most of all, he covered political campaigns.

The job required a lot of travel to political events around the country. Scott realized from the beginning that frequent flyer miles would be a perk of the job, so he set about figuring out how to generate as many as possible and get the most value he could from them. He studied up on the basics of mileage runs and earning points from credit cards, and soon he became a frequent flyer miles evangelist.

Before long, he realized that this compendium of information he'd collected about frequent flyer miles might be useful to others. As he puts it, many frequent flyer programs are purposefully opaque, because the airlines know that any unused mile or point is a savings to them.

Scott decided to start with combining his day job of writing with his side hobby of travel. He wrote a brief, explanatory e-book on how to generate and use frequent flyer miles. The book wasn't a best seller—it sold enough copies to buy a couple of beers a week, but that was about it.

Despite the book's meager sales, he enjoyed the process of research and writing about flight deals. Two years later, Scott was living what he calls "a terrible journalist life in Oaxaca, Mexico," where he freelanced for publishers back in the States.

ACTION PLAN

1. Select an attractive topic (cheap plane tickets!) that is potentially valuable, yet also misunderstood by a lot of people.

2. Set up a free or low-cost email list.

3. Invite everyone you know to join, and encourage them to spread the word.

4. Focus on finding and delivering great deals or other special information.

5. Introduce a paid membership option that provides additional, premium content.

6. Continue to research and publish deals every day.

FUN FACT One memorable deal featured a mistake fare that offered round-trip flights from the United States to New Zealand for just $390. Thousands of people jumped on it, and Scott's favorite story came from a couple in Seattle. They had deferred their honeymoon for years, not having much disposable income, but they took advantage of this offer to spend eight days in New Zealand.

> "Just because someone else has a business similar to your idea doesn't mean you shouldn't do it. You might be able to do the idea better, improve the customer experience, or just reach some of the 99.9 percent of customers who haven't heard of your competitor." —Scott

In the midst of all this travel writing, he'd developed a reputation among his friends and colleagues as a travel expert. This reputation was bolstered when he bought a nonstop, round-trip ticket from New York City to Milan for just $130. When he got back, dozens of friends asked him to let them know the next time he saw a fare like that so they could jump on it.

Rather than try to remember each individual person he was supposed to notify, he decided to make a simple email list and just let everyone know at once. He called it Scott's Cheap Flights.

Over the next eighteen months, that email list grew by word of mouth from a couple dozen friends to three hundred people, but it was still just a hobby. Everything changed when he posted a map on Facebook showing off the two-month trip he was about to take with his girlfriend. This trip consisted of thirteen countries, twenty-one flights, and twenty thousand miles—all for free using miles.

As luck would have it, a friend forwarded the map to a friend of hers at *Business Insider*, who thought it would make for an interesting article. The piece got a click-worthy headline—"This guy has gamed the airline industry so he never has to pay for a flight again"—and ended up going viral.

As a result, his sleepy email list for friends grew overnight from three hundred subscribers to more than five thousand.

This explosive growth was both a blessing and a curse. With so many subscribers, Scott would have to pay his email service for hosting costs. He enjoyed sending great deals to his friends, but he didn't really want to pay out of pocket to do so for *thousands of strangers*.

During that two-month trip, he thought about how best to monetize the opportunity. Should he put ads in the newsletters, or get paid for referrals to travel agencies?

He finally settled on a "freemium" model, where subscribers can join the basic list for free, but there's also a premium version with extra perks for those who pay a monthly fee.

This small newsletter continued to experience massive growth. Over the next two years, it grew to more than 275,000 subscribers.

The last time we spoke, Scott had 29,639 premium subscribers and 204,021 free subscribers (233,660 total). Thanks to a Black Friday promotion, he had generated $963,234 in sales that year, all from those premium members. The numbers are now substantially higher.

What's next? Well, he's still obsessed—in his words, he plans to "continue to scour for cheap flights like a hungry dog, improve the features and customer experience at Scott's Cheap Flights, and keep traveling the world."

These days, he can buy more than just a couple of beers with his profits.

CRITICAL FACTOR

Scott selected a topic that has widespread interest, and chose an extremely simple name ("Cheap Flights") for the project. He then focused on doing only one thing—delivering emails with flight deals—over and over.

LIFELONG GIRL SCOUT EARNS HER SIDE HUSTLE BADGE

After spending twenty-plus years as a Girl Scout and volunteer, a woman creates a series of resources for troop leaders. Selling at just $3 to $5 each, she earns up to $3,000 per month.

The Girl Scouts had been a big part of Jodi Carlson's life for over twenty-five years. For twelve of those years, she'd been a scout, and for the rest of the time she served as a troop leader. But when her son was born, Jodi decided it was time to step down from the position and focus the time on her young family.

Although she loved the challenge of her new home life, she missed the volunteering and organizing she'd devoted so many years to. She knew she couldn't commit herself to a schedule with lots of fixed appointments, like she'd have to do as a troop leader, but she still wanted a meaningful way to contribute to the scout community and inspire these young visionaries.

Her local troop was based in a small city in Ohio, located along the banks of Lake Erie. The year before her son was born, Jodi had created a website to share what the troop had been doing and to offer advice to other leaders around the country. She'd also written a short e-book that she offered for sale for $5—just hoping to cover the gas her car used to get to the meetings—and was surprised that after six months, people from the other side of the country were still buying it. She felt that if she could expand her product line, this site would be the perfect way to help the community *and* make some money to put toward her student loans. She called her upgraded project Leader Connecting Leaders.

Startup costs were a grand total of $16 for a domain name. Jodi was already paying for Adobe software for her day job as a designer, and she had access to a free hosting service. She was ready to go in just a few minutes.

Her first step to growth was to discover where the current traffic to her site was coming from, and how she could increase it. She added Google Analytics to her site and discovered that most of her visits came through Pinterest, from a few images she'd posted long ago.

This played right into her hands as a designer. Jodi created a new image for each of her articles and shared them on Pinterest. The few minutes she spent on this task allowed her to generate traffic for months after the article was initially shared.

NAME
JODI CARLSON

LOCATION
CONNEAUT, OHIO

STARTUP COSTS
$16

INCOME
$2,800/MONTH

WEBSITE
LEADERCONNECTINGLEADERS.COM

FUN FACT Jodi's mom was her troop leader for a long time, and the family converted their entire basement into the troop headquarters. They even decorated the house like the woods, using tree stumps for chairs.

> "I've tried many different things that have completely failed, but if I hadn't tried, I would have never known." —Jodi

She's also used the power of social media to market the business in other ways. By running competitions, hosting giveaways, and writing shareable articles, Jodi has been able to generate a lot of traffic through Facebook. These results gave her the confidence to try running ads for her products, but this strategy was met with more limited success.

Most of the information on the site is freely available. Visitors can download long-form articles, tutorials, and how-to guides that provide most of the information they need to run a successful and harmonious Girl Scout troop.* But Jodi puts a small price of between $3 to $5 on some of the more specific resources—activity booklets, printouts, and games—to help leaders solve specific problems in just a few clicks, and with a quick download from her site.

From these low-priced resources, Jodi is able to generate profits of $3,000 to $3,500 per month.

Two parts to her business have helped her the most: automation and an engaged mailing list. She spends four hours a month using tools to create and schedule social media updates that will go live even when she's not at the computer. She also sends multiple emails each month, providing extra information to her most loyal readers, letting them know about new articles, ideas, and products. Building this trust, she says, has been integral to her success.

The secret to profiting from a project with such low prices for each item is understanding the average scout leader's challenges. After twenty-five years in the Girl Scouts, she's been there and experienced them all. Creating products that would have solved her problems long ago, along with writing the copy in an empathetic way that connects with the struggles of other leaders, has allowed her to grow her business without needing to be pushy.

The best part of this success has been getting feedback from the leaders she's been able to help. Nothing gives her more motivation on the days she doesn't want to work than receiving a message explaining how her activity booklets have transformed meetings and excursions for the better. This is especially true when they come from towns and cities she's never heard of!

Jodi is now toying with the idea of starting a new side hustle to run alongside her current one. Whatever she does next, she plans to continue making useful products for Girl Scout leaders far and wide.

* Jodi notes that her project is not affiliated with or endorsed by the parent organization that oversees the Girl Scouts. She even pays full price for the cookies!

CRITICAL FACTOR

No one knew the needs of Girl Scout troop leaders as well as Jodi. By providing many free resources, she was able to build trust with other leaders around the country. They then looked to her for help with specific problems, gladly spending small amounts of money that added up to real dollars for Jodi.

PSYCHOLOGIST HELPS
STUDENTS MAKE THE CUT

After overcoming childhood barriers, this psychologist leveraged his educational success to help students gain entry to top schools.

Growing up, Shirag Shemmassian did not have it easy. Around the age of eight, he started exhibiting the symptoms of Tourette syndrome. Perhaps not surprisingly, he was mocked by his peers. The teasing, however, was not as tough for him as the lack of understanding and acceptance he experienced from his own Armenian immigrant family.

Shirag remembers one family dinner in particular where his dad wouldn't stop staring at him. Finally, his dad warned that if he didn't quit "this habit" of his, people would think he was stupid. "How will that reflect on our family?" he added.

Shirag stormed off, and these kinds of hurtful interactions went on for about a year until he was finally diagnosed.

Though at the time he didn't fully understand the effects the condition would have on his life, he sensed it would significantly impact him. And it did. During high school and college, Shirag's interest in mental health and psychology blossomed. He began to realize that he could translate his personal experiences with the disorder to help others.

Despite the early challenges, he went on to a high level of achievement. He studied human development at Cornell and attained a PhD in clinical psychology from UCLA. He was also able to graduate from both schools completely debt free. He now works as a clinical research psychologist, developing tests used to assess children for mental health conditions.

Based on this experience, his side hustle developed organically. While he was in school, his friends noticed his stellar track record of getting accepted and receiving funding from top schools. They began to ask for help with their own applications. He obliged, assisting them free of charge.

FUN FACT When Shirag learned that his wife was pregnant with their first child, he went on a mission to structure his business to rely less on him personally. After the birth, they spent five days in the hospital, and he was able to run the business by spending only a total of one hour on his phone each of those days.

NAME
SHIRAG SHEMMASSIAN

LOCATION
SAN DIEGO, CALIFORNIA

STARTUP COSTS
$3,200

INCOME
$74,000 IN YEAR THREE

WEBSITE
SHEMMASSIANCONSULTING.COM

"People look at mature businesses and don't realize that it took years to grow to their current states. It's like staring at a mountain and thinking you have to take a single leap to the top when you actually have to take one small step at a time. Eventually, you'll make it to the top." —Shirag

When those friends gained admittance to their dream schools, they started telling others, who also requested his services. As more and more people began knocking at his door, Shirag eventually decided to make the project official, launching Shemmassian Academic Consulting.

Though he knew very little about running a business, he didn't let that stop him. He dove straight into reading books and online articles about everything from business structure to sales and workflow. Between the training courses, books, and domain name registration, his startup costs totaled about $3,200.

He kept expenses low wherever he could, using a free Squarespace website and a free Mailchimp account. Even now, with a profitable business, his ongoing yearly costs are less than $2,500.

During the first full year, the company earned just over $1,200, and in the second year this jumped to $12,000. In the third year, the company's earnings surged to $74,000.

Admissions consulting is a competitive arena, but Shirag has managed to stay ahead of the game by speaking for free at high schools and colleges.

Available services, which include both advising and application support to prospective college students and graduate and medical school students, can cost his customers anywhere from $300 to $7,000.

The extra income has allowed Shirag and his wife to worry less about buying fancy coffee or staying in nicer hotels when they travel. It's also given him peace of mind that if he ever loses his full-time job, he could still support his family through the business.

He currently invests at least twenty hours a week into the project, providing consulting and completing various administrative tasks. Though he admits he could probably spend less time on it, he's always seeking ways to grow the business and reach more students. He's brought on two consultants to help, and will soon add a third. He says his goal is to never turn away a student who wants support.

So far, Shirag and his team have supported more than two hundred students through one-on-one support and online courses. Their track record is impressive. For college, 90 percent of students have gotten into at least one of their top three choices, and for med school, over 90 percent have gotten into at least one US school.

While the students are acing their exams, Shirag is earning extra credit from his second income.

CRITICAL FACTOR

Mastering the admissions game is a skill that requires strategic thinking and action. Shirag has proven success in helping people gain admission to top schools, both for himself and for others.

PE TEACHER RUNS LAPS AROUND MEMBERSHIP SITE

A teacher starts a blog to serve other teachers. After selling a series of individual products, he switches over to a membership model.

NAME
BEN LANDERS

LOCATION
COLUMBIA, SOUTH CAROLINA

STARTUP COSTS
LESS THAN $500

INCOME
$45,000/YEAR

WEBSITE
THEPESPECIALIST.COM

Ben Landers is a physical education (PE) teacher in Columbia, South Carolina. With two master's degrees, including one in educational leadership, Ben is both highly qualified and passionate about his job.

There's a lot more to being a good PE teacher than just playing sports. He says that teaching students the right lessons empowers them to be stronger, healthier, and more confident. It also helps them make better decisions.

A few years ago, Ben started thinking about how he could help more students. He wanted go beyond his own school and even his school district, so he started a resource blog for teachers. It began as a way for him to reflect, answer common questions, and provide materials to help teachers out.

He originally thought he would try to sell reports and online courses to make it sustainable, but he reworked that plan as he went along.

Side hustle success often comes by drawing from a couple of different skills and combining them in some way. In addition to his passion for education, Ben has been a part-time videographer off and on since he was in college. Since he already had some equipment and was comfortable using video, his startup costs consisted mostly of buying a domain, getting website hosting, and setting up an email newsletter service.

The first year he focused on writing and creating other content to get his name out as an authority among PE teachers. He also learned how to write and publish digital products. Even though his primary focus that year was growing the blog, he still made enough from his first report sales to pay for the costs of the site and break even.

FUN FACT One of Ben's free resources, "The Conflict Corner," became unexpectedly popular. It was about using a management system to teach kids to resolve their own conflicts instead of always complaining about them to the teacher. Some schools have even adopted it as a school-wide initiative.

"Try to go for a hustle that's a win even if you lose. I'm glad the PE site is profitable, but it's also great to help other teachers." —Ben

When he got his first sale notification, he was on the treadmill at the gym. He immediately took a screenshot on his phone and texted it to his wife. Ben had put hundreds of hours into that $27 sale, but he felt like he had finally begun to unlock the power of the internet.

Next, he made a big change that allowed him to earn a lot more than just $27. He realized that in the long-term, selling one-off reports for a low price was not a great revenue model. He made a shift and decided to create a membership site, where teachers would pay annually for access to resources.

Immediately upon making that shift, he also started to make an actual profit from the business. He began with a "beta" launch and offered it to early users for $97 a year. Then, once he got a few kinks worked out, he launched the official membership at $149 a year.

He currently has around four hundred members, which are now his main source of income for the project. He also makes money from the guides that he still sells at a lower price. Altogether, in year two he made about $11,000 from this project. In year three, he made $45,000—a fourfold increase.

Earning so much money on the side is great by itself, but it also led to another huge benefit for his family. Because of the new program, Ben's wife was able to leave her job to come home and raise their young daughter.

That change wasn't possible on his teacher's salary alone, but the extra income gave them the boost they needed to feel more confident. Also, his wife got inspired along the way—she's now working her own side hustle, providing day care for their friends' children.

 CRITICAL FACTOR

Ben is both highly qualified and passionate about his topic. Business-wise, making the switch from selling reports to a monthly membership model brought him more predictable income.

CONSTRUCTION INSPECTOR EARNS $200,000 HELPING STUDENTS PASS EXAMS

A teacher turned construction inspector aces his exams and creates a series of courses to help others entering the field.

NAME
GABRIEL KRAMER

LOCATION
SALT LAKE CITY, UTAH

STARTUP COSTS
$2,200

INCOME
$200,000/YEAR

WEBSITE
SICERTS.COM

Gabriel Kramer's side hustle story began after a big career transition. A former high school teacher who had burned out due to the lack of support from administrators—an all too common story—Gabe had started a new job as a construction inspector. He'd heard about this opportunity from a cousin, who helped him get a job as an entry-level inspector.

To advance in the industry, you have to earn certifications by passing exams. The more certifications you have, the more money you can make. From his background in education, including a master's degree he completed independently, Gabe had good study habits. In his first year, he studied for and passed several exams. Even beginning in the entry-level role, that year he made more than he did as a teacher.

Over the next few years he continued to gain experience, take more exams, and increase his earning potential further.

This brings us to his next step, and the side hustle that would eventually exceed the earnings from both jobs. In this industry, *SI* stands for "special inspector," a certain kind of construction inspector, and *certs* is short for "certifications." Gabe's hustle would be called, appropriately, SI Certs.

To get SI Certs up and running, he offered equity to two friends, Dee and Chris. Dee worked as an internet marketer, while Chris was an experienced Photoshop hobbyist. Finally, he got Dee's brother, Allan, to build the site. He says that having these three partners on board from the start was a huge help, because it meant he could focus on his core skill of course creation.

One of the main skills of inspectors is reading building plans. To help his students learn, Gabe shipped physical plans to them that complemented the online teaching. He even added his best teaching notes right on the plans. This teaching aid was unique to the industry. There were a few other people teaching cert study courses, but no one else was sending out physical plans.

"Add value where your competitors are lacking. If you do this in different ways, you'll have a greater chance of success." —Gabe

Video marketing was another strategy that was little used by anyone else. Therefore, after he created the first course, Gabe shot videos that covered material from the first exam entry-level employees are required to take. He uploaded the videos to YouTube, and the SI Certs channel has produced a steady stream of traffic over the years. It recently reached three hundred thousand total views.

SI Certs was a success from the start. Every year since beginning, Gabe and the partners have averaged at least 60 percent revenue growth. Four years in, they passed six figures in revenue. A big part of this success was because Gabe continued to create more courses, usually around one each year. Many of his students have become repeat customers, and the business continues to benefit from organic search results, as well as all those people who come from YouTube.

Gabe still works 9 to 5 in the construction industry, having switched roles a couple of years ago to take on a marketing director position. He enjoys the job and isn't thinking about working on SI Certs full-time, but he still invests a few hours each week to continue growing it.

The business is on track to pass $200,000 in annual revenue, and growth doesn't seem to be slowing down. Brick by brick, he's building on a sturdy foundation.

CRITICAL FACTOR

Passing tests leads to higher income, so students are highly incentivized to study and succeed. Gabe's proven courses can be a no-brainer investment for construction inspectors who want to get ahead.

FUN FACT   In addition to individual courses, SI Certs offers several "bundled" options where customers can receive a discount for purchasing multiple courses. This strategy is highly effective in increasing sales.

NYC JAZZ MUSICIAN TUNES UP
$40,000 A YEAR BLOG

A musician finds financial freedom by growing an online community focused on teaching people how to play jazz.

NAME
BRENT VAARTSTRA

LOCATION
NEW YORK, NEW YORK

STARTUP COSTS
MINIMAL

INCOME
$40,000/YEAR

WEBSITE
LEARNJAZZSTANDARDS.COM

Brent Vaartstra worked as a jazz musician, playing gigs around New York City. Like many musicians do, especially in expensive cities, he also had a number of other projects to make ends meet.

But over the past two years, his day job has become what had been his main side hustle—a website and podcast called *Learn Jazz Standards*. It helps musicians get tips, advice, and resources for learning and playing jazz, and it makes money from selling e-books, play-along tracks, and an online course.

The website was the idea of a friend of his named Camden. Camden had started with a basic, quickly thrown-together template, and worked on it for a few months before becoming too busy to continue.

Camden still liked the idea of providing musicians with online resources, and wanted to continue somehow. He thought of Brent because he was then in college studying for a bachelor's degree in jazz performance and

CRITICAL FACTOR

As Brent began creating products and focusing more attention on the blog, it blossomed from something that provided pocket money to a real asset paying thousands of dollars each month.

"The financial freedom has been amazing. It's taken me from being a struggling musician to feeling secure. No more worrying if I'll get enough gigs next month or not! Yet I still get to be doing what I love, talking about and working on jazz and music." —Brent

needed some extra income. Camden offered to pay Brent out of the ad money the site was making to continue putting up educational posts.

It wasn't a jackpot, but it gave Brent some pocket money while he was in school. He eventually became more invested in the site, accepting a fifty/fifty partnership to take over operations. Camden and Brent were now making more ad money, and they'd started selling play-along tracks for people to practice with.

The extra $500 to $600 a month he earned was important to Brent as a struggling musician. He began to think of ways to increase the site's revenue even further. As part of a transition, he eventually bought Camden's half of the business. Camden's other career commitments were too demanding for him to contribute, and *Learn Jazz Standards* had become Brent's primary focus.

It was fun having a friend to collaborate with, but the change opened up more doors for him. He started releasing e-books and planned to produce a full course. With increased attention and the added income that came from working solo, his monthly income soared to a livable wage. He then redesigned the site and outlined an ambitious plan for growth.

The best part is seeing how the years of hard work have finally paid off. After several months of work, he launched that first e-course, and in the launch month alone he made $10,000. He was amazed that so many people would sign up simply because they trusted the website. For Brent, it was truly gratifying.

He also says that the financial freedom has been incredible. It's taken him from a struggling musician to feeling secure. There's no more worrying if he'll get enough gigs next month to pay his rent. Yet he still gets to do what he loves, talking about and working on music . . . just with the security of having most of his bills taken care of.

FUN FACT Unlike almost every other story in this book, Brent didn't actually start this side hustle—he acquired it from someone else.

ORGANIC CHEMIST MASTERS EDUCATIONAL ALCHEMY

After hitting a number of career dead ends during a recession, a chemist charts a new course offering online tutoring.

NAME
JAMES ASHENHURST

LOCATION
NASHVILLE, TENNESSEE

STARTUP COSTS
MINIMAL

INCOME
SIX FIGURES/YEAR

WEBSITE
MASTERORGANICCHEMISTRY.COM

After earning an undergraduate degree in chemistry, James Ashenhurst spent a short spell in graduate school . . . but it wasn't meant to be, at least not at first. The best part was getting to go on a six-month study abroad trip to the Middle East.

When he got back home, he started applying for jobs, but nothing came of it. Frustrated with his situation, he moved to Montreal to spend the summer. With no friends or work, he was free to wander about, and he paid attention to how he liked to spend his time. It turned out he spent a lot of time going to the library and doing the problems in organic chemistry textbooks.

It occurred to him that he should spend some time developing this skill. He enjoyed it and was good at it. Furthermore, it was a potentially lucrative career. He joined a lab at the local university, ended up earning a PhD in organic chemistry, and then did a postdoc at MIT.

At this point in the story, our organic chemist was on track to get a position in industry or academia, but then the 2008 economic recession arrived. His job applications went nowhere. He did another postdoc, moved to Israel for a while, and tried starting a business that also went nowhere.

Once again, he spent a lot of time in the local library working through problems in notebooks. That's when he came up with the idea of tutoring organic chemistry online. At the time, almost no one was doing such a thing.

Several people close to him were skeptical. They asked, "Who would ever want to be tutored online?"

James ignored them. Over the next few years, he earned a good living doing online tutoring—but that's not really what this story is about. The online tutoring was still a lot like a day job, even though he worked for himself.

In his spare hours, he worked on a related project: a free WordPress blog on organic chemistry. He wrote articles and then used the articles to get

CRITICAL FACTOR

Medical students in need of help passing their chemistry courses are a recurring market. Every year, tens of thousands of them enter new programs—and most of James's material remains relevant over time.

search traffic. Over time, this project would become increasingly important.

Two things happened next. First, as he built up the repository of articles and posts, the blog got enough traffic that requests for tutoring came streaming in without him having to seek people out. That was a major accomplishment of its own.

But then, something else happened that ended up being even better. After talking to enough students through thousands of hours of sessions, James had a firm grasp on their common struggles. He also knew that there weren't many solutions for them outside of personalized tutoring.

That's when he started creating digital products in the form of detailed guides and reports. Anyone could buy them and study on their own. They'd pay less than they would for an individual session, and James could get paid without being physically present.

To start, his students told him they had a hard time keeping all the "reagents" straight in organic chemistry—so the first product was an e-book called *The Reagent Guide*.* It was a basic PDF, nothing complicated, and he did little marketing for it. He only had one hundred people on his email list at the time, but when he wrote to offer them the guide, ten of them bought it.

That opened his eyes, and he began making more study guides for other common problems that students experienced. To do this, first he'd make sure he fully understood the problems. Then he'd create solutions for them and put them in guides available for purchase on his website. He built out his library of products slowly—let's say *organically*— and month by month, more and more people bought the guides.

James now has two young kids at home, and once the youngest arrived, he began renting a small office at a coworking space so he could focus during the day. He talks about being surprised by two things.

FUN FACT James first created the site with North American students in mind, but has been surprised to see how many visitors are international. About one-third of them are from India, for example, and he even had a group of readers from McMurdo Station in Antarctica.

* From James: Think of reagents like "ingredients" in a kitchen. Students kept forgetting when to use oregano, when to add the basil, whether the recipe called for garlic, and so on.

> "One of the most important decisions I ever made was to take two to three months and move to a new city, live like a hermit, and see what I would do to entertain myself. That was very useful experimental data." —James

First, *the fact that he can make a living writing*. His college double major in English and chemistry worked out. He gets to think and write about a subject he loves, and he doesn't have to answer to anyone except his readers. (He also says that he's always hated committees, so avoiding them completely is a huge plus.)

Second, *the reports he receives from his students and readers*. Many of them tell him that they wouldn't have passed the course or have gotten an A if it were not for his website. He also hears from former students who are now in medical school.

Meanwhile, the website continues to grow. It was recently ranked as the tenth most visited chemistry website in the world, with 1.2 million monthly page views. It provides a healthy six-figure source of income—and, yes, much of that income arrives while he sleeps.

Looking back, James is grateful for the forks in the road that led him to where he is now. He's glad he wasn't able to get a job at first, because his extended time of exploration provided the foundation for everything that came afterward. He's also glad he began online tutoring during a time when such things were very new.

He's especially glad he didn't listen to those people who said "that won't work." Finally, he's proud that he decided to try a new form of monetization by creating study guides for his students.

Sometimes your strangest experiments lead to your greatest discoveries.

How to Create an Online Course

Sharing your knowledge can be one of the most powerful and profitable models for making money on the side. How do you do it?

First, you need the right topic. Choose something specific, and focus on benefits. It doesn't matter if your course has forty-eight different modules and a voice-controlled system that will give you daily affirmations. It matters if it will make your customer a better person, solve a big problem for them, or otherwise improve their life. Craft everything around these needs!

Next, you need the right platform. How will you deliver your course material to customers? There are a lot of options for this, both simple and not-so-simple. I include some of our current recommendations at the site below.

Last—but definitely not least—you need to spend time and energy on understanding your ideal customer, and knowing how to communicate with them. This is the essence of successful marketing: building relationships, making promises, and keeping them.

For more, visit SideHustleSchool.com/courses.

VI

Bring People Together

Have a knack for producing events or experiences? Use the power of community to connect people while getting paid.

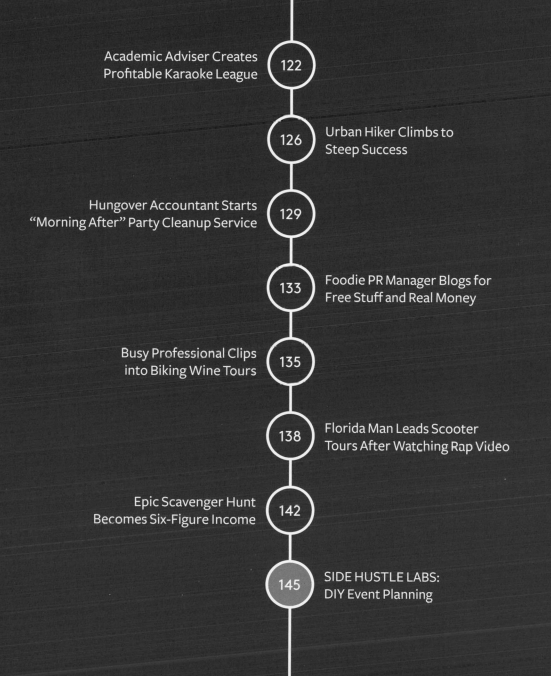

Academic Adviser Creates
Profitable Karaoke League

122

126

Urban Hiker Climbs to
Steep Success

Hungover Accountant Starts
"Morning After" Party Cleanup Service

129

133

Foodie PR Manager Blogs for
Free Stuff and Real Money

Busy Professional Clips
into Biking Wine Tours

135

138

Florida Man Leads Scooter
Tours After Watching Rap Video

Epic Scavenger Hunt
Becomes Six-Figure Income

142

145

SIDE HUSTLE LABS:
DIY Event Planning

ACADEMIC ADVISER CREATES PROFITABLE KARAOKE LEAGUE

A Washington, DC, man uses his entrepreneurial skills and vocal chords to turn a profit while cultivating a community.

NAME
JESSE RAUCH

LOCATION
WASHINGTON, DC

STARTUP COSTS
$20,000

INCOME
$45,000/YEAR

WEBSITE
DISTRICTKARAOKE.COM

About five years ago, Jesse Rauch was living in Washington, DC, and working as an academic adviser. In his free time, he competed in a weekly kickball league, where he says he had a "eureka" moment.

It happened while he was out one night after a game, having a few drinks at a karaoke bar. As he was sipping vodka and belting out "Sweet Caroline," he suddenly had an idea: Why not take the design of a social, competitive league, and apply it to karaoke?

He shared his epiphany with a friend and ruminated on it a bit in between songs. But he says it only sank in that the idea had potential when he woke up the next day—less influenced by the vodka—and *still* thought it was a good idea.

In his day job at a local community college, Jesse says that even though his students challenged him, he hadn't felt he was flexing his creative muscles. He wanted to make something of his own. And what could be more fun than competitive sing-alongs?

Jesse set to work on launching District Karaoke. Its design was similar to a sports setup, where teams of up to eight people would sign up to compete against each other in one-on-one and group karaoke matchups. Then everyone in the bar, regardless of whether they were involved in the singing or not, could vote on the winners using a web-based app.

When he opened registration, Jesse was able to fill all forty-eight available spots for the league in just six days. He officially kicked off the business the following month, using his thirtieth birthday as motivation. In addition to his friends, his new customers came to the party, which helped build early momentum.

FUN FACT The friendly competition of Jesse's karaoke league can inspire some notable performances. One night, a performer pole-danced on an elected official who was serving as a judge at the City-Wide Finals. Another night, a performer sang a song by Sia in the style of the Swedish chef from the Muppets, staying in character the entire song.

District Karaoke now runs three ten-week "seasons" every year, including playoffs and finals, with each division made up of six teams. They consistently fill almost all available spots, which have grown to two hundred per season.

Jesse's initial startup costs were low, as he used outside karaoke DJs that were paid for by the bars. But he soon realized he wanted a bit more control over the league in order to grow it. He invested about $20,000 to license the music, purchase equipment, and build the voting technology. The investment quickly paid off, since the business has been profitable since the first season.

In an average year, District Karaoke brings in $90,000 in revenue and makes about $45,000 in profit. The business makes this money from individual registration fees, payments from the host bars, and sponsorships.

To get the word out, Jesse relies on the performers themselves as his salespeople. Through their efforts, District Karaoke was able to expand from one to four nights per week.

To save money, he avoided developing a native app for phones—which is not only pricey and time consuming but also requires agreements with the Apple Store and Android Market—and instead built a simple, web-based voting site that would work on all smartphones.

However, while he did save money, he had to make up for it with his time. At the outset, Jesse poured thirty to forty hours each week into District Karaoke, all on top of his day job. He was young and motivated, and wanted to build on his idea. Now, after bringing people on to manage daily operations, he only has to devote ten hours or less each week.

In addition to part-time staff, Jesse engaged league members to help on a volunteer basis through a community board. His goal in recruiting helpers wasn't just to lighten his load. Instead, it was part of the ethos behind his vision. He wanted members to feel more invested in the league and to build a strong sense of community.

His hypothesis was that people are always looking for other people who share their interests, as a way to find friends and build professional networks. And if someone can creatively do this connecting and curate a positive experience, people will pay for it. This sense of community also has the benefit of keeping people engaged and returning, thereby ensuring a loyal customer base.

District Karaoke has now expanded to Baltimore, Chicago, New York City, and Los Angeles. Its members have sung exactly 10,236 songs, with the 50 most popular songs sung more than 1,200 times in competitions . . . including popular favorites "I Will Survive" and "Don't Stop Believing."

For Jesse, this side hustle has produced several positive changes. He's been able to switch day jobs, a move he credits to the new skills he gained through running District Karaoke. He's been able to save money for vacations. Best of all, he's been able to find true love. That's right: this side hustle came with some major secondary benefits!

One night while hosting a District Karaoke happy hour, Jesse says he looked to his right and saw the most beautiful woman in the world. They talked, danced, and sang, and he tried his best to impress her. They're now engaged to be married—and naturally, they even have a special karaoke song.

CRITICAL FACTOR

No one had ever started a competitive karaoke league before—and with its abundance of twenty-something working professionals, Washington, DC, was the perfect place to begin. It also helped that Jesse was a natural connector, enthusiastic about working with volunteers and helping competitors have a good time.

URBAN HIKER CLIMBS TO STEEP SUCCESS

A project manager turns a passion for her city into a substantial side income, while getting plenty of exercise along the way.

NAME
ALEXANDRA KENIN

LOCATION
SAN FRANCISCO, CALIFORNIA

STARTUP COSTS
$114.36[*]

INCOME
$50,000/YEAR

WEBSITE
URBANHIKERSF.COM

* Alexandra keeps detailed records. She spent $99 on a premium website hosting account and $15.36 on a set of 250 business cards.

San Francisco–based Alexandra Kenin has a flexible job as a project manager and editor for a fully remote company. It's a dream gig in the sense that she's able to set her own schedule—allowing her to go back and forth from focusing on those job responsibilities to building something for herself.

The company is in the tech industry, but Alexandra's side hustle is completely different. It's all about getting outdoors, showing city-dwellers and tourists a lesser-visited part of the city that includes scenic hills and hiking trails.

She calls it Urban Hiker SF, and Alexandra caters to small groups as well as private and corporate events. Thanks to that flexible schedule, she's able to offer the tours any day of the week, even in the middle of the day. She also coordinates with Match.com to offer special dating hikes.

To get the word out about her new business, Alexandra made a five-step plan:

1. Reach out to companies like Airbnb to see if she could offer tours to their guests (they said yes!).
2. Meet with other tour providers to see how they got their businesses started.
3. Offer free and discounted tours so that she could attract customers and get reviews.
4. Reach out to her network to see if people worked at companies that wanted to do team-building activities.
5. Join her local visitors bureau to meet other people in the industry.

FUN FACT   One challenge of an outdoor business is having to cancel tours due to rainy weather. Normally, this only happens a few times a year, but in the winter of 2016 the rain was out of control. It was the wettest winter since rainfall has been tracked starting in 1895! Thankfully, business picked up again when spring arrived.

"Anyone who lives in a city could create a tour business. It costs virtually nothing to start! All I spend on each hiking tour is my time, and the income is almost all profit." —Alexandra

Since she started in 2012, Alexandra has hiked with over five thousand people from around thirty countries. Depending on the season, she brings in between $2,500 and $8,000 per month, peaking in July. She also now has four to five contractors working for her, depending on the season. To complement the business, she wrote a hiking guide, which has sold more than seventy-five hundred copies.

All she spends on each hiking tour is her time. She has a few annual costs (insurance, visitors bureau membership, web hosting), but aside from those, there are no fixed costs associated with running a tour. That means that anytime she runs a tour, it's almost all profit.

If you're passionate about where you live, you can turn sharing your city into a way to make money. Alexandra says that anyone who lives in a city could create a tour business, at least if they like the idea of walking and talking with groups.

You first want to make sure there's a substantial number of visitors coming to your city each year. Then, see if there's anyone else leading the same kind of tour that you envision. It helped Alexandra that San Francisco gets eighteen million visitors a year, but no one else was leading an urban hiking tour.

After five thousand people and counting, she's now leading the way.

CRITICAL FACTOR

Most people associate San Francisco with cable cars and chocolate factories, but there's also a great outdoors with scenic hills and trails easily accessible from the city. Alexandra leaves the city tours to other companies and focuses entirely on her "urban hiking" theme.

HUNGOVER ACCOUNTANT STARTS "MORNING AFTER" PARTY CLEANUP SERVICE

Feeling queasy after a night of hosting a party, this Australian accountant dreams up an unusual cleaning service that becomes a media sensation.

Drinking too much on a night out can have its consequences. You might wake up the next morning with a ton of regret and a wicked hangover to match. Most people in that situation just want to pull the covers over their head and wait for the storm to pass.

James Hookway, a full-time chartered accountant from Western Australia, had a different experience. For James, it was while he was hungover after a Christmas party that he came up with a crazy idea that changed his life.

He and his wife had thrown the party. The next morning, they lay in bed, dreading the inevitable cleanup process. While procrastinating about when to start the job, they began talking about how great it would be if there was a service that would clean up after your party—and maybe even bring you breakfast in bed.

After having a good laugh about it, they dragged themselves out of bed, made their own breakfast, and got to removing all traces of the night before. But the idea stayed with James . . . and like a fine wine, actually got better with age.

Fast-forward to six months later, and the concept still excited him. After conducting some research, he learned that although there were a lot of cleaning services out there, none of them marketed specifically to the hangover crowd. In fact, there wasn't much differentiation at all—they were all generic companies with boring branding.

James decided to test the concept. To keep things simple, he created a Facebook page describing the proposed service and shared it with his friends and family. The name for the page almost wrote itself: he called it Hangover Helpers.

NAME
JAMES HOOKWAY

LOCATION
PERTH, AUSTRALIA

STARTUP COSTS
$25,000[*]

INCOME
$45,000/YEAR

WEBSITE
HANGOVERHELPERS.COM.AU

FUN FACT The cleaning industry is worth around $4 billion annually to the Australian economy. That huge amount of money means there are over sixty-two thousand people employed as contract cleaners. It's no wonder that there are literally thousands of cleaning companies across the nation.

* Arguably, his true startup costs were less than $1,000. The $25,000 investment in a website and better cleaning gear only happened after James had established the business as a winning concept.

What happened next was like popping open a bottle of champagne on New Year's Eve.

Perhaps it was the perfect name, the concept itself, or maybe the right person just happened to share the page. Whatever the cause, what followed was one of the wildest weeks of his life.

Print journalists from major publications, TV shows, and radio stations from all over the country contacted him for interviews. James had reached national exposure in less than two weeks, and everyone wanted to talk to the creator of such a comical (yet useful!) idea. This is something most larger companies are never able to achieve, despite expensive and time-consuming campaigns.

With all that free marketing, it was inevitable that customers would arrive faster than a headache after too many gin and tonics. And that's exactly what happened.

His first booking came in that very week. James picked up basic cleaning products, a "Ghostbuster style" vacuum cleaner, and some food supplies for the breakfast.

He found the house in a state of total chaos, but that didn't faze the new founder of Hangover Helpers. It meant he was able to get some "before" and "after" photos to showcase the type of work he was capable of. After the cleaning was done and the party hosts had enjoyed their breakfast burritos, James knew this could be a viable side business.

With the first job completed after a successful launch, he decided to build more of a brand around Hangover Helpers. This meant graduating from a simple Facebook page to an official website.

James figured that an investment in a professional-looking brand and website would be important, and he was meticulous in how he set it up. He wanted visitors to be able to fill out as many details as possible in order to get a detailed quote online before booking the service. That way, he could cut down on the administrative work and make the business much more efficient to run. This was especially important because he was still working at his job as an accountant.

Two years after starting, he had performed more than 250 "cleans" and earned $45,000, without spending a single cent on advertising. Business comes entirely through word of mouth and his social media presence on Facebook.

CRITICAL FACTOR

There are thousands of cleaning companies in Australia, but only one that caters to the hangover crowd. The unique idea brought James a ton of media attention and launched his business.

He's cleaned up after everything from dinner parties all the way to full-blown extravaganzas that the cast of *The Hangover* movies would be envious of. Sometimes he's shown up with people still asleep on the couches, and vacuumed around them. He once arrived at a party that was still raging early the next morning. It's all in a day's— or a morning's—work.

The biggest, messiest party he's seen achieved a scale of its own. A party of about 350 college students took place at a mansion while the parents were out of town. The backyard was the size of a football field, and there was so much mess left over that James had to call in reinforcements from a trash removal company. Even the helpers had a hangover after that one.

After operating successfully in Perth for two years, James expanded the service to Melbourne with the help of some dedicated cleaning teams on the ground. Although it isn't making enough to pay all the bills just yet, James hopes that in the future he can expand to more cities and go national across the rest of the country. At that time, he hopes to be able to quit his day job and go all in on Hangover Helpers.

Raise a glass to this nonconformist accountant. He's helping the party hosts of Australia recover, one hangover at a time.

"Find a niche market and develop a business strategy that is new and will be remembered. Make sure you can capture your audience's attention straight away with a clear message of what you do, who you are, and why." —James

FOODIE PR MANAGER BLOGS FOR FREE STUFF AND REAL MONEY

Two friends get paid to post photos of their lunch on Instagram. No, really! (And then one of them takes over the business, while working with more than 450 brands.)

By day, Alexandra Booze worked as an account manager for a public relations firm in Washington, DC. On nights and weekends, this foodie turned food and lifestyle blogging into a profitable side hustle.

It started with a project she shared with her friend Karen. Whenever Alex would visit Karen in New York City, they would always go out to eat somewhere new and interesting. It was during one of those nights when they were looking for their next meal that they decided to document all their fun foodie adventures. If you've ever wondered how to get paid for posting photos of your lunch, keep reading.

After a month of thinking about what their name should be, they launched East Coast Contessas. What started out as just friends and family liking their photos of food quickly turned into over one thousand followers.

For several months, they visited small bakeries, coffee shops, and food trucks and offered their services—reviews and social media campaigns—for free. With this attitude, they were able to feature a lot of different businesses. They also attended conferences, dinners, and festivals. Their goal was to meet chefs, concierges, and other food influencers. In other words . . . they hustled!

Once she realized there was a market for their reviews, Alexandra invested in some equipment so she could produce better media than what they were doing with their phones. She bought two cameras and a few interchangeable lenses. By keeping her eye out for sales, she only spent $1,300 on equipment that was worth at least $4,000. The new gear allowed her to create even better photos and video. Meanwhile, her consistent networking helped spread the word about their services.

To kick off the next year, Alex and Karen made a list of all the brands they wanted to partner with. They then reached

NAME
ALEXANDRA BOOZE

LOCATION
NEW YORK, NEW YORK

STARTUP COSTS
$1,300

INCOME
$25,000 IN YEAR THREE

WEBSITE
EASTCOASTCONTESSAS.COM

ACTION PLAN

1. Identify a goal and a strategy: What do you hope to achieve in working with brands, and how will you help them enough to justify your fees?

2. Build the project on a shoestring budget. Spend as little as possible on gear, online services, and whatever supplies you need.

3. Be willing to work for free or in exchange for something else . . . at first. Use the initial gigs to establish credibility and then pitch paying clients.

4. Be specific about what you offer to provide. "Social media promotion" doesn't give potential clients much info on what they'll actually receive. "Three dedicated posts to our five thousand followers in your local area" is better.

"Be open to new ideas and working with smaller brands. Everyone starts somewhere, and even smaller brands with limited budgets can still produce quality ideas and products." —Alex

out and pitched each brand personally. Since both of them came from media backgrounds, they already had a good handle on how to craft engaging narratives that would be interesting to potential partners.

They also knew that research was key. They spent time learning everything they could about a brand before making an offer. This level of research also helped Alex and Karen figure out how the brand would work with East Coast Contessas.

Their efforts paid off when they landed their first paid partnership with a national wine company. They leveraged that partnership and kept pitching to other brands on their list.

When it came to pricing, they offered multiple packages depending on the brand and situation. For some brands, it made sense to just do social media promotion for $300 per photo posted to their Instagram account. For other brands, social media promotion plus an editorial write-up on their blog at $1 per word was a better approach.

For brands that wanted to go all in, they'd offer social media promotion, an editorial write-up, *and* a promo video, which started at $400 on top of the other fees. They priced all these packages using three factors: the size of their audience at the time, the size of the company they were pitching, and the amount of work required.

In their second year of the project, they brought in $15,000—then in the first *half* of the third year, it was more than $17,000.

The East Coast Contessas eventually realized that the restaurant industry had a lot of crossover with the hospitality industry. They then started branching out to boutique hotels and mid-size national chains.

Before long, Alex and Karen were staying for free in fancy hotels. During those visits, they'd feature not only the rooms and amenities, but also the hotel bar or restaurant—a natural tie-in. This led to them receiving offers for press trips, where all of their costs were covered, as well as partnerships with tourism boards.

Alex and Karen eventually parted ways as business partners, with Alex continuing and Karen moving on to do other things.

Since launching three years ago, Alex has partnered with nearly 450 brands from the food and beverage, fashion, and beauty industries. And with dozens more partnerships lined up, she doesn't have plans to slow down anytime soon—even as she moves to Prague to begin a new day job.

BUSY PROFESSIONAL CLIPS INTO BIKING WINE TOURS

A marketing executive sees an opportunity to meet a tourism need in an up-and-coming wine region.

Erin Bury didn't think she had time for a side hustle. As a partner in a creative communications agency, as well as a frequent speaker with the National Speakers Bureau, she had a lot on her plate. But she also had an idea that wouldn't go away.

Erin had grown up visiting Prince Edward County, an up-and-coming Canadian wine region about two hours outside of Toronto. Her dad eventually moved there, and as an adult she continued to visit every summer with friends. They all loved touring the wineries—and they noticed that while there were limo tours available, *there were no bicycle tours.*

Erin knew this was a popular activity offered elsewhere. She also believed that if she didn't enter the market, someone else would. As she put it, "If your idea keeps you up at night because you know you'll be annoyed if someone else does it before you, it's a good sign that you should pursue it."

NAME
ERIN BURY

LOCATION
PRINCE EDWARD COUNTY, ONTARIO

STARTUP COSTS
$20,000

INCOME
$100,000 IN YEAR TWO

WEBSITE
THECOUNTYWINETOURS.COM

FUN FACT Safety first! On each tour, cyclists stop at four or more wineries—but only one per hour, and each stop is limited to four tastings. The guides also provide bottled water and snacks along the way.

So a couple of years ago, and working with two of her best friends, Erin started the County Wine Tours. The first step to launching a bicycle tour business was figuring out a route that had enough wineries within cycling distance. Erin approached wineries on the potential route, making sure to find backup options in case of busy days or to accommodate any special requests.

When selecting wineries, she considered their offerings to make sure there was a good variety of tastings, an affordable cost, and the right location—both in terms of being close to each other and also close to a fixed starting point. The region has a converted rail line for walking, jogging, and biking, so Erin also wanted to include part of that trail in the tour.

With all these considerations in mind, Erin selected five primary stops and a number of backups for their guided wine tour.

Once the route was in place, the next step was to get some bikes. Luckily, a family member worked for Giant Bikes, the world's largest bicycle manufacturer, so Erin connected with her to select a cruiser bike with custom accessories that would be comfortable and really stand out on the road. She purchased ten bikes, helmets, baskets, and repair tools.

Branding and marketing came next. Since Erin and her two cofounders all work in marketing, they had an advantage. They focused on a few key areas, first and foremost being search engine optimization (SEO) and Google AdWords, since most people start planning their wine weekend getaways by searching for a few specific phrases.

Setting up their TripAdvisor profile was another must for their business. They also invited members of the media to the area to take a tour, and partnered with a local bed-and-breakfast to invite their guests.

CRITICAL FACTOR

Bicycle tours to wineries operated in plenty of other regions, but not in Prince Edward County. Meanwhile, there were plenty of tourists coming to town. Erin put two wheels together and created the first-ever bicycle tours of the region.

But just because they're pros doesn't mean they did it all on their own. As Erin said when we talked, "It's impossible to do it all yourself. Whether you have cofounders, a virtual assistant, a freelancer or intern, or some other resource, having someone else to help you as you go will be imperative."

She took her own advice, working with a freelance designer to create their logo, branding, website, and all marketing collateral. They also brought on an accountant to handle financial forecasting and accounting.

One thing Erin *didn't* have to worry about was who was going to lead these guided tours. Erin's dad and stepmom are both enthusiastic wine drinkers, as well as experts on the local area. They eagerly signed up to be part of the adventure.

After a lot of planning on weekends and evenings, the County Wine Tours spun into business. The tours are priced at $95 per person, and so far they've been completely booked up on weekend days. They also offer midweek tours, with anywhere from two to ten people each.

With up to a dozen inquiries coming in daily, Erin and her cofounders are excited that their great idea has gotten so much traction so quickly. Their biggest problem at this point is managing demand on popular days.

With the framework in place for public tours, they've also created private tours that people can book for a birthday party or bachelorette party, as well as corporate tours that companies can use as part of a retreat. Oh, and for those who prefer beer over wine, they now offer a brewery option.

Erin's favorite tour is one she led herself. She hosted a private trip for her friends, which she assumed would be a special way to share her new project with them. But at the last tour stop, it became even more special when her boyfriend surprised her by proposing. The winery staff was in on it, appearing with sparkling wine the moment she said, "Yes!"

Though it made for an excellent photo op, Erin now has to manage expectations: "I make no guarantees that future tours will include a proposal!" she says.

While it's clear that there's lots of room for expansion, they plan to ride out this season with their current setup, and then decide how many tours to add for next year.

"It's impossible to do it all yourself. I work on the business during the evenings and on Sundays, and I've outsourced functions like customer service, marketing coordination, and accounting so I can focus on the high-level stuff." —Erin

FLORIDA MAN LEADS SCOOTER TOURS
AFTER WATCHING RAP VIDEO

A corporate refugee relocates to Florida and kicks off a new hustle leading adult scooter tours.

NAME
JORDAN CROWLER

LOCATION
FLORIDA PANHANDLE

STARTUP COSTS
MINIMAL (HE TRADED SERVICES FOR THE BIKES)

INCOME
$50,000/YEAR

WEBSITE
KICKBIKE30A.COM

Jordan Crowler wears tank tops and a pair of board shorts to work most days, but five years ago he was working a typical job as an art director for a major corporation in Dallas, Texas. Wanting to break free from the golden handcuffs, Jordan worked his way into a full-time remote position. He had the goal of moving his wife and two young daughters to their dream destination—a little stretch of paradise in the Florida Panhandle called 30A, where *The Truman Show* starring Jim Carrey was filmed.

Not knowing a soul on 30A, and having to support his family, he decided not to tell his employer that he was moving. The company he worked for was going through a big merger, with layoffs happening left and right, and Jordan had already endured all sorts of corporate bullying and harassment. He still did his job well, but in the back of his mind, he knew the clock was ticking until a more permanent change would be required.

Being a resourceful person, he looked around his newfound paradise for new opportunities. One thing he noticed during his research was that bikes, skateboards, and walking were the preferred methods of transportation. It was far easier than dealing with parking, and the weather was almost always nice.

Not long after that, Jordan had what he calls his "Aha!" moment. Browsing on YouTube, he stumbled upon the music video for John Macklemore's "Thrift Shop," in which the artist undertakes an anthropological exploration to a number of secondhand stores in search of formerly unwanted items.

In parts of the video, Macklemore is seen riding on an old-school scooter. Jordan began to wax nostalgic about his early days spent meandering about on his old mongoose scooter. Chasing that nostalgia, he started looking for something similar to the scooter of his youth, but after some quick research, he realized that most scooters were just not as awesome as he remembered (a common problem with nostalgia).

But then he discovered a company called Kickbike, which takes all the best aspects of scooters and bikes, combining them into a single recreational product. Based in Helsinki, Finland, Kickbikes has been

FUN FACT Jordan is shifting the focus of his side hustle from tours and rentals to the fitness aspect of Kickbikes, introducing a class called "Kickbike Kardio." This class is much less time-consuming than the tours, and allows him to spend time growing other aspects of his business.

> "It's a cliché, but 'fake it till you make it' worked for me. I had to become the highest level expert on my product in the country, starting from scratch. Sometimes, to get the job of your dreams, you have to dream up the job, hire yourself, and then quickly prove you belong there." —Jordan

a growing sensation through much of Europe for over twenty-five years. They call themselves the "Porsche of the scooter industry"—perhaps a bit of a stretch, but they do have a passionate fan base.

Despite their international success, Jordan had never seen a Kickbike in the United States. He couldn't believe that this fad hadn't caught on yet, so he began to research the company. What he found was that the owner of Kickbike America actually lived *right there in Florida*, just a few hours away in Orlando.

Jordan drove down for a meeting, and asked if they could come to an arrangement that would lead to him being able to use the bikes on 30A. He felt that the business had a lot of potential for growth, so he offered to assist the owner in building up his brand presence.

With years of experience in web design and marketing, Jordan proposed a trade—he'd completely revamp the Kickbike US website and manage his marketing campaign for him. In return, the owner would give him some Kickbikes and a commission on all online Kickbike sales in the United States.

Before he knew it, Jordan was heading back to 30A, feeling victorious. He was towing a U-Haul containing his first twenty-five Kickbikes!

The real work began when he arrived home. His vision was to turn this truck full of Kickbikes into the next big thing, in the next big destination.

The 30A road runs along a coastline dotted with a dozen vibrant little beach communities that each boast their own unique vibe and flavor. Jordan thought the Kickbikes would provide the perfect vehicle for a fun, active tour that would enable people to get "off 30A" and see another side of this incredible place he called home.

Following the exposure that the area received when *The Truman Show* came out, this thirteen-mile stretch of road that had previously been a well-kept secret was quickly becoming a major tourist destination. But despite the growing tourism trend, *no one* was offering tours of the area.

Jordan had spent two full years exploring every inch of his new home—the rare coastal dune lakes, the state forests and parks, and all of the accessible trails, in addition to every business and street in each town. He'd made himself into an authority of the area, and he used his knowledge to create customized tours.

Getting his Florida business license and liability insurance was easy and inexpensive, but finding retail space in the area was much more of a challenge. Space was technically *available*, but it wasn't cheap.

Not one to be dissuaded, Jordan started out by operating off the back of his truck in parking lots, and leaving some of his Kickbikes parked in high foot-traffic areas with flyers detailing how to get in touch with him to schedule.

Jordan strategically tailored his tours based on the fitness level of those who signed up. Kickbiking is more fitness intensive than bicycling, so he tried to feel out the expectations of his customers in order to ensure that it was a positive experience for everyone. Some tours sold better than others, so as time went on he focused on those and dropped the more experimental ones.

He also developed relationships with local businesses, and several of them ended up allowing him to use their shops as official starting points for the tours. This was a win-win, bringing new business to the shops, while allowing him to forgo paying for a rental space.

These days, the Kickbike side hustle is well past the kickoff point. Jordan ended up leaving his remote-work position to freelance as a web developer, and his tours and commissions are bringing in an additional $3,000 to $5,000 a month.

He's now thinking about what comes next. Maybe he'll roll his way into markets where the adult scooter trend hasn't yet kicked its way down the road.

CRITICAL FACTOR

The Kickbike brand is the "Porsche of the scooter industry" in Europe, but it's largely unknown in the United States. After relocating to a stretch of the Florida coastline popular with tourists, Jordan was determined to bring Kickbikes to the masses.

EPIC SCAVENGER HUNT BECOMES SIX-FIGURE INCOME

An event planner creates a competitive scavenger hunt game that takes place across Boston. Can you really make money while having so much fun?

NAME
CHRIS DAMIANAKOS

LOCATION
BOSTON, MASSACHUSETTS

STARTUP COSTS
$150

INCOME
SIX FIGURES/YEAR

WEBSITE
CASHUNT.COM

Chris Damianakos runs a scavenger hunt in Boston, Massachusetts. To understand where this *seriously fun* project began, we have to go back to the late 1980s when teenage Chris was on a family trip in Greece. It was there that he first witnessed a scavenger hunt being put on by an Italian tour group. He fell in love with the idea of playing a competitive game with other people, using the world as a game board.

Chris had grown up putting on tournaments and shows for his friends, and when he got back to the United States, he designed his very first hunt. In the movie version of Chris's story, he would have gone straight from there to creating his own company.

Instead, he finished high school and continued on to college, where he majored in marketing. After college, he got a series of jobs in event management, both as a freelancer and contracting for companies. But he never felt fully fulfilled.

So a number of years later, he came back to the scavenger hunt idea that he loved so much when he was a teenager. As another passion project, he created an elaborate, six-hour long hunt for his friends and family. They loved it! A friend that was in marketing couldn't stop talking about what a great *business* this would be.

Chris then spent a few months redesigning the hunt so that it could be played in two hours instead of six—the theory being that not everyone would be up for a six-hour hunt, no matter how awesome it promised to be. He then launched his new venture, which he called Cashunt.[*]

This project began in the dark ages, more than a decade ago, when social media was just getting off the ground. Chris decided to place ads in the wedding parties section of a local newspaper, to see if he could attract bachelorette and bachelor parties.

[*] Everyone thinks the name refers to a cash prize, but it's actually short for Chris, Areti (his wife's name), and Super Hunt.

FUN FACT The scavenger hunt has now expanded internationally, with a new location that opened up on the island of Crete in Greece.

The plan worked, as his first group scavenger hunt was a bachelor party. He was simultaneously excited and petrified since he had never done a hunt for the general public before. He charged them $30 per person with an eight-person minimum . . . and the group was thrilled!

That first year he did five games and made a couple thousand dollars. Since his initial investment was so low—the newspaper ads, materials for the game itself, and his time—most of what he made was pure profit.

During that year, he also landed a wireless provider as a corporate client. The company asked him to customize the scavenger hunt for their employees. It took some figuring out, but after that first experience, he created a blueprint to make customization for future corporate clients easier.

Even without specifically pursuing corporations, he continued to get one or two corporate clients a year, who used his scavenger hunt as a team-building outing. Since he customized scavenger hunts for each company, he charged them more per person and had a minimum of 10 participants instead of 8, with a cap of 250.

Over the next few years, Chris kept advertising in newspapers. Because this was a side hustle and he wasn't dependent on the income, he enjoyed making the game as epic as possible. For example, he designed a fully interactive game that used the city of Boston as the board. Players start off with a comic book that has some initial challenges in it. They have to decide as a team how they're going to get the most points before the two hours are up.

Sometimes challenges lead to point cards, sometimes they lead to other challenges or scannable codes that send them to an online puzzle. At one point, he even created a prop that looked like a real newspaper. Players had to find it, and then use it to complete the challenge. As Chris described it, "I wanted to make it as much like one of those reality TV shows as possible, so people could get that experience for an afternoon."

Chris continued to put on more and more scavenger hunts and saw his revenue increase steadily, solely through word of mouth and newspaper ads. Four years after starting, his annual, part-time income was up to $30,000.

And then his business started to take off even more, but not because of anything he did directly. Review sites like TripAdvisor and Yelp had gained momentum, and all of a sudden he was getting excellent reviews, furthering his word-of-mouth marketing in a more technological way.

> "If you want to start a side hustle, don't listen to the noise, listen to yourself. And be prepared to put in the time! This isn't like an office job where you just clock in and clock out." —Chris

As his reputation on review sites grew, so did the business. He finally decided to jump into Cashunt full-time. Not only had his revenue gone up, but the increased volume of interest by way of phone calls, emails, and interactions on social media (which was now much more common) served as further confirmation.

Once he decided to focus all his attention on the business, he started increasing the number of games in the Boston area. He invested in technology to add in additional interactive elements. Over the years, the prizes also got better, with each winner now receiving a medal.

He switched to a commercial bank account to process credit card payments, and stopped running newspaper ads in favor of online ads. He updated his website, bringing it forward nearly a decade into present-day standards.

Over the years, Chris had been approached a few times about franchising Cashunt in other cities. He always deferred, instead making one-day round-trips to other cities himself for corporate clients. But soon he was flying back and forth to Chicago so often that the commute was getting impractical. When he was once again approached about franchising, he finally considered the idea.

He flew to each city to meet with the interested parties, scoped out the area, and entered into collaborative partnerships with existing tour companies in five different cities.

It's been quite the journey since that first six-hour hunt Chris made for his friends. He's now making well over six figures a year. He has one other full-time employee working with him in Boston, and facilitators in several other locations. He also has plans in the works to expand further.

Oh, and he's still having a lot of fun.

CRITICAL FACTOR

A successful scavenger hunt is made up of two critical qualities: fun and organization. Chris brought both of them to Cashunt, refining the process along the way and continuing to improve from gig to gig.

DIY Event Planning

In some ways, producing a successful event is like developing an online course: you need a reason to bring people together, and the right venue or space for them to meet.

But a conference, meetup, in-person class, or other event has at least one big difference: a fixed deadline that comes with other unchangeable variables. If no one signs up for your online course on ballroom dancing, you can try again later. But if no one shows up at a physical venue you've booked, you have a bigger problem.

Right from the beginning, you'll need a clear plan for how you will attract people to your event. This should include an easy way for them to sign up (and pay in advance whenever possible) so that you know what to count on.

If you can avoid paying for a venue for your first event, do so. Community centers, schools, and religious institutions that are often empty throughout the week can be good options. In some cases, bars and restaurants will be happy to host your group, especially if you commit to spending a minimum amount on food and beverages there.

Make a simple projection of how many attendees you'll need for your event to be successful. Of course, you'll want *more* than the minimum standard of success, but this way you'll have a baseline goal.

Perhaps most important of all: When it comes to events, publicity matters a *lot*. Shout it from the rooftops!

For more, visit SideHustleSchool.com/events.

Get Crafty, Get Paid

If you have a penchant for a paintbrush or a love of making pottery, you might be able to turn your creations into money—just like the people in these stories did.

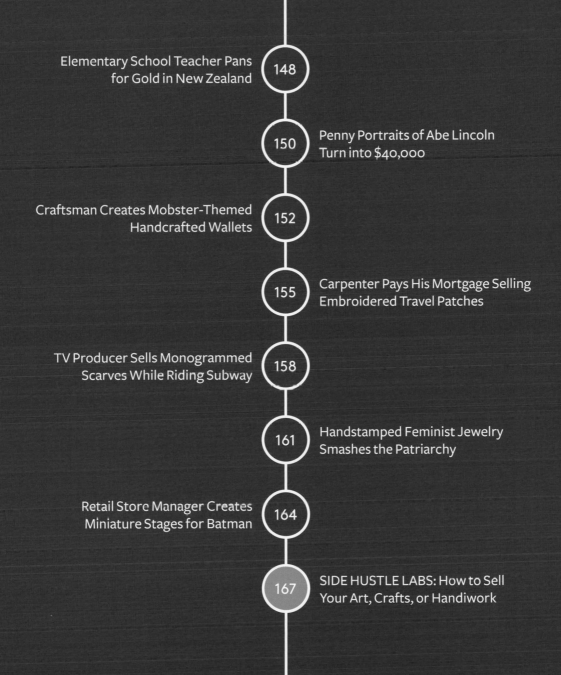

Elementary School Teacher Pans
for Gold in New Zealand — 148

Penny Portraits of Abe Lincoln
Turn into $40,000 — 150

Craftsman Creates Mobster-Themed
Handcrafted Wallets — 152

Carpenter Pays His Mortgage Selling
Embroidered Travel Patches — 155

TV Producer Sells Monogrammed
Scarves While Riding Subway — 158

Handstamped Feminist Jewelry
Smashes the Patriarchy — 161

Retail Store Manager Creates
Miniature Stages for Batman — 164

SIDE HUSTLE LABS: How to Sell
Your Art, Crafts, or Handiwork — 167

ELEMENTARY SCHOOL TEACHER
PANS FOR GOLD IN NEW ZEALAND

After changing continents, an elementary school teacher finds true love, goes panning for gold in New Zealand, and ends up making an extra $40,000 in a year, working mostly on the weekends.

NAME
ALEX MOORE

LOCATION
WELLINGTON, NEW ZEALAND

STARTUP COSTS
$4,000

INCOME
$40,000 IN YEAR ONE

WEBSITE
GOLDPANPETE.COM

ACTION PLAN

1. Apprentice with a master jeweler or other craftsperson.
2. Make your first jewelry and learn as you go.
3. Specialize by crafting something unique. Some of Alex's best sellers are rings featuring different "house seals" from Game of Thrones.
4. Find the right tourist market. Pay close attention to what sells. Chances are, that's what you should focus on.
5. Shift to online sales. In the long run, you'll be able to reach far more people than selling locally.

For the past twelve years, Alex Moore has been an elementary school teacher. Originally from St. Louis, Missouri, he taught in the area for several years before moving overseas to London to continue teaching and to play rugby.

While in London, he met his future wife, Paula. Once he visited her homeland of New Zealand to meet her family, he knew it was a match made in heaven—and not just with Paula, but with the country of New Zealand too.

On that first trip, Alex had a crazy idea. He'd heard it was possible to pan for gold in parts of the country, and his goal was to find enough gold to make his wedding ring. He spent about twenty to thirty hours pursuing this goal, but in the end he only found about two grams of gold.

You need around twenty grams to make a ring, so after all that work, he was only 10 percent there. Still, when he got home, he took the gold he'd found to a master jeweler, who melted it down into his future ring. It was that process that led him to the side hustle that would change his life.

When talking to the jeweler, Alex learned that he taught jewelry making on the side. On the spot, he signed up for lessons. He continued these lessons off and on for the next two years while he was teaching. After he'd learned enough, he was able to start making a few pieces of his own and selling them on Etsy.

This took place for a few more years until he moved to New Zealand with Paula and their young family. Their new home base was Queenstown, a huge tourist destination that's known as the adventure sports capital of the world.

Right on the banks of the gorgeous Lake Wakatipu, the Creative Queenstown Arts and Crafts Market is held weekly, drawing in hundreds of tourists from all over the world. It was at this market that Alex began to get a lot more serious about his jewelry making.

Alex took on the moniker "Gold Pan Pete," and now sells both online and to tourists visiting the market. Most of his sales take place at the market, but he tends to get repeat customers who order more jewelry from him once they return home.

During an average week, he makes about $800 in net income, or approximately $40,000 in a year. To be fair, he needs to be on-site selling at the market for eight hours on Saturday, and then spend another six to eight hours a week in his home workshop once his kids go to bed.

Still, for $40,000 a year, it's worth it. He's currently expanding his online presence and hoping to develop more relationships with shops around the globe. This will allow him to work less or make more money, or both.

FUN FACT Alex uses the moniker "Gold Pan Pete"—but there is no Pete. "It just has a nice ring to it," he says.

"I was getting burned out on being a school teacher. Now I can afford to reduce my amount of teaching days, and still look forward to going to work." —Alex

 CRITICAL FACTOR

Alex sells at a big, international market that draws visitors from all over the world each weekend. Many of those visitors see his work at the market, then go home and place an online order.

PENNY PORTRAITS OF
ABE LINCOLN TURN INTO $40,000

An investment broker earns an above-average return on
an unusual art project.

NAME
MAURY MCCOY

LOCATION
AUSTIN, TEXAS

STARTUP COSTS
$800*

INCOME
$40,000 SO FAR

WEBSITE
PENNYPORTRAIT.COM

*and another $8.46 in
pennies for a model . . .

Do you have an extra $8.46 in pennies? Maybe you could put it to use
creating a portrait of Abraham Lincoln. At least that's what Maury McCoy
from Austin, Texas, would suggest. Maury works in the investment world,
and spends much of his week pitching large endowments, foundations,
and pensions. In industry terms, he's what's known as an independent
third-party marketer.

But that's his day job. When he's not at the office, Maury sells an
Abraham Lincoln portrait kit that can be filled in with 846 pennies. The
idea came about when he read a story about a father and son in Florida
who had created a giant, wall-size portrait of Abe Lincoln made out of
pennies. He loved the concept, but looking at the final portrait, he thought
their execution left a little to be desired.

He'd also been curious about the side hustle world, having
previously tried different projects ranging from producing
video games to helping out with his wife's crafty creations—
and even unsuccessfully launching an app that he describes
as "a neat but unprofitable learning experience."

Looking at that story about Honest Abe, he kept thinking
about ways he could improve the image quality and also
make it smaller. He couldn't resist tinkering: within fifteen
minutes on his computer, he had a mock-up in Photoshop
that looked decent. Then in the nature of Photoshop
editing, "about thirty-eight versions later," he finally had
one he was satisfied with.

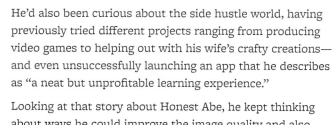

FUN FACT Why does the United States still have the penny?
A lot of people think it should be phased out. In 2007, the price
of the raw materials to make a penny *exceeded the face value,* so
there was a small risk that coins would be illegally melted down
for resale. It now costs about 1.4¢ to mint a penny.

At the time, he had no idea if anyone else would be interested in it. He didn't really do any market testing. He just thought it was a fun project, and figured he'd give it a try.

To get it going, he had to put down more than just pennies—he placed a print run of two thousand units of his new Abe Lincoln template. The order size was this large because the printer set-up cost $800 whether he printed one copy or one thousand, so he figured he might as well get the cost per unit as low as possible.

He called his creation the Penny Portrait, and the pitch was simple: "Create a portrait of Abraham Lincoln—completely out of pennies!"

A buddy of his bought the very first kit, which helped him confirm that the online check-out system worked properly. To make his first real sales, he sent out a number of emails and posted on various message boards and forums. There were multiple target markets, so he dabbled a bit with them all. His early sales depended almost entirely on the effort he put into it, which was enjoyable at first but then seemed like a lot of work.

Fortunately, as time went on, sales began to happen more naturally. He also listed the Penny Portrait on Amazon, which has been a good source of consistent sales over time.

Maury makes a profit of around $10 per unit, and to date he's sold well over four thousand Penny Portraits. In the beginning, he jokingly said to his wife that he wanted to be able to make enough to buy a Lincoln automobile from selling Lincolns made from little Lincolns. Before too long, he'd accomplished that goal.

Not bad for a penny-pinching project!

"As much as I love passion projects, you need to make sure there is a way to turn a profit for the effort you put in. Fortunately, this project has been both enjoyable and financially rewarding." —Maury

CRITICAL FACTOR

It's a fun project that people often do with their children or grandchildren. And the penny probably won't be around forever...

CRAFTSMAN CREATES
MOBSTER-THEMED HANDCRAFTED WALLETS

After receiving custom requests from friends and family, a leather craftsman launches his own line of leather products.

NAME
PHIL KALAS AND DAN CORDOVA

LOCATION
CHICAGO, ILLINOIS

STARTUP COSTS
$5,000

INCOME
MULTIPLE SIX FIGURES/YEAR

WEBSITE
ASHLANDLEATHER.COM

By day, Phil Kalas works in development and operations at Horween Leather Company, a 114-year-old tannery in Chicago, Illinois. Working around leather all day is what inspired him to start his side hustle.

He's constantly surrounded by hundreds of sheets of different-colored and textured leather, and he wanted to create something he could use and appreciate every day. He started by making leather wallets and bags for himself out of the most unique styles of leather he came across. Soon, his friends started admiring his handiwork and wanted items for themselves.

After a year of receiving compliments and requests, Phil and his good friend Dan Cordova—who's also in the leather business—decided to try making and selling their handcrafted leather products online.

Since leather products require specialized tools and materials, there were some substantial startup costs involved in getting their new business off the ground. While they tried to keep costs as low as possible by working out of Dan's garage, they still had to purchase leather, hardware, sewing machines, hand tools, and books to keep educating themselves. All of this ran them around $5,000.

One area where they were able to save money was in marketing—they put in very few paid marketing efforts, relying instead on word of mouth and their connections in the leather business.

They created a website and got a bit of organic traffic through some very basic search engine optimization (SEO) efforts. It was through those efforts that they got their biggest sale that first year. A large retailer in Asia placed a wholesale order through their website, which launched them with over $50,000 worth of wallets and accessories sold that year. In Phil's words, "It was exciting but exhausting. I stayed up late many nights and worked weekends to fill their wholesale order."

FUN FACT Phil and Dan decided to name their wallets after Chicago gangsters, with names like "Bugs Moran," "Fat Herbie," and "Tony the Ant."

> "If you want to do something similar, create something that you love and make it the highest quality you can. And then double the price you think that you should charge." —Phil

They started simply with just one wallet, a cardholder, and a purse that has since been discontinued. Each year or so, they add a new wallet style and a new accessory. Six years in, they now have eight wallet styles, plus belts, key cases, passport holders, and their own line of leather care products.

They caught a big break when the owner of the tannery they work for started up a specialty leather store in Chicago, and decided to stock their goods. With his expertise and authority in the leather industry, it gave Phil and Dan's new business a boost in credibility.

As time went on, the marketing tactics for Ashland Leather have become more sophisticated. They now run their website through Shopify, publish a newsletter announcing weekly deals, and produce daily posts featuring their favorite leathers and manufacturing techniques.

Another profitable strategy has been partnering with Massdrop, a company that cultivates communities where people with common interests can learn together. They've sold hundreds of wallets through this partnership.

They've also done some collaborations a little closer to home. For example, the Chicago Comb Co. wanted a leather sheath to cover one of their products. That product quickly took off and has resulted in an ongoing partnership, with thousands of comb sheaths made and sold.

These localized and virtual efforts have paid off in a major way. It wasn't long before they outgrew Dan's garage and needed to find a new place to work. Luckily, a space behind the tannery was available and they moved everything there, where they still work today.

Their first year in business, they had around fifty visitors per day to their website and just over $50,000 in sales. Now they consistently have over five hundred visitors a day with a conversion rate of 1.5 percent, for about $350,000 worth of merchandise sold annually.

While that sounds like a lot, their material costs are substantial. They also brought on two more craftspeople to help create the products. Finally, Phil's brother Matt helps with managing production and customer service.

As much as they love the extra income, Phil and Dan also love that they get to create something that people are excited to buy. They enjoy the challenge of figuring out how to overcome new business hurdles—everything from choosing the best online store to how to tell the story of the leather and convey the right color with photography.

Ultimately, the community they've created with their craftspeople, customers, and partners is what motivates them to keep creating products.

CRITICAL FACTOR

There's no magic shortcut to making a high-quality leather product, but the consistency that Ashland Leather displays through its daily posts and weekly newsletter helps them with continued visibility.

CARPENTER PAYS HIS MORTGAGE SELLING EMBROIDERED TRAVEL PATCHES

Tired of look-alike flag patches, this carpenter and frequent traveler creates his own designs, selling them to fellow backpackers and collectors.

By day, Mike Lecky works as a carpenter in Montreal, Quebec. His side hustle is Vagabond Heart, a company making vintage-inspired travel patches for people to sew on their luggage.

When Mike was younger, he worked as a graphic designer and book editor. After becoming a carpenter, he missed some of the aspects of a desk job where he could sit down in clean clothes and work on a computer. But he didn't want to leave his current job . . . he just wanted the best of both worlds.

He started his project so he could get his hands dirty during the day and then work on the computer in the evenings. It's essentially the opposite of people who have desk jobs and take on more DIY work as a hobby.

Mike also likes to travel. He packs light, not wanting to bring a bunch of stuff home with him. His one consumer indulgence is collecting patches for his backpack, like many other travelers do, and for years he was disappointed with how they looked. The most common patches were boring country flags or other designs that looked like they came from a cheap souvenir shop.

He wanted something that had a bit more style—patches with a hip, modern look but that included an unmistakable nod to the 1920s and '30s era of luxury travel. Not only was Mike unable to find anything like that while traveling, he couldn't even find it online when he got home. So he decided to make them himself.

To get things going, Mike had a designer in mind—someone he'd found on Tumblr years earlier when working on another project. Next, he needed a manufacturer. He found about twenty embroidery shops on the online

NAME
MIKE LECKY

LOCATION
MONTREAL, CANADA

STARTUP COSTS
$1,500

INCOME
$1,000+/MONTH

WEBSITE
VAGABONDHEART.CO

FUN FACT Mike says his stomach makes a lot of his travel plans for him, and by far the happiest it's ever been was in Oaxaca, Mexico—a beautiful, smallish city surrounded by great produce-growing regions. It's also the home of mole sauce and mescal.

business directory Alibaba and requested quotes from them all. His main consideration, other than price, was to find a company that offered a small order size. He wanted initial orders of just fifty pieces of each design.

Startup costs were low: $1,000 to have the patches designed and $500 to have them manufactured. The two months of planning and setting everything up was his least favorite part of the process, especially when he had to put money in with no idea if this would work or not. But he decided in advance that if necessary, he could afford to lose the money. He set a firm boundary to only spend the $1,500, and he found that this strategy reduced the stress.

Once he had his patches ready, he began to sell them on both Etsy and a Shopify site he'd made. Etsy sells cute, hip, and handmade items, and Mike found that he got a lot of traffic through organic searches. After he put his store up, it fell to the back of his mind, so he was pleasantly surprised when he got that first ding on his phone announcing a sale. The patches sell for $7, about the price of a pint of beer, so when he made his first sale, he went out after work and promptly "reinvested" the profits.

Mike made $75 his first month and $150 his second, and then he started marketing his patches using Etsy Promoted Listings, which are easy to

CRITICAL FACTOR

Backpacking patches haven't been updated for decades. Mike's designs present a modern look that pays homage to the classic era of luxury travel.

turn on with the click of a button. The service lets you pay to have a particular listing show up more prominently in search results.

By the fourth or fifth month, Mike was pulling in over $1,000 a month in sales from this strategy, a minimum number that continues to this day. His side hustle pays for his mortgage!

In addition to patches, Mike started selling pin versions of his designs because people were asking for them. He also began working with a wholesaler who sold similar products. They have a network of stores that buy from them, and the patches are now found in a number of shops across the United States and Canada. Finally, he's trying out a new way of selling by hosting a booth at a Patches and Pins expo, the largest "flare event" in the United States. This expo is attended by fans, artists, retailers, and wholesalers.

With such a big world to cover, Mike's goal is to keep expanding the Vagabond Heart collection from his current twenty-four designs to at least fifty in the near future and eventually one hundred. And, of course, he's planning more trips to find or create more patches.

"The best part about customer orders is trying to imagine the trips they've been on. Someone will order a Vancouver patch, a San Francisco one, and a Los Angeles one, and you can almost see them driving down Highway 1 along the West Coast." —Mike

TV PRODUCER SELLS MONOGRAMMED SCARVES WHILE RIDING SUBWAY

In pursuit of a handmade income source, this TV producer experiments with different items until she discovers what customers like the most.

NAME
KIRSTEN LA GRECA

LOCATION
HOBOKEN, NEW JERSEY

STARTUP COSTS
$250

INCOME
$120,000/YEAR

WEBSITE
WWW.ROSA.GOLD

Kirsten La Greca was a television casting producer at a big production company in New York City. Her side hustle, which recently became her full-time work, is called Rosa Gold. It's a handmade scarf brand that gives back—trying to wrap the world in a little more love, as she likes to say. She donates a percentage of profits to Pencils of Promise and DonorsChoose because she's passionate about education, especially for young girls.

Rosa Gold blossomed out of an Etsy store she opened as a testing ground for different ideas that were swirling around her head. She'd come up with an idea, order some sample materials, and then post a listing. She'd only produce that item again if it was getting a lot of views, favorites, and orders. Etsy taught her how to listen to her customers, and she'd pay attention to requests for custom orders, especially if two or more people asked for something.

While in college, Kirsten had spent her nights and weekends working as a merchandiser, so she knew that putting items that weren't selling on a mannequin or even just moving them around could lead to them flying off the shelves. Since Etsy is entirely online, she decided to use the same concept by updating product images for items that weren't selling well.

Monogrammed blanket scarves were the product that stuck. After a few years of occasional selling, she decided she wanted to go bigger than Etsy. She still lists products there, but she also migrated everything to its own site,

ACTION PLAN

1. If you're a crafty person but aren't sure what kind of crafts to sell, follow Kirsten's model: try a few different things and see what works.
2. Browse Etsy to see what's selling, and make a list of possibilities.
3. Start with at least two different ideas so that you can compare each part of the process: the making *and* the selling.
4. Over time, see both what you enjoy most *and* what people respond to most.
5. Eliminate the less interesting and less profitable ideas. Do more of what works, and begin to specialize in that.

FUN FACT Kirsten recently funded a special-needs teacher's supply list that would help the teacher's students monogram items and sell them to other students and parents. It was a perfect fit.

"My biggest mistake by far was not starting sooner. I let this idea of 'trying something' swirl around in my head for far too long! I was scared of ALL the things: failing, putting myself out there, losing money, etc. I took baby steps . . . and little by little, doing the best I could with what I had, a business was built." —Kirsten

added additional items (including bandanas and T-shirts), and started to build it into a brand.

Startup costs were low. She spent just $250 at first, and then grew the project as organically as possible. Her inventory increased as her sales did, so growth was gradual for the first few years. As it grew into a real business, she began to upgrade to better machines and make other investments.

When she first started, Kirsten bought wholesale products to resell, but she wanted to design her own, so she tested out manufacturers she found online. She started with a lot of cold emailing to scarf factories all over the world, and eventually found suppliers she preferred.

Because scarf sales are seasonal, Kirsten can sell as little as $1,500 of product a month and as much as $10,000 to $20,000. She's trying to incorporate more nonseasonal products, and recently launched summer blanket scarves to increase sales in the warmer months. She was able to negotiate low minimums with the factory for those, so it wasn't a huge risk, and she's waiting to see what happens—because after all, trying new things is how she built this business.

One day, Kirsten was on a train heading to work in Manhattan and received a flurry of notifications indicating that she'd sold $1,000 in scarves in a very short period of time. By the time she exited the train and walked ten minutes to her office, she'd sold another $1,000. While silently freaking out at her desk, she checked her website analytics and saw that the deluge of orders was coming from a radio mention on a popular morning show.

That day was crazy. She was sitting at work watching her phone explode, all while getting bombarded with customer messages and phone calls. By 9 a.m., she was completely out of inventory. She crafted an email to buyers saying there'd be a two-week wait to receive the order—but only one person canceled.

Kirsten's goal was to turn her side hustle into a full-time job, so she invested her profits into the business, upgrading and enhancing each element. One big lesson: Kirsten understood from the beginning that good photos were important, but she made a mistake in not having them done with a white background. This meant that she couldn't be included in a lot of product gift guides, which can make a big impact on sales.

After making enough improvements and increasing sales to a sustainable level, Kirsten left her job to go all in. She continues to experiment, keeping an eye on what works best.

CRITICAL FACTOR

Kirsten didn't know from the beginning that she was going to focus on scarves. Instead, she tested out different ideas, offered them for sale, and noticed what customers responded to the most. Over time, she began to specialize.

HANDSTAMPED FEMINIST JEWELRY
SMASHES THE PATRIARCHY

An Arkansas feminist finds a way to give voice to her beliefs, one handstamped bracelet at a time.

Stacey Bowers works as a communications coordinator for an arts education nonprofit in Little Rock, Arkansas. On the side, she sells "handstamped feminist jewelry," as well as some tote bags, shirts, and enamel pins. Stacey started her shop, Bang-Up Betty, as a hobby, but it's grown into a solid brand that brings in at least $3,000 a month in net income.

Bang-Up Betty isn't Stacey's first side hustle. In first grade, she resold magazines from school to her neighbors. She's also done freelance graphic design, marketing, and writing gigs while working other jobs. When she worked for a magazine and wasn't allowed to write for other publications, she sold funny greeting cards she made by hand.

The new project began when Stacey made jewelry for holiday gifts in the form of copper bracelets with four-letter acronyms such as OMFG and STFU. When her gift recipients were enthusiastic, she listed the bracelets for sale. Design ideas kept coming to her, and she got better and better at bringing them to life. As a next step, she decided to build her own website.

At first, the website was merely informational, with all her sales coming through Etsy. She designed it herself, which involved staying up long nights chatting with the Squarespace customer service team so she could figure things out without having to hire a web designer. A friend took portraits and initial product photos for the site, and Stacey borrowed a camera to take more.

Eventually, she converted the site to an online shop. She wanted people who wore her designs to say they got them from Bang-Up Betty, not from another site or platform.

FUN FACT Everyone thinks Stacey's name is Betty, but Betty is actually her cat's name. Also, he's a boy. "It's a long story," she says.

NAME
STACEY BOWERS

LOCATION
LITTLE ROCK, ARKANSAS

STARTUP COSTS
LESS THAN $500

INCOME
$40,000/YEAR

WEBSITE
BANGUPBETTY.COM

"Be original. Don't take someone else's dream and make it your own. And be flexible. Your hustle will evolve in mysterious ways!" —Stacey

Among others, her designs have included these favorites:

- A "Smash the Patriarchy" shopping bag
- A George Michael heart pin
- A necklace that simply reads "Hot Mess"

Stacey's materials range from chains and charms to rings and brass, and she gets them from more than a dozen suppliers. She stays on top of logistics by keeping her supplies in clear containers so she's never surprised by being out of something. In fact, her workspace is cleaner than the rest of her home. "It has to be for me to maintain order and peace while surrounded by a million little things that I have complete responsibility for," she says.

Finding the best suppliers was a process of trial and error. Stacey says she ordered a lot of bad chains before she found suitable ones, and stocked the wrong size metal before she figured out what she really needed. When she decided she wanted to branch out into apparel, the process was much smoother because she relied on a local printing business run by a couple of friends.

The jewelry making itself is an organized process, consisting of stamping, polishing, drilling, assembling, and packing. Stacey makes a lot of items per week, but she breaks down the steps over several days so she doesn't feel completely overwhelmed.

As long as it's not the Christmas season, Stacey can maintain a healthy balance of work, side hustle, and play. In December, she's in full panic mode, waiting for the light at the end of the tunnel. That light arrives in January, when sales return to normal and she can take a big payoff for all of her hard work.

In a recent year, Stacey made more than $40,000 from Bang-Up Betty. She also purchased her first house, thanks in part to the extra money she makes.

Last but not least, she's taken advantage of opportunities to give back. She recently donated 100 percent of the proceeds from a "Strong as Hell" bracelet to the Arkansas Women's Outreach. She also came up with a line of enamel pins for a website called The Outrage. Sales of the pins benefit the ACLU and other progressive causes.

She's taking a stand for her beliefs and building something for herself at the same time.

CRITICAL FACTOR

These pins and earrings with a mission have a clear target market that is both a demographic and a psychographic. Bang-Up Betty's buyers tend to be millennial women who identify with progressive causes. By marketing specifically to them, Stacey stands apart from many other sellers making similar items.

RETAIL STORE MANAGER CREATES MINIATURE STAGES FOR BATMAN

A man's accidental side hustle fulfills a long-held dream to make movie sets—just not in the way he first expected.

NAME
JASON HUOT

LOCATION
KANSAS CITY, MISSOURI

STARTUP COSTS
MINIMAL

INCOME
AT LEAST $500/MONTH

WEBSITE
**INSTAGRAM.COM/
MISCHIEF_DIORAMAS**

During business hours, Jason Huot manages a large retail store. His climb in the retail sector took him from Kansas City to Chicago to the Mall of America for companies like Fossil and Eddie Bauer. After eight years, he returned home to settle down.

Jason had grown up using his hands and imagination to fix cars and houses alongside his dad. He was also a huge movie fan, fascinated in particular by anything miniature. He'd imagined himself making miniature sets for the movie industry, but set the dream aside to become a star in retail.

He didn't set aside his love of movies or miniatures, however. He discovered the world of one-sixth-scale miniature figures from movies and television, where collectors purchase mini-replicas of popular superheroes and action stars. Batman was his favorite.

The process of creating the figures requires a long back-and-forth between the studios and the companies who create them. The figures have to be as exact as possible, especially in Asia, where this is a billion-dollar business. The manufacturers typically post preproduction photos of the characters online, and then take preorders from fans. It's common to wait six to nine months for delivery, with limited runs.

Collecting sixth-scale figures isn't a cheap hobby. The figures range from about $150 to well over $1,000. With such an investment at stake, Jason thought that collectors could do a better job in displaying their prized figures. Most of the time, the figures are placed on stands, as if in a museum.

Jason felt that the figures deserved more—after all, many of them were based on superheroes. He wanted to place them *in a scene from their movie*. Working in his off-hours, he started building sixth-scale miniature movie sets.

His Kansas City basement became his studio. He loved building things again, just as he'd done as a kid. He also enjoyed the process of sourcing objects to replicate different movie scenes. The plumbing and electrical aisles at home improvement stores became an adventure in reimagining how one thing could be used for another, and the wires inside thrift store radios added a nice touch.

By coincidence, one of the country's top distributors of sixth-scale figures, Timewalker Toys, was only three blocks from Jason's home. The staff there encouraged Jason's interest in designing dioramas, and featured one of his scenes at a comic convention.

Jason's excitement over his dioramas inspired him to post photos of them on Instagram. This caught the eye of other collectors, who asked him to create scenes for them. His first commission was for the "Holding Cell" scene from *The Dark Knight*, which prompted four more of the same order within five days from other customers who saw the photos. His basement became an assembly line.

FUN FACT A tiny amount of lead is traditionally used to make miniatures. When the New York State Legislature enacted a bill outlawing its use, the community protested. After months of back-and-forth, the governor signed a bill that exempted miniatures from the law.

"It feels so good to be using my hands and creativity to make things. It balances out my life perfectly." —Jason

Because all figures are twelve inches tall, Jason knows the exact proportions for each scene. It usually takes him two weeks to a few months to complete a diorama, and he often has a waiting list that stretches to four months or longer. Collectors are used to preorders and long wait times for the figures themselves, so they don't balk at waiting for their scenes.

Jason collects a deposit to secure a customer's place in line. Once he begins building a diorama, he sends photos to the customer as the scene is created. While he invites input from buyers, he makes it clear that he has final creative license. He demonstrated this when a customer wanted to increase the length of an item by two centimeters. Not possible!

Once a scene is completed, Jason sends it to the customer. He asks them to place the figure in the scene, take a photo, and post it on Facebook. This is the official "reveal," and once he sees the figure in the set he designed, the scene is a wrap.

Jason's dioramas cost an average of $300, and he admits he could probably charge more without upsetting customers. He doesn't want his side hustle to take over all of his personal time, so he's content to let customers find him through referral. In fact, until recently he didn't even have a website, taking all of his orders as a response to requests on Instagram.

After making more than one hundred miniature stages, he finally decided to set up an online store. He's got something to plan for: Jason and his wife are expecting their first child, and his side hustle profits are going toward a much-needed savings fund.

His big dream of making miniature movie sets ended up coming true, just in a different way than he expected. He now has that basement assembly line, something to look forward to after work, and a moneymaking side hustle.

How to Sell Your Art, Crafts, or Handiwork

If you like to get crafty, there are lots of places online where you can sell your creations. The key is to go where the buyers are, not just where a lot of other artists and makers hang out.

If you're not sure where your buyers might be, start with Etsy, the world's largest marketplace of handcrafts. And keep these tips in mind:

- Great photos go a long way: Not a photographer? Ask a friend with a good camera to help. Include multiple shots from different angles. And if you're selling clothing or jewelry, include images of how it looks on someone.

- Tell a story: Whenever you have the chance to sell something, you also have the chance to write a description. Make it a good one! Go into lots of detail and tell people why you made whatever you're selling.

- Respond quickly to inquiries: If possible, a one-hour response time is best. It builds trust and confidence ... and it also encourages buyers to make a purchase. Don't give them too much time to wander off and find something else they like better.

- Ask for reviews: Follow up with customers and ask them to review you on the site they purchased from. This makes a big difference, especially in the beginning. "Social proof" matters a lot—we want to know that other people like us were happy with their order.

For more, visit SideHustleSchool.com/crafty.

Automate Your Income

"Earn money while you sleep" is the ultimate promise—and for these people, it's part of their daily routine. These stories illustrate how working smarter, not just harder, can help you create systems that will pay out over and over.

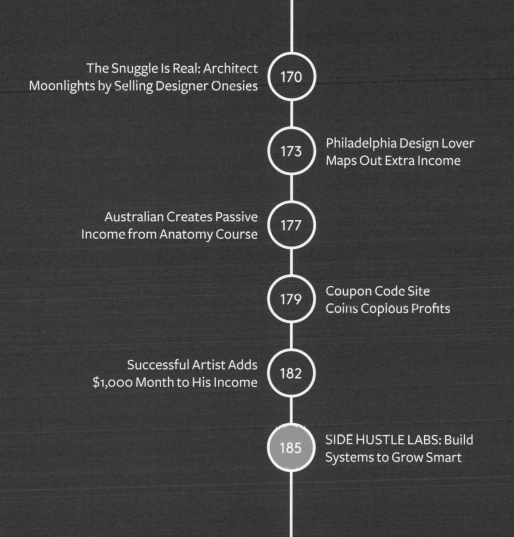

The Snuggle Is Real: Architect
Moonlights by Selling Designer Onesies — 170

173 — Philadelphia Design Lover
Maps Out Extra Income

Australian Creates Passive
Income from Anatomy Course — 177

179 — Coupon Code Site
Coins Copious Profits

Successful Artist Adds
$1,000 Month to His Income — 182

185 — SIDE HUSTLE LABS: Build
Systems to Grow Smart

THE SNUGGLE IS REAL: ARCHITECT MOONLIGHTS BY SELLING DESIGNER ONESIES

An architect creates minimalist, typographic onesies and T-shirts for his own kids—then turns it into a profitable side hustle, without stocking any inventory.

NAME
GERALD LAU

LOCATION
SYDNEY, AUSTRALIA

STARTUP COSTS
MINIMAL

INCOME
$1,000+/MONTH

By day, Gerald Lau is an architect in Sydney, Australia. He's a fan of clean lines, lots of white, and simple typography. Like a lot of people, he enjoys his job, but also wants to diversify his income.

He had previously tried a couple of projects that didn't work out. The first was selling designer stationery and homeware online. Since he handled his own inventory, it was hard for him to find time to keep up with stock, fulfill orders, and do the marketing needed to grow the business.

Next, he tried doing interior design gigs on the side, but it felt just like working overtime. His architecture job often requires long hours, and he needed a gig that he could fit into the cracks of his day.[*]

Gerald is a regular listener to *Side Hustle School*, and an episode about print-on-demand businesses caught his interest. It inspired him to develop an idea he had to create timeless, minimalist T-shirts for kids. He named his new idea the Typo Tees.

Startup costs were cheap: a domain name and a Shopify subscription, which helped keep the running costs low. He used a third-party service called Printly that would take care of all the printing and shipping. All of his products are made in the United States and they ship worldwide, choices Gerald was able to make when he set up his online shop.

But what would he sell? He knew he had to stand out somehow. Gerald decided to specialize in *alphabet onesies and T-shirts*, featuring the first letter of a kid's first or last name.

The initial results were as lackluster as his previous attempts, and nothing much happened. It took a few weeks before Gerald got his first order, for six shirts. That was

ACTION PLAN

1. Print-on-demand is easy to start, yet hard to master. To stand out, experiment with different ideas.

2. Identify your product: What will you sell? People who are successful at it tend to "niche down" like Gerald has done.

3. Choose a service that will print and ship your orders. In addition to the one mentioned in this story, there are many other options.

4. Once you have a supplier, build a basic website using Shopify or another platform.

5. When orders come in . . . do nothing, because your print-on-demand supplier will handle it all. Nice!

nice, but not nice enough to suggest that the project would continue long term—especially when that customer wasn't happy with the shirts and wanted her money back.

The mishap got worse when his supplier wouldn't give Gerald a refund, and he had to pay for it from his own pocket. Plus, he forgot to ask for the shirts back before refunding the customer, and she never returned them. Oops.

Gerald learned from the experience, put it in perspective, and moved on. At first, he was worried that something was wrong with the printer. But then he decided that quality wasn't the problem; it was just an unhappy customer. He had done his best in choosing a partner and decided to continue with them. If any other problems developed, he could always look for a different printer later.

One of the best things about print-on-demand is that there's no need to stock any inventory. Products are printed as people order them, and if you're the seller, you may never even see them. This gave Gerald the ability to expand his designs *with absolutely no cost.*

All he had to do was post new designs and see what people put in their shopping carts. He added simple, typeface-inspired graphics that featured playful messages with a clean aesthetic.

As he broadened his designs, more people began buying the onesies and shirts . . . and, fortunately, these customers were happy with the product.

FUN FACT Gerald was inspired by an episode of *Side Hustle School* that featured a man who provided for his family with five different side hustles. He's decided to attempt a similar feat, and is now on the hunt for his next project.

* It's usually important to do something different for your side hustle than you do for your day job. You want it to be work that brings you energy, not tires you out.

They loved dressing their kids in something that was personalized for them, like the first letter of their name. Gerald also added companion onesies and shirts to encourage multiple product purchases. One customer favorite is a onesie that reads, "The Snuggle Is Real," with a companion T-shirt for moms and dads that reads, "The Struggle Is Real."

Next, he added a customizable feature to his site. A customer can choose from five fonts and put in any message they would like. Thanks to the wonders of print-on-demand, the turnaround time from order until shipping is only twenty-four hours.

Gerald says the best part of having a side hustle like the Typo Tees is getting photos from happy customers and their kids wearing those onesies and T-shirts. He advises anyone thinking of going into online clothing sales to be sure they do something different to stand out. It's a saturated market, and anything you can think of has probably been done before in some shape or form.

He also advises you not to expect a positive return overnight. These kinds of projects tend to need time and experimentation. The struggle— or the snuggle—is real, but the rewards can be worth it.

PHILADELPHIA DESIGN LOVER
MAPS OUT EXTRA INCOME

A neuroscientist turned marketing manager moonlights as an artist, selling original paper-cut designs with very little marketing.

After what she calls a strange career jump from neuroscientist to marketing director—along with a few bad breakups along the way—Emma Fried-Cassorla found herself in the midst of an existential crisis. She loved her new job, but felt a strong urge to make something that showed off her artistic side.

In order to jump into extracurricular creative activities, Emma set herself a challenge: she'd create a paper-cut map of the city of Philadelphia.[*] She'd spent a lot of time with a scalpel performing experiments as a neuroscientist, and felt her skills would transfer perfectly.

For the next three months, Emma spent her evenings and weekends working on what she called her "4 × 3 project." She documented her progress on a blog, *Philly Love Notes*, and through its associated Instagram account. Once the project was completed, and on the recommendation of a friend, she scanned the finished work into her computer.

NAME
EMMA FRIED-CASSORLA

LOCATION
PHILADELPHIA, PENNSYLVANIA

STARTUP COSTS
LESS THAN $500

INCOME
$35,000/YEAR

WEBSITE
PHILLYLOVENOTES.COM

[*] A paper cut involves making precise incisions into paper to remove all the sections of paper that don't look like what you're trying to make. See the photo of Emma's map (page 174) for an example.

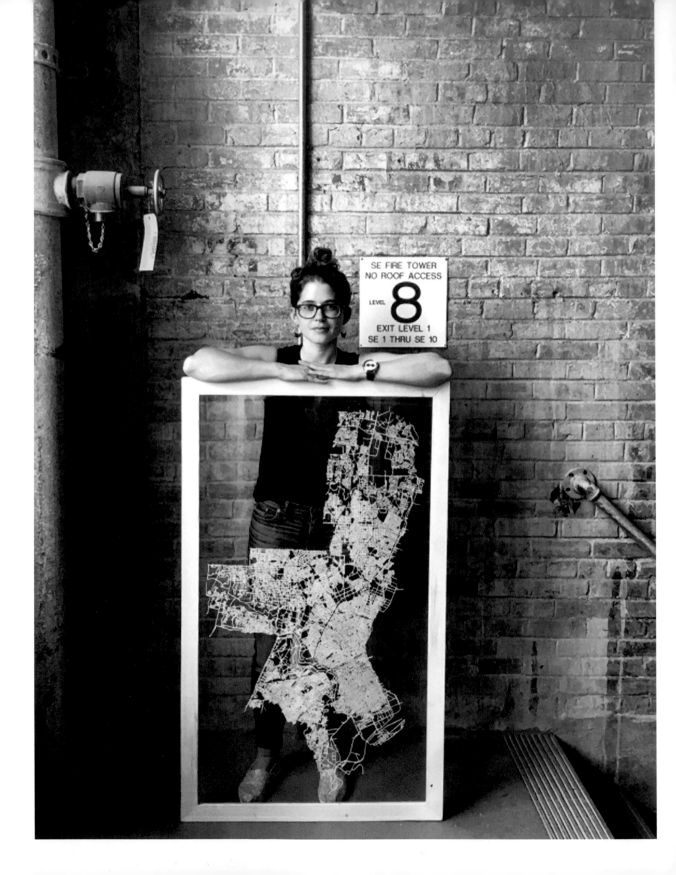

Little did she know that this labor of love would go on to become a project that earned tens of thousands of dollars a year in mostly passive income.

In the following weeks, Emma generated some buzz around the project by offering a giveaway people could enter to win the original map. She also shared the smaller maps she'd made for friends by laser-printing her design into pieces of wood. The response was overwhelming, and people began requesting their own custom maps through comments and direct messages.

To manage her business and the sudden influx of orders, Emma took her new craft business online, setting up shop and using the same name as her blog. She says that Etsy is the only real tool she uses to run the business, because it lets her handle both the front and back ends of her business in one easily accessible interface. On the one hand, it's a storefront she can refer people to with a simple link. On the other, it allows her to process and manage sales. And being a scientist at heart, she also has a manual spreadsheet that she maintains as backup documentation.

Custom maps make up around 95 percent of Emma's monthly orders. But while for most businesses *custom* means a lot of extra work, Emma has managed to refine it to a relatively painless process.

The original design that she scanned onto a computer forms the basis of all her orders. It's essentially a customizable template, and she can edit it, chop it up, and change it around to meet the needs of any custom order—all without having to spend any more months hunched over a piece of paper. She takes these custom files to her local art space, NextFab, where they're printed onto pieces of wood and then sanded down to be ready to ship.

She's got it down to a weekend ritual that she completes nearly every week of the year.

The ease of this process helped Emma keep her startup costs extremely low. She invests $129 into her NextFab membership per month, an additional $15 to $35 per hour for laser time, and nominal amounts for the

"I think that when you focus too much on it being a business, you get too caught up in business plans, debt, marketing plans, and so on. For me, it's a passion project. I don't rely on it, and if it went away, I wouldn't be too sad." —Emma

FUN FACT Emma's first sale was a trade with a street artist. She swapped a map for a faux sign saying, "Dream Big." Seems appropriate for what this project has become!

wood or craft paper for each map. Each piece will then retail in a range of $50 for the smallest size and $350 for the largest, with a small premium for a custom order.

The main marketing channel for her work has been Instagram. She has more than fifty-five thousand followers, which she's attracted through curating a feed solely about Philadelphia. Here she shares photographs that local people and travelers love, and uploads images of her maps once every two weeks. Whenever she does, she always sees an immediate spike in sales.

The second biggest driver of sales is word of mouth. Because of the uniqueness of her designs, she has a constant stream of people coming to her to see how much it would cost to have their own map made. This means that, aside from that biweekly social media update, Emma puts little effort into getting her maps in front of new customers. At some point, they just started to sell themselves.

Since her initial three months of work several years ago, the sales of these maps has earned her an average of $35,000 annually. Because she views her side hustle as a project and not a business, Emma has been able to avoid the need for constant expansion. That said, she would like to organically grow her brand and its designs to other cities.

If you've got a request, check out her shop and let her know where you live!

AUSTRALIAN CREATES PASSIVE
INCOME FROM ANATOMY COURSE

He didn't know much about human anatomy, but he created the definitive online course to help med students master its vocabulary. After making no updates to it for four years, it still brings in $800 a month.

For the past eight years, Mike Benkovich in Sydney, Australia, has earned an average of $800 a month for a project he's barely touched since first creating it. He hasn't improved it, and he hasn't done much to maintain it . . . it just keeps paying out, month after month.

The project is an online audio course that helps medical students memorize the human anatomy. Mike didn't make the course because he was a med school student himself, or because he was especially knowledgeable about anatomy. He made it because he thought other people might be interested in paying for it.

Here's how he did it.

Before actually creating the product itself, he wrote a pitch for it. The pitch explained the benefits of the product, as well as the problem that it would solve. In short, he promised to help students learn through mnemonics, without having to come up with potentially hundreds of them on their own.

Then, he tested the offer. He made a one-page website with a few stock images, and included a mailing list at the bottom where interested students could sign up to learn more.

When they signed up, they received a message: "Unfortunately, we are upgrading Anatomonics right now, so it is unavailable for order. We will email you shortly once the system has relaunched."

The entire purpose of the testing site was to see if people would really be interested in the product. But of course, he didn't have a product at that point—he had to make it![*]

FUN FACT There are more than seventy-five hundred parts of the human body—no small number to keep up with when you're studying medicine.

NAME
MIKE BENKOVICH

LOCATION
SYDNEY, AUSTRALIA

STARTUP COSTS
MINIMAL

INCOME
$800/MONTH FOR 7+ YEARS

WEBSITE
ANATOMONICS.COM

[*] Notice the order of these events. He didn't start with making the product; he focused first on clarifying who it was for and then verifying the existence of a market for it.

"I got the idea by going to the Google keywords tool and typing in 'memorize.' One of the suggestions was 'memorize anatomy,' so I went from there. After brainstorming a few ideas, I decided that combining anatomy mnemonics with audio could be a good approach." —Mike

To do this, he got creative. He hired two people from a freelancing website, a researcher and a voice-over actor. The researcher's job was to collect the data that the voice-over actor would then record. Mike reviewed everything before the actor recorded it, and he also updated the site to accept payments from customers.

The whole process took about two months. Once it was ready, Mike went back to his initial test audience and offered them the product for sale at a 50 percent discount. There were just thirty people in that group, but ten of them took the deal, earning him $600.

That was a great start, and to make sure the customers would keep coming, he made a series of short online videos. He also posted some articles about anatomy on the site over the next few months, improving its Google rankings and drawing in new students. Before long, he was making at least a few hundred dollars a month, with almost no marketing and minimal customer support.

A few months later, he made a very smart decision: he added price tiers, giving customers three options to choose from when purchasing the course. This one action increased his average order by $25 without affecting the conversion rate, and he was soon earning $800 a month without much effort.

So what did he do next? Did he get more serious about the business, growing it to six figures by working on it night and day? Nope . . . he got bored and moved on to other projects. It happens.

But *before* he got bored, he arrived at this plateau that has never changed, at least not significantly, in all those years. The business is somewhat seasonal, because students are more active in their studies during certain times of year, but the annual income is consistent. His profit margin is virtually 100 percent, because there are almost no expenses now that the product has been made.

At the time we profiled him, it had all added up to something like $67,000 that arrived over time. And, of course, the payments *continued* to arrive month after month.

It was an incredible return on investment for something he'd known nothing about when he started.

CRITICAL FACTOR

Mike's anatomy course served a specific group of people that didn't have access to anything similar. It's also an evergreen topic—not much changes in the world of anatomy from year to year!

COUPON CODE SITE COINS COPIOUS PROFITS

A marketer for a retail company sits on a domain name for more than a decade before finally turning it into a website that earns ongoing affiliate commissions.

Ever search for an online coupon code? Many people have . . . and a lot of them have been frustrated by codes that are expired or otherwise inactive.

Enter Antonella Pisani. Her side hustle was a long time coming: twelve years to be precise. That's when she first bought the domain OfficialCouponCode.com. At the time, she was working in marketing for a major retailer and saw a growing number of people making money through that retailer's affiliate program. She had grabbed the domain because she wanted to cash in on this revenue stream herself, with a coupon site that was more customer friendly than average—one with no expired deals or codes that didn't work.

However, the project wasn't meant to be, at least not for a number of years. She was so busy with her day job that she didn't have time to do anything with it, so it just sat there. Then, four years ago she happened to mention to some coworkers that she owned the domain—and they basically told her she was crazy for not doing something with it.

Right around this time, Antonella had also decided to strike out on her own and start a digital marketing agency. She took some time off to travel as she transitioned to working for herself, and during the trip she made a plan to finally build the site.

The first thing she had to do was decide on a platform. After testing out a few options, she settled on a WordPress coupon theme that had all the features she was looking for, with plenty of room to grow. She did a lot of customization as she built out the website, mostly using free and paid plug-ins. She hired a friend to design her logo for a few hundred dollars and slowly started creating a more polished brand.

NAME
ANTONELLA PISANI

LOCATION
DENVER, COLORADO

STARTUP COSTS
$15,000

INCOME
$45,000/YEAR

WEBSITE
OFFICIALCOUPONCODE.COM

ACTION PLAN

1. To be successful with this kind of project, you'll need two things: relationships with affiliate managers, and traffic that will click their links.
2. Review some other coupon code sites. Identify merchants or directories and request approval to list their links.
3. Find a source that provides updated coupon codes on a regular basis. It's also possible to search for codes on your own (it just takes a lot of time).
4. Build your site and attract traffic! This is easier said than done, of course, but ultimately it's the only key to success with a project like this. If you can figure it out, you're in business.

With the base website in place, she needed a way to import and maintain deals that didn't involve her manually inputting data. Again, she did some testing. After trying a few free plug-ins, she opted to pay for a feed service that provides real-time information.* At anywhere from $500 to $2,000 per month, the service doesn't come cheap, but it has real people behind it testing each offer and providing quality content.

From there, it was time to start applying to be an affiliate with as many retailers as possible. As Antonella shared, "The affiliate industry is a chicken or egg game. Retailers won't let you into their programs if you don't have traffic or sales on the network, but it's tough to get traffic and sales without good retailers. It really didn't matter that I had just come off of being an executive at several large companies, I still had to do a fair amount of groveling early on."

Eventually, she made her way onto multiple affiliate networks, and now works with half a dozen of them.

Once she had her first affiliate partnership set up, she wanted to invest in a copywriter to help build out content for various store pages. But that got expensive quickly. Luckily, she learned about Fancy Hands, a US-based virtual assistant service, and was able to outsource some research and writing to them for much cheaper.

"All of the projects in my day job come with very large budgets. When you're on your own, you have to find inexpensive ways to accomplish things, and I think it makes you better at your job. I've had a tremendous amount of fun getting my hands dirty again, and learning to think in a more scrappy way." —Antonella

The goal was to strike the right balance between providing useful content and discounts for customers while also ranking well in search engine results. Oh, and she needed to do it all without burning through a ton of cash.

With the key elements in place, Antonella was ready to get the word out, which started by using social media to tell her friends. With her background in corporate marketing, she also knew to distribute press releases to media outlets. This tactic worked well and ended up getting her press on sites like Engadget, Entrepreneur, and the Street—all of which drove high-quality traffic to her website.

FUN FACT The project began when Antonella was on an extended trip, and she built the website almost completely from the road and the ocean—both the Antarctica and the Arctic. She once even had to update the site from her cell phone in the Sahara desert.

* The service is called FMTC, which stands for For Me to Compete.

A more unique marketing tactic was especially helpful. She ran a scholarship contest for undergraduate students, both to give back and promote her new business. Each year, one student is awarded a few thousand dollars, and Official Coupon Code gets some great press in a variety of different media outlets.

For all her efforts, Official Coupon Code cleared five figures in net income during year one. While she spent a fair amount of money getting the website set up and paying for the content to flesh out the site, that initial investment has more than paid off. The next year, she saw more than a 300 percent increase in both traffic and referral fees.

Antonella knows that the key to generating more revenue is continually updating the website with custom content, new links, new deals, and new retailers. That's why she's happy with her decision to use a service to help her update all that data.

Since this is purely a side hustle for her, Antonella thinks of the website as a long-term investment, and a nice source of income for her frequent trips. Her focus has now shifted to a new project, and this one can continue to pay dividends even as she does other things.

It took more than a decade, but she's glad she decided to dust off that domain name and put it to work.

CRITICAL FACTOR

It's frustrating to search for deals online, only to find coupon codes that don't work. Antonella's site promises "no expired codes," generating loyalty in an industry where most visitors are merely clicking around with no intent to return.

SUCCESSFUL ARTIST ADDS
$1,000 A MONTH TO HIS INCOME

An artist uses his love of whimsical drawing to create a side hustle selling everything from autographed prints to coffee mugs with his designs on them.

NAME
MARC JOHNS

LOCATION
VICTORIA, CANADA

STARTUP COSTS
$0

INCOME
AT LEAST $1,000/MONTH

WEBSITE
MARCJOHNS.COM

From his studio on beautiful Vancouver Island, the artist Marc Johns creates and sells artwork all over the world. You may have seen his whimsical designs online or in shops. And because of an unexpected decision he made a few years ago, you may see those designs on someone's phone case.

A few years ago, Marc noticed he was getting lots of emails asking the same question: "Where can I get an iPhone case with your artwork on it?"

Marc is a decidedly low-tech guy. His first response to the queries was "What's that?" . . . because he didn't even own a smartphone. He

ACTION PLAN

1. Are you an artist? Do you have prints or other work for sale? If yes, keep reading.
2. Make an account with Society6 or a similar platform.
3. Upload high-quality images of your artwork or designs.
4. Select which items you want customers to choose from: T-shirts, phone cases, or others.
5. Let your customers, fans, and online followers know that the shop is open! Include a link on your website and anywhere else people might find you.
6. You probably won't make a ton of money, but you might make some . . . and once you're set up, there's not much more you need to do for it.

RAINBOW TYPES

regular

bold

light

italic

extended

condensed

marc johns

lightning bolt cats are better than regular cats.

marc johns

repeatedly turned down the requests, but as they continued to arrive in his inbox, he began to look into doing something about them.

That search led to a site called Society6, a print-on-demand service focused on the arts community. With Society6, artists can upload designs, and customers can purchase them whenever they'd like. The business behind the site handles all the fulfillment, so once you've uploaded those designs, your work is done—at least theoretically.

It's important to note that as a successful artist, Marc already had his own online shop where he sold prints. So why would he create a profile on this other platform? Well, in short, he didn't want to be in the business of making phone cases. But if his fans wanted to buy them, and someone else was able to easily make them, why not?

Marc signed up with Society6, added some artwork, and began to let people know that those long-desired phone cases were now available for purchase. And his fans started purchasing—not in droves, but steadily.

FUN FACT Learning to sell his designs on phone cases led to another unexpected side hustle: teaching others how to do the same thing, through a self-directed course he created.

"Before I started selling on Society6, I thought people would only be interested in art prints. I couldn't imagine my work on products. The lesson I learned: listen to your audience. You are not your audience." —Marc

CRITICAL FACTOR

Marc's designs were already popular, but he'd never thought about putting them on phone cases. By delegating sales and production to a company that handles the entire process, he was able to make more money with very little effort.

Whenever he made a sale, he'd get a notification. That was fun for a while, but then he also liked the thrill of turning off the pings and just logging into the site once in a while to see how much "bonus money" he made.

That's the key to this project: it's not a full-time income; it's bonus money. A significant commission is taken by Society6, but again, making phone cases isn't part of Marc's mission. The fact that he can make them available and earn royalties on them is good enough.

Marc likes the fact that Society6 pays out royalties every month, no matter how small your earnings are. If you make $2, they'll send you $2. Even payments like those can feel empowering, especially when you're not doing much work for them.

Even better, after he experimented a bit with different designs and pricing, Marc now makes a lot more than $2—he's consistently bringing in more than $1,000 a month from this additional source of income. The process happens without him doing anything at all, and he continues to focus full-time on his real career as an artist.

He also finally got his own smartphone.

Build Systems to Grow Smart

What are business systems? Simply put, they are tools, protocols, or workflows that allow your business to operate without your direct involvement.

In the case of Mike's passive income anatomy course (pages 177–78), students automatically receive access to the files after making a purchase. They also receive an email confirmation, which serves as a receipt and reminds them where they can go to start studying. If the students didn't get access automatically, Mike would have to manually send each one a message whenever he received an order—an inefficient process for everyone involved.

You might not be able to build a completely automated business, and you might not want to—if you're doing client work, for example, you'll still need to spend time with clients. The point is that *the more systems you build, the less time you'll spend doing the same tasks over and over*. Also, if you choose to grow the business at some point, systems will be key in allowing you to serve more customers.

For more, visit SideHustleSchool.com/systems.

IX

See the World Without Going Broke

If you don't want to be confined to a desk, how about living in an RV or jetting out on a series of one-way plane tickets around the globe? For those looking for a room with a view, preferably one that someone else pays for, read on.

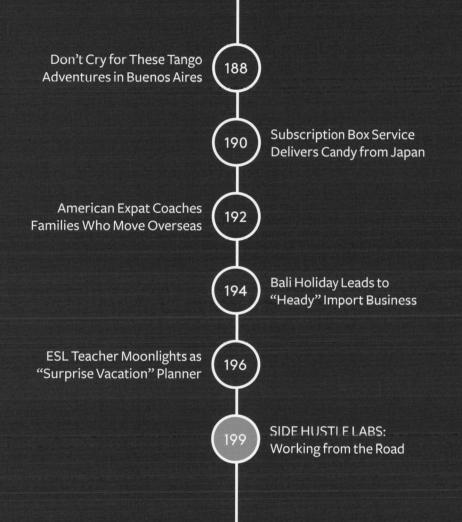

Don't Cry for These Tango
Adventures in Buenos Aires
188

190
Subscription Box Service
Delivers Candy from Japan

American Expat Coaches
Families Who Move Overseas
192

194
Bali Holiday Leads to
"Heady" Import Business

ESL Teacher Moonlights as
"Surprise Vacation" Planner
196

199
SIDE HUSTLE LABS:
Working from the Road

DON'T CRY FOR THESE TANGO ADVENTURES IN BUENOS AIRES

After traveling to South America, an American woman falls in love with tango and creates a group experience to teach others.

NAME
SASHA CAGEN

LOCATION
BUENOS AIRES, ARGENTINA

STARTUP COSTS
MINIMAL

INCOME
$15,000/YEAR

WEBSITE
SASHACAGEN.COM

Sasha Cagen is currently living and working in Buenos Aires, Argentina—but she didn't start out there. She first discovered the city several years ago while on a long trip around South America.

From the moment she saw tango on display in a public square, and then danced a beginner's version of it the same day, she knew there was something special that spoke to her. Then she practiced more and took lessons back at home in California. She attributes the dance with helping her gain confidence, improve her relationships, and even get in the zone with her writing.

When she moved to Buenos Aires, she planned to "live tango at the source" and get a deeper experience of the whole culture. It was while she was there that she had a bolt of inspiration. She wanted to design a weeklong experience to share with other women what she had learned over the last few years of dancing. Before she returned to the United States for an extended visit, she checked out hotels and found an instructor to teach the actual tango lessons.

Back in California, Sasha created an all-inclusive experience that would facilitate this deep-dive into tango that she'd experienced. The $2,195 fee includes pre- and postcoaching sessions with Sasha, private lessons with the tango teacher, and four *milonga* outings, where dances are held through the night.

Sasha encourages everyone to stay at the same hotel, to further encourage the group bonding. She also includes group outings to help build community—they all go shoe shopping and have a few shared meals.

"Tango teaches you things in a way that you might never learn any other way. The amount of self-awareness and insight a person can gain through studying tango is immense." —Sasha

FUN FACT Sasha's clients range in age from twenty-eight to seventy. One of her favorites, a sixty-year-old woman who had recently divorced her husband of thirty-five years, came on a Tango Adventure trip to fulfill an item on her bucket list—to dance tango in Buenos Aires—and Sasha got to help her check it off the list.

Once she had the logistics figured out, and six months after the bolt of inspiration, she launched her sales page. She was soon back in Buenos Aires leading her first Tango Adventure experience with the five women who'd signed up.

That first group came just from marketing to her own email list, from her primary business as a life coach for women. In fact, for a while that was her *only* marketing. Eventually, she started getting tango clients from different sources.

The money she makes from her tango hustle isn't enough to live on, but it's helped to supplement her lifestyle and allowed her to focus on her writing. The original costs of moving to Buenos Aires have long been offset by the lower cost of living in Argentina, as compared to California.

Beyond getting paid for something she loves to do, Sasha enjoys connecting with the women that go on her trips. She imagines that when she releases the memoir she's been working on, women who read it will want to travel to Buenos Aires and experience tango for themselves.

For now, she's happy to let things evolve organically and see how each of her projects might support the other in the long run.

CRITICAL FACTOR

Many women who come on Sasha's trips are in search of adventure or rediscovery. The sense of experiencing the world as part of a group is important to them, and they might not take a trip like this solo.

SUBSCRIPTION BOX SERVICE
DELIVERS CANDY FROM JAPAN

An expat living in Japan searches Tokyo for the most unique candy he can find, and then ships it to subscribers worldwide each month.

NAME
BEMMU SEPPONEN

LOCATION
TOKUSHIMA, JAPAN

STARTUP COSTS
$0[*]

INCOME
$40,000 TO $75,000/YEAR

WEBSITE
CANDYJAPAN.COM

* Bemmu made his website himself, and only purchased the candy for his first shipments after he had received a batch of orders.

When you go to Japan, be sure you see the cherry blossoms and the shrines of Kyoto. And before you leave, take time to visit a local convenience store. It's not just where you go for a soda, it's an immersive cultural experience. You can find everything from fully prepared meals to a kimono for formal occasions.

On your way into the store, you might also notice the vending machines. In Japan, vending machines are a tourist attraction of their own. Among many other options, you can pick up your choice of dozens of kinds of candy.

But if you can't make it there right away, there's another way to experience this magical land . . . and it's all because someone decided to try something fun and unusual.

Nearly a decade ago, Bemmu Sepponen moved to Japan from his native Finland. He had met the woman who would become his wife when she came over as a foreign exchange student at his university. After moving abroad to be with her, he worked remotely for an employer back in Finland, but he also had a lot of spare time. He wanted to create a second income, and before long he hit on an idea: Why not sell Japanese candy to people outside of Japan?

Not only was it a great idea, he also chose a great model for this hustle: instead of one-off sales, he set it up as a subscription box service. For $29 a month, shipping included, Candy Japan would send people two boxes full of interesting and unconventional sweets that could only be found in the Land of the Rising Sun.

"I started Candy Japan with the idea of mailing Japanese sweets to subscribers around the world on a twice-monthly basis. It worked! Hundreds of people signed up, and we kept sending them crazy Japanese candy for years." —Bemmu

Starting out was easy. Being a programmer, he made his own website, and he didn't invest in inventory. He only went out to purchase the candy whenever orders came in, so the entire project funded itself.

Just as the candy is ever-renewing, so too are his subscriptions. They didn't arrive all at once—they came over time, slow and steady, until he grew to more than three hundred people paying that $29 a month.

In addition to subscriptions, he also offers gift purchases of a single month, or even a whole year. This has been a great boost to his ongoing monthly subscribers, and for a while he had income of $15,000 a month from the project. It's slowed down a bit since the peak, but still brings in at least several thousand dollars a month.

Bemmu has tried a lot of different things to market Candy Japan. One of his most successful marketing attempts came from a post he replied to on Reddit. Someone asked, "What is the most ridiculous thing available on the internet for $25 shipped?"

Bemmu replied, "My subscription box of candy from Japan is just $4 more than that. It's pretty ridiculous."

His website received two thousand visits over the next few days, and more than thirty new subscriptions. That one post resulted in him earning an additional $10,000 that year.

FUN FACT You might think that Bemmu would run out of candy options after a while, but candy in Japan is serious business. There are more than forty different Kit Kat flavors alone.

 CRITICAL FACTOR

It's candy from Japan! And even if you don't want to subscribe for yourself, it makes for a fun gift.

AMERICAN EXPAT COACHES
FAMILIES WHO MOVE OVERSEAS

After living in multiple countries with a family, a technical writer creates a service to help other people interested in having a similar experience.

NAME
JEFF PARKER

LOCATION
HALIFAX, CANADA

STARTUP COSTS
$300

INCOME
$10,000/YEAR

WEBSITE
EXPATYOURSELF.COM

Jeff Parker is a technical writer and textbook author who works at home. As for where he lives, it's kind of a long story.

Jeff is American by birth and passport, but he now resides most of the time in Halifax, Nova Scotia. He met his wife, Maylia, while they were both living in South Korea more than twenty years ago. Since then, Jeff and Maylia—and eventually their two children—migrated around the globe to a lot of different spots. They lived in the Czech Republic, back in the United States, and then in Denmark and Germany. And that's not all— long ago, Jeff served in the military and was stationed in the Middle East.

All these experiences gave him a different perspective than a lot of people have, especially those who haven't traveled as a family. Jeff believed that while he's been fortunate, his experience didn't need to be extraordinary—most families can do what his has done. He also knew that many of them *want* to, but just don't know where to start.

Some parents perceive that living abroad or extended travel is something for young people or couples without children, when in reality there are also many families who strike out to see the world and describe it as a life-changing experience.

If this sounds like the makings of a side hustle, well, it is!

For a long time running, Jeff's friends (and friends of his friends) would call or email him to ask questions. When he

ACTION PLAN

1. It's much easier to be a coach who provides an easily understandable service. "Helping families master the transition to living overseas" is ideal. What can you offer?
2. Speak with three to five people who meet the target market—people who could benefit from your offer. Ask them in detail about their questions, needs, fears, and concerns.
3. Create a workflow for a consulting session. Plan for each session to have clear outcomes for the client.
4. Make it simple for people to sign up. Create a one-page website that includes an option to take payment right there.
5. Follow up with clients after the session with a list of notes and further recommendations.

FUN FACT When planning to move abroad as a family, Jeff recommends a three-month plan from decision to move. Of course, some people may take longer or shorter, but in his experience, this is the time frame most people need to sort out jobs, housing, and schools.

and his wife were out in a group, the topic would come up, often becoming the whole focal point of the conversation. Jeff did a number of informal chats and meetings, but people had more and more questions.

At some point, he grew frustrated. He liked to be helpful, but he also had a job and a family of his own. Finally, he realized he could keep being helpful—he could always provide quick answers for free and compile some basic info on a website—but for those who were serious about moving overseas, maybe a personal consultation was just what they needed.

One riddle he had to solve was how much to charge for the service. He started at $50 an hour, and then went to $75, and ended up at his current rate of $150 an hour. You can communicate a lot of information in a focused, hour-long call, so there's real value for the customer, and at that rate it's also worthwhile for Jeff.

This side business now brings in more than $10,000 a year entirely through that coaching, which Jeff does apart from his regular work as a technical writer. His next step is to diversify, since there's only so much time he can devote to coaching sessions.

In pursuit of that goal, he's creating an email series that will provide a ton of specific, helpful info that doesn't require him to be on the phone for an hour. Depending on their needs and preferences, clients can choose whether they want the written information or a real-life session.

Back when he was traipsing around eastern Europe, or stationed in the Middle East during his military service, there wasn't a strategic plan to eventually turn it into a business—Jeff was just enjoying the process.

He had no idea those stamps in his passport would eventually be so valuable.

> "The first time I charged money for helping a family overseas, I couldn't stop smiling. It clicked because I realized that this is something people are willing to spend money for." —Jeff

CRITICAL FACTOR

Many people with families would love to move abroad, even if just for a year or two, but naturally they have many questions and concerns. Jeff is an expert and understands their needs. If you're in that situation and considering a major move, a session with him is an easy purchase.

BALI HOLIDAY LEADS TO "HEADY" IMPORT BUSINESS

Fascinated by Balinese culture and sensing an opportunity, this San Francisco native imports and resells an unusual set of items.

NAME
MICHAEL SINDICICH

LOCATION
BALI, INDONESIA, AND SAN FRANCISCO, CALIFORNIA

STARTUP COSTS
$10,000

INCOME
$30,000 IN ONE YEAR

WEBSITE
BALISKULLS.COM

For account executive Michael Sindicich, his vacation to Bali was a way to break free from a series of stressful, seventy-hour San Francisco work weeks. He needed to find a little corner of the world where he could relax. One night, taking a stroll among the Indonesian markets and boutiques, he happened upon a stall filled with Balinese carved cow skulls—and instantly fell in love with their unique and intricate designs.

At $80 each, these high-quality skulls were a real bargain . . . but they came with a headful of problems. Because of their size and delicate nature, you couldn't just pop them into your suitcase. Doing some further research, Michael found stories of people who had been stopped at customs and had the items confiscated, even though they were perfectly legal. So instead of buying local, he figured he'd wait until he got home and try to order one online instead.

Before we go on, you might be wondering how these skulls are sourced. Indonesia is predominantly a Muslim country, but Bali is where most of the Hindu minority lives. Cows are considered sacred in Hindu culture, and the skulls are taken from animals that have died of natural causes. They are not killed in order to use their skulls for art—instead, it's a process of using every part of the animal.

Once Michael was back in California, a few Google searches revealed that the skulls were retailing for over $300 in the United States—a full $220 more than he'd seen in Bali! Right away, he was struck with an idea for his next side hustle. He knew he couldn't be the only traveler in the world who'd wanted to bring back a skull from their Balinese holiday.

Michael spent the next few weeks in between his job responsibilities scouring the internet, trying to find a company in Bali to help him import the skulls. He had almost given up when he turned to YouTube to watch videos of local artists. In the descriptions of one of the videos, he found

> "Find a good product you can make margins on, assess the market need, find a reliable supplier, and speak with them on video call. Then order small to start, and stay lean." —Michael

FUN FACT The Balinese use a 210-day calendar called the Pawukon. It consists of 10 weeks composed of 10 days each. This special calendar isn't used in the rest of Indonesia, which can sometimes lead to confusion.

a blog, which led him to a company. Using LinkedIn, he found the owner of the company and sent him a message to propose a new partnership.

After a few messages back and forth, they came to a deal. Michael ordered one hundred hand-carved skulls for $10,000 . . . and then began to play a nervous waiting game.

He admits that sending such a large amount of money to someone he barely knew on the other side of the world was scary and potentially reckless. But after a few months of waiting, the shipment arrived, and he had his first batch of stock ready to sell.

Over the next few weeks, Michael began to create a marketing campaign for his unique works of art. He put together a website using the brand name Bali Skulls, and started an Instagram feed to bring the skulls back to life through social media. He also invested a small amount of money in advertising, trying to maximize his visibility. Lastly, he found spaces at local markets and events to promote the skulls in person.

Within a month of receiving his first shipment, Michael had made his first sale for $300. Since then, he's gone on to make up to $3,000 in sales of the skulls in one week. When we last spoke, he predicted that he'd have no trouble selling the rest of his inventory within the year.

His next steps are to increase the visibility of the online store, as well as spread the word through local markets in San Francisco. He's also targeting interior decorators and retailers.

It looks like this side hustle has already got a good head start—or is it a skull-rattling success?

CRITICAL FACTOR

Getting Balinese art direct from the source can be a customs and logistics nightmare. Michael figured it out for a niche product, and is able to help himself while also helping local artists.

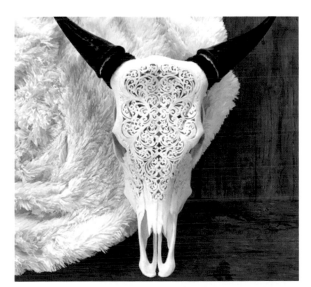

ESL TEACHER MOONLIGHTS AS "SURPRISE VACATION" PLANNER

An elementary school teacher creates a service-for-hire to "whisk away" travelers to surprise destinations.

NAME
CHARLOTTE MCGHEE

LOCATION
CHARLOTTE, NORTH CAROLINA

STARTUP COSTS
MINIMAL

INCOME
$25,000 IN REVENUE, $5,000 IN PROFIT IN YEAR ONE

WEBSITE
EXPLOREWHISKEDAWAY.COM

Charlotte McGhee is an English as a Second Language (ESL) teacher at an urban elementary school in Charlotte, North Carolina. Until two years ago, she had never had a side hustle.

She didn't know how to create a website, decide on pricing, or market herself—but she knew that she loved planning travel for people. She was good at it, and she noticed that other people often didn't know where to start when planning a trip. And while she would happily pass the time looking up options and sample itineraries, other people didn't want to sit in front of a computer for hours after work to do all the research.

Still, she'd only helped friends, and only for free, until one weekend when she and her husband were sitting in a bar in Savannah, Georgia, on a quick weekend trip that she'd planned. Naturally, she'd plotted out all sorts of activities and spots to explore in advance.

Before the trip, she'd been pondering the idea of starting a trip-planning service. Her husband looked at her and said, "You know, you should really do this."

So she did.

The service is called Whisked Away Surprise Travel. Charlotte created a simple website where prospective clients complete an intake form. The form asks about their budget, travel dates, and which region of the world they'd like to travel in. They also note any preferences or "wish list" items.

Each client gets a completely customized trip to a surprise destination in the region of their choice. It's just ten minutes' work for the client, but then Charlotte spends around ten hours per trip doing all the research and preparing a detailed plan.

FUN FACT One of Charlotte's clients was traveling alone, and her mother was concerned—so Charlotte took the mother out for coffee. She says that all she did was listen, but by the end of the visit, the client's mom felt reassured.

Two weeks before they leave, clients receive an email detailing (a) what time to arrive at the airport, (b) what to pack, and (c) what the weather will be like.

One week before, they get a surprise envelope with their entire itinerary inside: flights, accommodations, restaurant recommendations, and activity suggestions. Charlotte is hard core—she recommends that clients wait to open it until they get to the airport!

Clients pay the total amount of their trip up front when they book. For example, if someone wants to take a weeklong solo trip to Latin America, those prices start at $1,500. The price includes both the travel expenses and Charlotte's planning fee.

Her very first clients were a couple who wanted to celebrate their honeymoon with surprise travel. Charlotte got the notification of payment on her phone while she was at a school celebration with her colleagues . . . and screamed out loud. When she showed it to everyone, it started a great conversation about going after things you are passionate about.

As business slowly grew, clients came in through referrals. That first couple referred their wedding photographers (also an engaged couple) and *they* booked a surprise honeymoon too.

In her first year, Whisked Away brought in $25,000 in revenue. Most of that total was used to pay for clients' travel, Charlotte's own travel, and some small marketing costs. Net income was around $5,000.

Having someone else book your vacation isn't for everyone. For some of Charlotte's clients, the trip she books is their only one of the year. If you enjoy planning, or if you don't like surprises, then Whisked Away is probably not for you. On the other hand, if travel planning stresses you out and you're open to new experiences, it could be the perfect fit.

When she was starting out, Charlotte was impatient to book those first clients. A friend of hers said something that stuck with her: "You aren't selling $50 shoes. People aren't going to wake up in the morning and decide to buy a surprise trip on a whim. Give it time."

"In the first few months, read everything you can and hustle it out. But once you have your project in place, try to sit back and let things play out a bit. Surrender a little!" —Charlotte

That friend was absolutely right. What she's selling is not only a big-ticket item, but it's also something that people purchase with no idea of what they're going to get. She's had to build trust with her clients, and also find the right people in the first place.

No travel plan survives contact with the battleground of real travel, but Charlotte has learned to make adjustments in response to conditions on the ground. For example, during that first year, a client used Whisked Away to book a solo trip to Latin America. Charlotte was excited because Latin America is her favorite region. The client had also just finished her yoga teacher training, so she sent her to an amazing beachfront spot in Cartagena, Colombia. It was perfect . . . or at least, it started that way.

Three days into the stay, Charlotte got an email letting her know that the electricity had been out at the hotel for forty-eight hours. Apparently, the city was working on the grid where the hotel was located. Charlotte got the client rebooked in a different place and she was happy, even referring another client who booked right away after she came home.

The experience was a reminder that there are some things with travel that just can't be controlled. Even for a person who loves to plan, being able to respond to changes can sometimes be just as valuable.

Next, Charlotte wants to reconsider her pricing to make sure she's being fairly compensated for her time. Profit of $5,000 in year one isn't bad at all, but for this to be sustainable, she'll need to make more. She plans to keep working with immigrants in the school system for her day job, while growing Whisked Away and serving more clients.

She's also recently added an option for gift card purchases—perhaps a good holiday gift for someone out there in need of a surprise vacation.

Working from the Road

For more than fifteen years, I've had a location-independent lifestyle where I can do almost all of my work from wherever I am. This doesn't mean I don't have a home—it just means that frequent travel is a big part of my life, and I've learned to incorporate it into everything else I do.

It's harder than it looks. Based on reality, not a promise of brushing sand from your laptop while you work from the beach, here are some tips that might help.

- Set yourself up for success: If you're trying to see the world, you need to see the world—and not everything can be a priority. Give your work the attention it deserves, no matter where you are.

- Be intentional about what you hope to accomplish: When there's a lot happening or if you're just easily distracted, you need to have a specific idea of what needs to get done. Otherwise, *nothing* will get done.

- Let go of material things and obligations wherever you can: Life is all about choices. Ask yourself, "What can I let go of?" Don't obsess over what pair of socks you should pack for your two-week overseas trip. Trust me on this: you can buy socks *all over the world*. (I know, globalization is crazy!)

- Capture pockets of time wherever you can: Always carry a notebook with you, and take advantage of downtime. Make a "ten minute list" of things you can accomplish in a short period of time—while riding the bus, waiting at the bank, or whenever you only have a few minutes before dashing for an airport shuttle.

For more, visit SideHustleSchool.com/travel.

Eat, Drink, and Be Merry*

Cookies, coffee, ice pops, and beer—these stories really take the cake.

*We thought about calling it "Eat, Drink, and Deposit Money in Your Bank Account," but it didn't have quite the same ring.

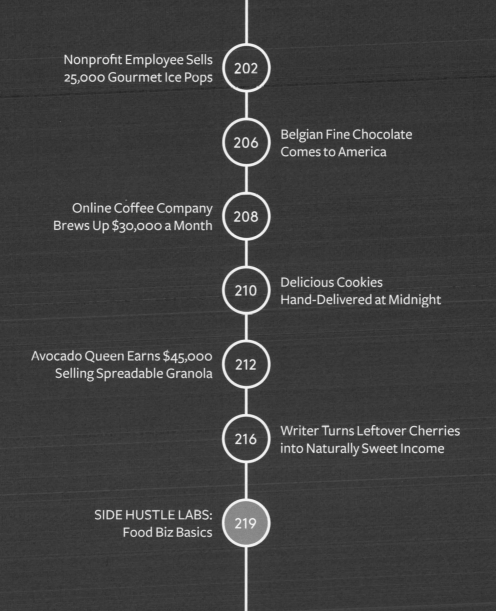

Nonprofit Employee Sells
25,000 Gourmet Ice Pops

202

206

Belgian Fine Chocolate
Comes to America

Online Coffee Company
Brews Up $30,000 a Month

208

210

Delicious Cookies
Hand-Delivered at Midnight

Avocado Queen Earns $45,000
Selling Spreadable Granola

212

216

Writer Turns Leftover Cherries
into Naturally Sweet Income

SIDE HUSTLE LABS:
Food Biz Basics

219

NONPROFIT EMPLOYEE SELLS
25,000 GOURMET ICE POPS

A Texas couple's bucket list challenge turns into a full-time hustle making and selling ice pops throughout the state.

NAME
CAROLYN PHILLIPS

LOCATION
FORT WORTH, TEXAS

STARTUP COSTS
$2,000

INCOME
$80,000 IN YEAR TWO

WEBSITE
ALCHEMYPOPS.COM

Carolyn Phillips and her husband, Wiley, created a list of thirty things they wanted to do before they turned thirty. They framed the list and updated it regularly by placing stickers next to the items they completed. But as the stickers started to add up, one item remained stubbornly sticker free—Carolyn's goal to start a side hustle.

Around this time, they threw a party at their house. In a fit of inspiration, Carolyn decided to create *alcoholic ice pops* using a bottle of vodka and some items that she'd picked up from the farmers' market. Living in Fort Worth, Texas, anything that can be used to beat the heat was likely to go over well, and gourmet pops were essentially the cupcakes of the sweltering Southwest.[*]

Carolyn's boozy pops were a juicy success, and it occurred to her that this might be the project she was looking for. Not only could she make them using whatever seasonal ingredients were available at the time, ice pops in general were also wildly popular across multiple demographics. And despite the success that this frozen treat was having in other major cities, it was relatively nonexistent in the Dallas–Fort Worth area.

So she began to experiment from her kitchen with different flavor profiles and combinations. When she wasn't working her 9-to-5 job in donor relations, she spent every free hour on her new side hustle, which she called Alchemy Pops.

Her friends would come over to try out new flavors of pops and take a "pop quiz." For her birthday party, she made herself more boozy pops.

FUN FACT At one point, Carolyn ordered equipment from Brazil and listed her home address as the delivery location. She got a call from the company the day before it arrived, confirming that there was a loading dock for the eighteen-wheeler that would be delivering it. After making some frantic calls, she was able to get permission from a company down the street from her to deliver the equipment there. A kind employee then drove the equipment to her house on his forklift.

[*] "Popsicles" is a trademarked term owned by Unilever. Generic terms include ice pops, ice drops, icy poles, and freezer pops.

And she started frequenting her local farmers' market to ask questions. Through those visits, she learned what was in season and unique to the greater Texas area.

Some of her first flavors came straight from what she learned at the farmers' market—watermelon basil, cantaloupe mint, and blackberry lemonade. In addition to all the in-person research, she also created social media accounts and tried to post consistently about her new research project.

By the end of the year, Carolyn was convinced that she wanted to pursue Alchemy Pops more seriously. She bought a domain name, signed up for PayPal, and got a business bank account. She then volunteered at a local food festival. Her goal was to talk to a bunch of chefs in one place and ask if anyone had extra kitchen space they would rent to her. Only one said yes, but that was all she needed.

After the holidays, she moved the operation from her home kitchen to a commercial kitchen in a local bakery. This meant she had to get liability insurance and upgrade the type of pop molds she was using. She also bought her first "pop cart" for $500 from Craigslist, which brought her startup costs to around $2,000.

The next spring, she booked her first event, a charity car wash, through a family friend. The event benefited a young girl with cancer, to help the family pay medical bills. In Carolyn's words, "It was such an amazing feeling to not only set up on-site as a business, but also as someone there to help out. That's when I first realized the potential of using my business to give back to others, which I later dubbed our Pops for a Cause program."

From that charity event, she got her next gig catering a wedding three hours away from her home. She had to figure out how to make and store enough pops, and then transport them three hours in the car without any of them melting. She pulled it off, and kept the momentum going.

Alchemy Pops rolled these successes into a successful crowdfunding campaign that summer, raising over $8,000 from more than one hundred supporters. Carolyn used that money for kitchen equipment, an outdoor tent and banner, more freezers, and more molds. That first full year, between events, catering, and the Kickstarter campaign, she made over $15,000, all while working on weekends and evenings.

CRITICAL FACTOR

Ice pops are the new cupcakes! Carolyn was the first to focus on the Dallas–Fort Worth market, which has warm temperatures much of the year.

Carolyn wanted to make the jump and turn her side hustle into her full-time focus. But before she quit her job, she created a spreadsheet of all the money going in and out of her family's personal and business accounts. After getting a detailed accounting of their overhead, she realized that they weren't huge spenders.

Since Alchemy Pops didn't have a brick-and-mortar establishment, most business expenses went toward maintaining the mobile food carts that she used to sell on the streets of Fort Worth, as well as the energy it takes to keep all of those pops nice and cold. Thanks to those mobile carts, Carolyn can still make sales year-round through in-person pop-ups, events, and corporate catering.

The next step was figuring out how many frozen pops she would need to replace her full-time salary, and how long it would take her to get to that number. The direct costs for each pop are around 25¢ to 30¢ each (including the wrapper, stick, and ingredients), and she turns around and sells them for $3 to $4 depending on the ingredients. In setting her initial pricing, Carolyn surveyed the landscape of the market and set up the business to where Alchemy Pops wasn't the least expensive seller, but not the most expensive either.

In year two, she sold more than twenty-five thousand pops and brought in roughly $80,000 in sales, with about $1,350 to $3,000 each month as net income. Not only that, but the business was growing. Once she had all those numbers in front of her, it was a much easier decision to quit her job.

The move to running Alchemy Pops full-time meant that Carolyn could focus all her efforts on expanding her pop empire. It also meant more freedom and flexibility. While she admits that she works more hours now than when she had a 9-to-5 job, what she's lost in hours, she's more than made up for in living her life. For example, she and Wiley took a month off to travel in New Zealand and Australia. They had to plan the trip around his job, but her schedule was easier: she just didn't take on any events that month.

In year three, Carolyn hit a new milestone: she made more in one month from Alchemy Pops than she had made in all of year two. And she's not slowing down. She recently opened her first brick-and-mortar store, right on Main Street in downtown Fort Worth. She already has plans for new products, additional locations, and even an idea for a brand-new side hustle.

Finally, she can also put a sticker next to "start a side hustle" on her 30 Things Before 30 bucket list.

"Don't try to be perfect, be personable. Don't pretend to know it all, embrace the fact that you don't. Pick one person to ask. Pick one thing to try. And before you know it, you'll have your next step, and then the one after that." —Carolyn

BELGIAN FINE CHOCOLATE COMES TO AMERICA

After living in Belgium for thirteen years, a Louisiana freelancer returns home and starts a hustle making fine chocolate.

NAME
JEFF SLAUGHTER

LOCATION
SHREVEPORT, LOUISIANA

STARTUP COSTS
$1,500

INCOME
$5,000+ (SEASONALLY)

WEBSITE
CHEZSLAUGHTERCHOCOLATE.COM

"When people sample my chocolate, they can instantly taste the difference. I enjoy being a chocolate ambassador for Belgium!" —Jeff

The small country of Belgium is well known for its delicacies, including french fries, beer, waffles, and chocolate. Jeff Slaughter lived and worked in the country for thirteen years before returning home to his native Louisiana.

While he was in Belgium, he became intrigued by the chocolate culture of the country. Not only is its chocolate delicious, it's also artfully made and well packaged. Jeff had the idea to bring some of this culture back and share it in America.

As a resourceful side hustler, he set out to learn how to make chocolate in the traditional European manner—but at first his quest led only to dead ends. He found two options, neither of which was ideal.

The first option was a two-year, full-time school, which would have been nearly impossible to fit in with his day job. The second was a short, three-day workshop from one of the Belgian chocolate companies. This sounded good at first, but as he dug deeper he learned that it was mostly for tourists and wouldn't really show him everything he needed to know.

FUN FACT Farmers' markets proved unprofitable for Jeff, but becoming a "personal chocolatier" at hosted parties and events has been far more successful.

Finally, he found an online program in Vancouver, British Columbia, Canada, known as *École Chocolate*. This three-month course came with a lot of reading material, video training, and graded weekly assignments. Although attending a course in person might have been more helpful, with the limitations of time and money, it seemed like the best option. The course exceeded his expectations and gave him the working rules to learn much more on his own.

Back in Louisiana, Jeff set up a small kitchen and began to make batches of artisanal chocolate, using the skills he'd learned through the course. Rather than open a chocolate shop, which would have been expensive and potentially risky, he decided to stay small and nimble.* He wanted to run the project seasonally, from November to March, so that he wouldn't compete with the heat and humidity.

Louisiana and many other states have what's known as a "cottage law," where you can sell certain foods that you make in your home until you reach a certain level of revenue. In Louisiana, it was $20,000 a year. At that point, you have to have a dedicated kitchen and receive regular inspections, but you don't have to worry about those things in the beginning.

When it came to marketing, Jeff had another novel idea. He decided to offer other services such as parties, workshops, and personal chocolatier services. Making chocolate can be a lonely venture, but the client interaction that comes with the events allows him to get out of his kitchen and spend time with others.

Jeff's chocolate hustle brought in more than $5,000 the first season, and then about the same the next. His long-term goal is to grow it to $12,000 a year, so that every month he has $1,000 in extra income.

There's no word on whether he's going to expand to making Belgian waffles.

ACTION PLAN

1. Learn to make legit chocolate.
2. Experiment with packaging. Appearances matter, and a luxury product needs to look good.
3. Set up shop online, offline, or both.
4. Add supplemental events, like a tasting party or Valentine's Day celebration.
5. Optional: Remodel your kitchen.

*He also said, "I don't want this business to run my life— I want it to fit into my life." This is a great philosophy for side hustling!

CRITICAL FACTOR

Jeff's passion for Belgian chocolate combined with his new interest in marketing is bringing buyers to his door. Not being reliant on this income for his livelihood, he can also experiment and have fun without feeling much pressure.

ONLINE COFFEE COMPANY
BREWS UP $30,000 A MONTH

Tired of the guilt associated with consuming coffee while pregnant and breast-feeding, a biomechanical engineer creates a line of coffee bean options that keep moms happy and babies healthy.

NAME
EMILIE SIMMONS AND SHARON PIECZENIK

LOCATION
COTATI, CALIFORNIA

STARTUP COSTS
$30,000

INCOME
$30,000/MONTH

WEBSITE
MOMMEECOFFEE.COM

Mommee Coffee is not your average cup of joe, and cofounder Emilie Simmons is not your average entrepreneur. She's a coffee lover, a biomechanical engineer at a medical device company, and a mother. Oh, and a couple of years ago, she set out to develop coffee options for moms everywhere.

It's a hustle that grew out of a need—because coffee is serious!

It all began when Emilie, at eight months pregnant, was planning a trip from San Francisco to San Diego. Already a parent to a two-year-old, Emilie could imagine the misery of a long car ride with a toddler. The idea of having one on her pregnant lap while flying wasn't any better, so she welcomed a solo driving adventure while her wife flew with their son to their destination.

In Emilie's words, the alone time "was like finding a unicorn." It gave her an opportunity to do some thinking, and her thoughts were fixated on coffee. She'd already been researching the impact of caffeine on a baby, both during pregnancy and while breast-feeding. Emilie came to the realization that for many women, drinking coffee during pregnancy is influenced as much by emotion and guilt as it is by data.

CRITICAL FACTOR

Moms like coffee, but many of them need to be choosy about drinking it because it can affect their baby's health. Mommee Coffee provides a variety of solutions while relating directly to the intended audience.

This led to her big idea: to source and roast delicious coffee specially geared to the unique needs of moms and moms-to-be. That blissful, eight-hour unicorn voyage provided the creative foundation of what would become Mommee Coffee.

Emilie connected with her friend, Sharon, who, after spending time in a cooperative community in Costa Rica, realized she wanted to shift her focus toward women's health. When Emilie mentioned Mommee Coffee, Sharon thought it was an intriguing idea and the perfect name.

They each invested $15,000. As they explored the world of coffee and developed their product, they focused on low acidity, as well as varying levels of caffeine. The finished product is organic, low acid, and offered in four caffeine levels: full caffeine, one-half caff, one-quarter caff, and decaf. Their coffee is decaffeinated using a water-processing technique rather than chemicals, to be on the safe side for pregnancy and breast-feeding.

A few months prior to public launch, Emilie and Sharon had friends and family test their product, website, and shipping process. They took to the streets to spread the word about Mommee Coffee, handing out information at farmers' markets, baby fairs, and to anyone who would listen.

Two years in, the business was selling approximately $30,000 of coffee each month. Emilie attributes the success to satisfying a true need—not just a need for coffee itself, but a need for moms to feel that it's okay for them to still want things that were important parts of their lives before they became parents.

In addition to the financial prosperity, one of the best parts of the hustle has been the out-of-the-blue emails from customers telling them how Mommee Coffee has made an impact. For example, one breast-feeding mom wrote to tell them about how her baby's skin had been constantly breaking out. Realizing it could be from acidic foods, the mom cut out suspect items like orange juice and coffee until there were no more breakouts. When she tried to return to drinking standard coffee, the breakouts returned—but then she tried Mommee Coffee, and her baby's skin remained healthy.

Since this is a side hustle, Emilie and Sharon have limited bandwidth. They like the idea of doing more local events, but want to be mindful of spreading themselves too thin.

The partners may expand further at some point, but for now the priority is to continue spreading the word about their current mission. Just because you're a mom doesn't mean you have to give up your precious caffeinated (or one-quarter caffeinated) ritual.

"Pick something manageable *and* something you are passionate about. Limit the scope as much as you can to start, because even something that seems small can take an enormous amount of work. Test your idea before making big investments. And have fun!" —Emilie

FUN FACT The amount of caffeine in a cup of coffee depends on many factors, including the type of bean, brew time, how many grounds are used, and whether it's brewed with hot or cold water.

DELICIOUS COOKIES HAND-DELIVERED
AT MIDNIGHT

A late-night craving evolves into a cookie-delivery service, spreading chocolate chip goodness throughout the land.

NAME
JULIA BALDWIN AND RICHARD KOTULSKI

LOCATION
PORTLAND, OREGON

STARTUP COSTS
$3,000

INCOME
$8,000/MONTH

WEBSITE
AFTERDARKCOOKIES.COM

Julia Baldwin and her husband, Richard, grew up in Portland, Oregon, but they spent the better part of a decade living in Philadelphia and New York City—cities where you could get anything delivered at any time of night, and there was always someplace open to get a snack.

When they moved back west, they realized that aside from pizza, Portland didn't have much in the way of late-night delivery options. One night, they were relaxing at home and were overtaken with a craving for cookies . . . but they were too tired to make them themselves. That was how the idea started: What if there was a way to make delicious cookies and bring them to people's doorsteps?

They talked about it for over a year before beginning to work on it. Richard, the head of customer experience at a startup, was coaching some students on the basics of entrepreneurship. He suggested that one of them look into what it would take to create a late-night cookie business.

That student ended up not wanting to take the idea anywhere, but Richard and Julia kept mulling it over until they decided to take their own advice.

Their first step was market research. They prepared a survey that went to students at two local colleges. Not surprisingly, students were responsive to the idea. This gave them the confidence they needed to figure out how to make it happen.

They called it After Dark Cookies. Julia was in the kitchen baking, and Richard stood by, ready to take cookies out for delivery. The first weekend they opened for business, two things happened that showed Julia and Richard they were on to something.

FUN FACT Julia recently took a phone order from a mother in Florida who wanted to send cookies to her son for his twenty-ninth birthday. Those kinds of experiences—the hugs from customers, the faraway orders to loved ones—have given her and Richard the fuel to keep going. The free samples don't hurt either.

Their first order came from a couple in Colorado with a friend in Portland who had just had surgery, and the faraway couple wanted to get something nice delivered to him. They Googled "Portland dessert delivery," and the brand-new After Dark Cookies site came up on the first page.*

Richard went out to deliver the order, but when he knocked on the door, nobody answered. It turned out they'd already gone to bed for the night. Richard called the friends in Colorado, who said to just leave the cookies by the door. He did as instructed, but it didn't feel right. When he got back home, he emailed the recipient to say that he wanted to deliver to them again the next night—at no charge. They were over the moon with gratitude . . . a buttery, sugary moon.

That same weekend, another customer was so excited that when Richard dropped off a delivery, she asked if she could give him a hug. He'd worked a lot of jobs, in restaurants and retail and all sorts of other industries, but had never gotten a reaction like that before. It was another moment when they thought, "Hey, there really might be something to this."

The goodwill and good baking continued. But even though the cookie kingdom is delicious, it's also a ton of work. Julia and Richard have full-time jobs, and they've been spending six nights a week working on their side hustle.

They're also doing this as a couple, a fact that they point out is enriching in some ways, but "character building" in others. Still, they're glad to be following their chocolate chip passion.

Can you change the world through cookies? Perhaps so, and even if not, they're still delicious homemade cookies brought to your doorstep.

"Question all the assumptions you tend to make. When you think about how much it would cost to do something, try to think creatively about how else you might accomplish it." —Julia

*Search rankings like these don't always appear so quickly, but in this case there was limited competition, so the new site shot straight to the top.

CRITICAL FACTOR

Who wouldn't want late-night cookie delivery? If this service doesn't exist in your town and you like to bake, maybe it's time to fire up the oven.

AVOCADO QUEEN EARNS $45,000 SELLING SPREADABLE GRANOLA

After documenting her recovery from unhealthy eating, this health tech worker turns a kitchen experiment into a growing business.

NAME
ALI BONAR

LOCATION
SAN FRANCISCO, CALIFORNIA

STARTUP COSTS
$40,000

INCOME
$45,000 IN SALES IN THE FIRST FOUR MONTHS

WEBSITE
KWEEN.CO

Ali Bonar, a product marketer for a health tech company, lives in San Francisco. Growing up, she was outgoing, had a bunch of friends, and played volleyball on her high school team. On the outside, everything appeared fine.

On the inside, however, she was developing an unhealthy relationship with food. People would marvel at how thin she looked. Ali would play it down, acting as if everything was okay . . . but it wasn't.

She'd starve herself all day, and then spend the night binge eating—which left her feeling guilty. She felt that she had no self-control. In fact, she had developed an eating disorder *while studying nutrition* at the University of California, Berkeley. Food was seriously stressing her out.

Shortly after college, she began documenting her journey of intuitive eating on Instagram, using the handle @avokween, because of her love of avocados. Her struggles with food persisted, and she tried a lot of different methods in search of lasting improvement.

Her breakthrough came when she shifted her focus away from worrying about how certain foods made her look and instead focused on how they made her feel. This changed everything. The "avokween" *began giving zero guacs*.

At the same time, her marketing job was leaving her creatively unfulfilled. As soon as she'd get off work, Ali would go home and tinker around in her kitchen. This was the place where she could exercise her

FUN FACT Ali's first launch almost never happened. Before she could officially share her Granola Butter with the world, she needed the approval of the food inspector. However, at the time, there was only *one* inspector in all of San Francisco, who was struggling to keep up with the amount of work on her docket. Ali worried that she wouldn't get approval in time—but after a flurry of emails, it finally came through the day before launch.

creative freedom. She felt alive and in control. She began experimenting with different foods, posting stories to her followers.

A self-proclaimed nut butter–aholic, Ali found herself putting peanut or almond butter spreads on everything. However, these tasty treats were taxing her digestion. Trying out alternatives, she looked for something that tasted good and left her feeling full.

It was while experimenting with a combination of granola and coconut oil that Ali stumbled upon a mysterious, buttery concoction. This spreadable gold was getting rave reviews from family and friends. Because of all the encouragement, Ali decided to kick things up a notch.

What started as mere kitchen experiments resulted in the founding of Kween Foods, a wellness company with the mission to empower women to reclaim their relationship with food. Her first official product? Granola Butter—the world's first *spreadable granola*.

It didn't happen all at once. There was paperwork to fill out and permits to obtain for a commercial kitchen space. It took her nearly four months to get through all the red tape. But there was also a silver lining—this four-month window allowed her to test and *retest* her product to get it just right. Ali tried nearly forty variations before she was certain that she had a winner.

She now says that her naiveté was an advantage—she simply didn't think it would take so long. If she knew in advance, she says, she might have been discouraged from starting.

Meanwhile, Ali's Instagram following had increased to over twenty-eight thousand followers in just over a year. The shift happened when she publicly shared her eating habits, including the struggles she encountered. Comments, likes, and messages began flooding in.

Ali was deliberate when it came to building this following. She attributes success to posting every single day, sometimes twice a day. Her followers loved her authenticity, seeing her hard work and her not-so-glamorous posts.

Leading up to the launch, Ali created a list of one hundred influencers that she wanted to send her product to. She broke down her targets into microinfluencers (under ten thousand followers), midtier (ten to fifty thousand followers), and high tier (over fifty thousand followers). When

CRITICAL FACTOR

Ali built her following by sharing honestly and posting consistently. Then, she spent a lot of time and energy developing an interesting product.

selecting influencers, she was careful to choose the ones who had high engagement and therefore a loyal audience base.

The influencers she reached out to consisted largely of people she had some kind of interaction with in the past. And she asked them to only post about her product if they loved it and really wanted to.

An additional perk of "working in public" was the immediate feedback she received when testing various brand ideas. It was like having an instant survey at her fingertips. For example, her followers helped her to pick the product name Granola Butter.* It also made her community feel more invested in her brand's success.

In the first four months of launching Kween Foods, business went on a steady climb resulting in $45,000 worth of sales. In addition to what seems like a bright financial future, the project has had a tremendous impact on her life in other ways. In her words, "Starting Kween has fulfilled me in ways that my full-time job couldn't. I've always had a creative streak in me, and didn't find myself fulfilled with my traditional marketing job. With my side hustle, I had freedom and control, which ultimately meant I was a lot happier."

Kween Foods is scaling quickly, and there might even be an opportunity down the road for Alis to pursue it full-time.

The avocado queen's reign is set to continue.

* She had a different idea at first, but the new name was clearly the "butter" option.

WRITER TURNS LEFTOVER CHERRIES INTO NATURALLY SWEET INCOME

After being diagnosed with diabetes, a food blogger creates a sugar-free line of ketchup alternatives.

NAME
ERIKA KEREKES

LOCATION
SANTA MONICA, CALIFORNIA

STARTUP COSTS
$15,000

INCOME
$5,000/MONTH

WEBSITE
NOTKETCHUP.COM

One summer day, Erika Kerekes took her kids to a pick-your-own cherry orchard. They ended up with so many cherries that they couldn't eat them all fresh. The kids were picky eaters and didn't care for jam—but the family *did* eat a lot of burgers.

Getting creative, Erika turned some of the extra fruit into an improvised version of cherry "ketchup." Everyone loved it! For the rest of the summer, she experimented with lots of different fruit recipes in her own kitchen. She'd feed them to her family, friends, and even the mail carrier, in an attempt to get honest feedback on her formulations.

Based on the response, by August she decided to turn her recipes into a side hustle. Her first step was reaching out to a food chemist who helped her figure out how to take a home recipe and turn it into a formula that a copacker could use in their facility.* This involved several rounds of testing to make sure the taste and consistency was perfect, and learning how to source all the fruit ingredients she needed.

Once she dialed in the product, Erika decided on the name Not Ketchup. She then worked with a graphic designer to create a logo and product labels. Finally, she purchased product liability insurance and found a copacker that would work with her on a small initial run.

With all that in place, by the end of the year Erika was able to have sixty cases of three different flavors of Not Ketchup produced. She estimates that it cost her $15,000 to complete these steps.

Erika is a writer for a nonprofit organization, and she knew a lot of food bloggers. She gave away about a third of her first production run to those bloggers, as well as to anyone else she knew who might help get the word out. They cooked up original recipes using her sauces, sharing them on their websites and social media.

* A copacker is a company that will make a food product in bulk for you, according to your specifications and recipes.

FUN FACT Erika's side hustle started because she had a ton of leftover cherries from a family fruit-picking outing, and her friends didn't like jam. This eventually turned into her line of condiments that she had to call Not Ketchup.

"I focus on my day job when I'm at work, but in between things—when I'm doing dishes, folding laundry, brushing my teeth, packing my lunch, or working out—I'm always thinking about my business." —Erika

She also used some of that first run to go to the Fancy Food trade show in San Francisco. While there, she met a reporter at the *Los Angeles Times* who interviewed her and wrote up an article about Not Ketchup. Erika knew that the reporter was going to ask where people could buy her products, so she leveraged the upcoming article to get stocked at a few local stores.

Month by month, she continued to get into more and more stores, including Sam's Club and Whole Foods. And by the second year, Not Ketchup was available on Amazon.

It was all starting so well, but then life threw her a major curveball. Erika was diagnosed with type 2 diabetes and realized she needed to make some lifestyle changes, including cutting out all added sugar. Within three months of snapping into action, she had reversed her diabetes. No small feat!

During this time, Erika realized that if she was trying to cut out sugar, other people probably were too. She decided to make a big shift from traditionally made fruit sauces (which included a lot of sugar) to condiments sweetened only by the fruit itself. As Erika shared, "That was almost a complete relaunch and took a tremendous effort, but I knew it was the right direction to take."

Her first no-added-sugar flavor, Tangerine Hatch Chile, was released on Amazon at the end of the year and instantly became her number one seller. A few months later, she released a no-added-sugar version of Cherry Chipotle, and sales for that flavor doubled overnight. With these successes under her belt, Erika decided to make *all* of her products without any added sugar. To help with this transition, she used a crowdfunding site called PieShell to successfully raise $15,000.

Erika fulfilled her campaign rewards and put the new flavors up on Amazon. This time she specifically focused her marketing efforts on paleo, Whole30, low-carb, and diabetic customers. To reach them, she used content marketing, social media, and pay-per-click advertising. Through all her efforts, she recently celebrated her biggest month of sales yet.

While she plans on continuing to grow the Not Ketchup brand, she also wants it to remain a side hustle no matter how big it gets.

CRITICAL FACTOR

Switching to a sugar-free line of ketchups was a huge transition, but the change allowed Erika to market to people with specialized diets. By narrowing her audience, she increased her sales.

Food Biz Basics

If your idea involves food, you might need to do more research than what's required for other projects. In most cases, you'll need a basic business license before selling to the public. In *some* cases, a visit from your local health inspector will be required.

One of your first steps should be to look into local "cottage laws," which may make it much easier for you to get started. These laws are on the books in many states, provinces, and areas. They allow people to sell certain food products without going through a complicated process of inspections.

The specifics of the laws vary quite a bit. In some places, you can sell up to a certain amount of goods before your business is required to operate under the same regulations that larger companies follow. In other places, what matters is whether or not you have employees. Do your own research to see if the answers help you decide how to proceed.

For more, visit SideHustleSchool.com/recipe.

XI

Do Good *and* Do Well

Don't choose between profit and philanthropy—

do both. You can do good *while* doing well.

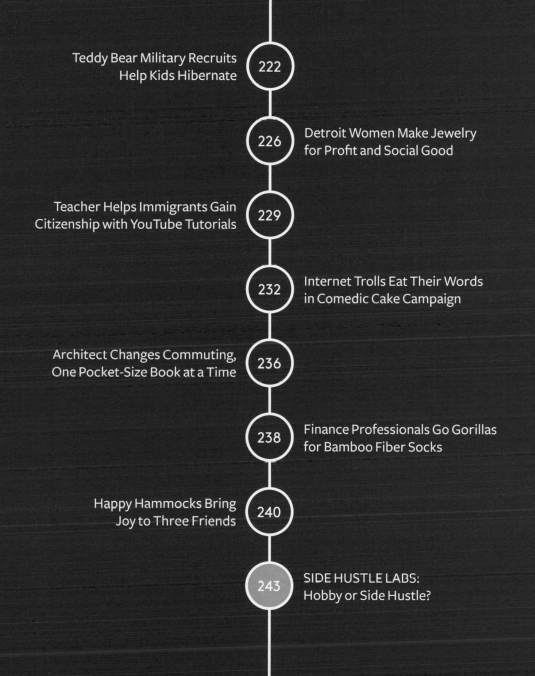

TEDDY BEAR MILITARY RECRUITS HELP KIDS HIBERNATE

An in-house ad executive turned teddy bear manufacturer creates a military-grade sleep system for children, earning $100,000 in sales and making a lot of people beary happy.

NAME
JUSTIN BAUM

LOCATION
WINSTON-SALEM, NORTH CAROLINA

STARTUP COSTS
$7,500

INCOME
$100,000 IN SALES ($15,000 PROFIT) IN YEAR TWO

WEBSITE
ZZZBEARS.COM

Before taking the job as creative director for the in-house advertising agency at Lenovo, Justin Baum was the lead writer of recruitment advertising for the United States Marine Corps. It was while working there that he was stirred by the men and women serving in uniform. He wanted to find a way to give back. Inspired by his own daughter's difficulty sleeping through the night, he had an idea.

Justin decided to bring home a teddy bear in a marine sweatshirt. He then told his daughter a story, introducing him as a marine bear who had protected the nation for more than two hundred years. "Now, he's ready to protect you while you sleep," he told her.

"Well, what if *he* falls asleep?" his daughter asked.

"He's a marine," Justin reassured her. "He would never fail at his mission!"

That night, she slept like a bear in hibernation. And if this worked for his daughter, he thought, perhaps it could work for other children.

He developed the idea of "Sgt. Sleeptight," a full-fledged military-grade sleep system that protects children from bad dreams, fear of the dark, and the nighttime anxieties that come from having a deployed parent.

This isn't your run-of-the-mill teddy bear. Sgt. Sleeptight comes equipped with a door hanger warning nighttime monsters that he's on guard, a

"Growing up, my mom used to tell me how good I was at everything—from drawing and baseball to brushing my teeth. I now realize it was a well-meaning lie. Nobody is good at everything. Be brutally honest in assessing your strengths and weaknesses, then get help. Find the people you need, put them to work, and stay focused on what you do best. P.S. I love you, Mom." —Justin

Sleeptight Oath to be read with your child before bed (which officially puts your bear on duty), *and* Silver Slumber Stars to be awarded after sleeping through the night.

He called his creation ZZZ Bears.

Justin's talents in copywriting did not lend themselves to direct knowledge of the teddy bear manufacturing world. So, he did what most of us do when we want to figure something out—he Googled it.

His searches led him to Alibaba, the gateway to manufacturing in the East. From there, he typed in "teddy bears," and the search results returned hundreds of manufacturers. Then, he narrowed his search to ones with experience making military uniforms. Finally, he found one willing to do a small run of two hundred bears.

Prototyping turned out to be easier than expected. Justin sent his manufacturer pictures of different styles of bears he liked. He'd snap a pic of a snout from one, a patch of fur from another, and on and on until he was satisfied with the final design.*

The bigger problem came when he sourced his first order.

His manufacturer came through in the sense that he didn't run off with the money. However, the quality was subpar . . . not *terrible*, but not great. These bears deserved greatness!

In order to scale his business, Justin needed a better manufacturer. He used the power of Facebook, connecting with another plush product designer who had just gotten his product into Walmart. They formed a friendship, and his new mentor referred him to his new manufacturer.

Justin then wrangled a graphic designer friend to design the logo and accessories (door hanger, Sleeptight Oath, and stickers). He built a simple and inexpensive website through Squarespace. And just like that, he had himself a fully functional e-commerce business. He was up and running . . . now he just had to sell those bears.

On a whim, Justin sent a message to the toy buyer for the Marine Corps Exchange, the directory of stores that sell to military members and their families. The buyer was impressed, and a week later she made an offer to stock them in the exchange. There was just one problem: she wanted the

FUN FACT   Justin once received a twenty-foot container from China at his front door and had to unload four thousand bears and carry them down his driveway into his house. The laundry room became the assembly room and his garage became the warehouse.

* It was the Frankenstein's monster of bears, except not nearly as creepy.

bears to be in a marine uniform, packaged in a retail box. In other words, she liked the concept, but not that first batch he had produced.

Despite the setback, Justin pulled it off. A year later, he got into the Navy and Coast Guard exchanges. Naturally, each one wanted bears in their respective branch's uniforms. The name Sgt. Sleeptight didn't work for them because neither the Navy nor the Coast Guard has sergeants. So, in addition to the new bears, Justin had to trademark new names as well. He dubbed his new creations Sailor Sleeptight and Coastie Sleeptight.

For a while, all was well. Justin's honey jar was full, and the bears were standing sentry in bedrooms across the nation. He was ready for the next step, and when he had the chance to meet with buyers from Target, he thought he'd found it.

After a single twenty-minute meeting with those buyers in a Miami hotel room, Justin had won them over. They loved the bears, or at least he thought they did. They agreed to stock them in five hundred of their stores, or at least he thought they did.

It turned out that getting his bears into Target wasn't all it was cracked up to be. Setting himself up as a vendor was highly complex, requiring lots of late-night Skype calls with his manufacturer in China. It felt, you could say, more than a little teddy-ous.

On the day his bears were supposed to arrive on the shelves, Justin called his local store to make sure they were available—and they weren't. Making matters worse, the store manager who took the call had no idea what Justin was talking about.

He then called another store and had a similar conversation. Then, in an act of tenacity, Justin hired three students from his local college to call *all five hundred Target locations* to see if the bears were displayed.

Turns out, a good number of stores hadn't even heard of them. Some stores had them in stock, but hadn't put them on display where anyone would see them. One store even discounted them on their first day.

As weeks went on, Justin kept checking sales numbers. Much to his disappointment, they continued to be poor. He realized that standing out in a big box store in the presence of other popular brands like Disney and Marvel was no small challenge. In a forest full of products, his brand of six bears remained off-duty—and he didn't have the marketing dollars to make a meaningful advance through enemy lines.

He decided to grin and bear it, changing focus to pay more attention to smaller boutique stores. As Justin described it, "Boutiques are smaller

CRITICAL FACTOR

Sgt. Sleeptight is a hard-working bear, awakening from his own hibernation to keep watch over kids as they sleep. Justin also gives back, donating bears to children who have lost a parent serving in the military.

and warmer. There are people there who can explain and sell your product to customers."

However, being on the shelves of Target did bring him some other opportunities. ABC's *The View* ended up doing a feature on ZZZ Bears, and Justin is convinced that his ability to get his product stocked in such a major national outlet gave the network confidence.

They were also interested in his mission to give back. Justin donates bears to children who have lost a parent in the line of duty through a partnership with TAPS, an organization for those grieving the loss of a family member who served in the military.

These days, Justin still relies on asking his audience for help. When he posts a question regarding a product he's developing, he typically gets hundreds of replies.

"This kind of research used to cost thousands of dollars, now it's practically free," he said. Plus, the interaction builds relationships, and his audience feels more invested in the success of ZZZ Bears.

On an annual basis, the project recently brought in just over $100,000 in sales with $15,000 in profit. Clearly, the lack of manufacturing knowledge was no bear-ier to entry in this market.

DETROIT WOMEN MAKE JEWELRY
FOR PROFIT AND SOCIAL GOOD

An attorney starts a jewelry company with a purpose, employing disadvantaged women in Detroit to help them transition from a life of dependence into one of self-reliance.

NAME
AMY PETERSON

LOCATION
DETROIT, MICHIGAN

STARTUP COSTS
$15,000 (PLUS A CROWD-FUNDING CAMPAIGN OF $25,000)

INCOME
$300,000 IN YEAR FOUR

WEBSITE
REBELNELL.COM

Originally from upstate New York, Amy Peterson relocated to Detroit after earning her law degree. She moved for a job as a sports attorney with the Detroit Tigers. Baseball was a big deal during her childhood, and she had always wanted to work in the sports industry. Every day is different, and she has no idea what will cross her desk.

Growing up, Amy's family was working-class. When she moved for the job, she chose to live in downtown Detroit, not the suburbs. She wanted to immerse herself in the city, with all its ups and downs.

The juxtapositions she encountered could be jarring. At the ballpark office, she worked on contracts with players who were paid $5 to $10 million a year. Meanwhile, just steps from her front door, she passed by a homeless shelter whenever she went for a run or walked her dog.

The contrast was unmistakable. Amy often stopped to talk with the women staying at the shelter, and she was inspired by their stories. For most of them, getting out of poverty wasn't a question of motivation— it was a question of opportunity.

As she continued on her run one day, she went past an old part of town near an old railway line. She noticed layers of graffiti coming off the walls. Back in college, she had paid for her education by making jewelry—and that day, she had a big idea.

Her idea was to combine each of these elements: to make jewelry from fallen graffiti, in a way that employed women from the shelter and taught them new skills.

FUN FACT According to Rebel Nell, Eleanor Roosevelt was "a strong, independent woman who stayed true to her beliefs, regardless of her husband's or public opinion." Amy and her business partner chose to name their new project after her.

Amy didn't want to go it alone, so she found a partner. Together, they chose the name Rebel Nell, a reference to Eleanor Roosevelt, and set up an Indiegogo campaign to raise funds. The campaign brought in $25,000, which helped them buy supplies and find a space.

Rebel Nell is a jewelry company with a purpose, one that employs disadvantaged women to help them transition from a life of dependence into one of self-reliance and empowerment. Everyone who works in the business is, or was once, transitioning from a women's shelter in Detroit.

Amy and her business partner, Diana Russell, teach the women how to make jewelry from that graffiti as a way to repurpose the city. The profits earned directly impact programs and services that help the community of women to lead self-sufficient lives. At Rebel Nell, they operate under a "teach a woman to fish" mentality.

Amy continues to work her day job as an attorney, even as Rebel Nell employs more than fifteen women at a time. And that's not all. Over the next five years, Amy hopes that Rebel Nell will continue its pattern of rapid growth (the business did $300,000 in sales in a recent year), while at the same time helping women who are ready for the next step in their professional path.

In fact, one of the women who worked for them recently launched her own business. Knowing that Rebel Nell provided her the tools she needed is both rewarding and motivational.

CRITICAL FACTOR

Rebel Nell blends art, commerce, and a philanthropic mission all in one. Whoever thinks you can't do all three should take a close look at their model.

TEACHER HELPS IMMIGRANTS GAIN CITIZENSHIP WITH YOUTUBE TUTORIALS

A stay-at-home mom and former teacher helps immigrants prepare for the US citizenship test through a series of YouTube tutorials.

When she decided to start volunteering as a leader for a literacy course, Danielle Fang was a stay-at-home mom with two kids. She had previously taught elementary school, but she also enjoyed working with adults, so the volunteer opportunity was a perfect fit.

During the course, she met a woman who was in the process of getting her US citizenship. Danielle did everything in her power to assist—researching the system, accompanying her to the interview, and even observing the swearing-in ceremony. Surrounded by the enthusiastic, soon-to-be citizens echoing the Oath of Allegiance, Danielle was deeply moved.

Soon after, she started volunteering through teaching civics, citizenship, and ESOL (English for Speakers of Other Languages) classes to help others through the same process. One of her first students was a Tibetan refugee who had escaped by walking through the Himalayan mountains to India before finally making it to the United States.

Listening to the student's story—and meeting others from around the world with similar tales—further inspired Danielle. She wanted to do more to help.

Danielle lives in the Washington, DC, metro area, which has a large immigrant and refugee population. She saw a great need in her community for the kind of support her classes were providing—but the courses usually ran for nine to twelve weeks, and each class was up to three hours long. Furthermore, many of the students didn't have time to make the full commitment. They often missed classes when they couldn't get off work or find child care, putting them at a disadvantage through no fault of their own.

FUN FACT   Danielle's YouTube channel now has twenty-five thousand subscribers and over nine million views. Every day, her videos are watched at least twelve thousand times.

NAME
DANIELLE FANG

LOCATION
WASHINGTON, DC

STARTUP COSTS
MINIMAL

INCOME
$2,000/MONTH

WEBSITE
ESSAGROUP.ORG

ACTION PLAN

1. Identify a topic that a lot of people are interested in. It helps to choose one that can be confusing or overwhelming—your goal is to simplify the information.

2. Outline a series of lessons. Make them long enough to be substantial, but short enough that viewers won't give up.

3. You don't need expensive equipment. Record the lessons using your computer's webcam and a $50 microphone.

4. Create a YouTube account and upload the first batch of lessons.

5. If your channel proves popular, outline and upload more lessons!

Danielle came up with a simple solution. She decided to post all the information and lessons on YouTube so that the students could catch up on their own time. And with that action, she also ended up starting an accidental side hustle.

The goal was to simplify the overwhelming process of US naturalization. Government websites can be confusing for the majority of people, even if you're a native English speaker. Danielle's new website and YouTube channel would guide students on everything from how to prepare for a citizenship interview to navigating the cumbersome application process.

Though she originally had no intention of making money off the videos, her husband quickly noticed the traffic the site was generating. At around one thousand visitors per day with an upward trend of two thousand each week, they decided to try monetizing the channel through YouTube's advertiser program.

They also increased the number of videos she posted each week, using the information she already taught in her classes, as well as information from government websites and experts. In less than a year, she was making a steady profit from visitors who clicked on the ads in the videos.

"I love that I am able to continue helping others and volunteer in the community without feeling guilty that I am not earning a salary for the household. Now I do both!" —Danielle

Startup costs were almost nonexistent. Danielle's website cost $12 a month. She purchased software for creating the video tutorials for less than $150.

Monetizing the YouTube channel itself was completely free. She made a Google AdSense account, connected it to her channel, and—voilà—at the end of each day, she could log in and see how much money she made.

The channel now generates around $2,000 each month with a nearly 100 percent profit margin. Best of all, this gain doesn't come at the expense of her students. All of them can watch each video for free, gaining a valuable education without cost, while Danielle gets paid through the partner program. It's a true win-win!

From her couch at home, Danielle invests about six hours a week when launching a new video, and about two hours a week to respond to questions from subscribers. There are now a few competitors, but she's been able to stay ahead of the game by providing the most up-to-date information about fees, regulations, and processes.

Even though her kids are now older, Danielle hasn't wanted to go back to full-time employment and give up on her community work. She says her side hustle has given her the freedom to volunteer even more, without feeling guilty that she's not earning an income for the household. She now has the best of both worlds.

The business has enabled her and her husband to make some large purchases, as well as start savings accounts for their daughters. It's also allowed Danielle to help the immigrant community financially, by purchasing books for her students as well as household items and clothing for arriving refugee families.

In the process, she's become a crusader for side businesses. She loves sharing her experience, and is hard at work convincing her friends that earning a second income for yourself—while giving back—is entirely within reach.

CRITICAL FACTOR

A difficult test meets a modern technology, and Danielle finds a way to get paid while providing a free service.

INTERNET TROLLS EAT THEIR WORDS
IN COMEDIC CAKE CAMPAIGN

After seeing a mean comment on Facebook, a woman realizes the absurdity of internet trolling and bakes up a hilarious side hustle.

NAME
KAT THEK

LOCATION
NEW YORK, NEW YORK

STARTUP COSTS
$230

INCOME
AT LEAST $1,000/MONTH

WEBSITE
TROLLCAKES.COM

One day in early 2017, Kat Thek was taking a mental break from her full-time copywriting work. She noticed something on Facebook that struck her as completely absurd. Someone had left a comment on Dolly Parton's fan page that said, "Your Mamma be so disappointed in you."

Kat looked at it for a good, long moment. For some reason, the comment just stuck out like a sore thumb. Why would anyone waste their time to insult a complete stranger like that?

It wasn't even a good insult. It was ridiculous, and also grammatically incorrect. Kat thought it was a strange impulse to want to attack someone with random, senseless Facebook trolling—especially so if it's someone like Dolly Parton.

A couple of days went by, but she couldn't stop thinking about it. At some point, the idea of a cake with the troll comment written on it popped into her head—something different than the usual "Happy Birthday" or "Get Well Soon" messages.

She baked the cake and wrote out the full comment ("Your Mamma be so disappointed in you") in icing on the top. She and her friends got a kick out of it.

"It's a weird impulse to be mean to a stranger on the internet, but to be mean to Dolly Parton is even weirder. It's like giving the middle finger to a rainbow—the rainbow doesn't care, and anybody who sees you do it just thinks you're crazy." —Kat

And then she leveled up her idea—*she would send the cake to the person who made the original comment*. After a little investigative work to find his address, she mailed off the cake along with a printout of his original insult.

The whole idea was fun, sarcastic, and gave everyone that Kat told about it a good laugh. She realized that other people might want to call out their internet trolls with cakes, so she bought a domain, built a basic website, and officially launched Troll Cakes Bakery and Detective Agency.

She priced her service at $35 for a cake, and $60 for a cake and the detective work to find the troll's address. If she couldn't find the address of the person leaving the comment, she would just cancel the order and issue a refund.

After buying some supplies and setting up the site, Kat's total startup costs were right around $230. At first, she thought she'd have to buy special shipping boxes to fit her cakes, but that ended up being a nightmare. Not only was it difficult to find the right box at the right price, but the shipping costs would be different for every cake.

She eventually realized that it would be easier to make her cakes fit the USPS Flat Rate boxes (with protective padding, of course), rather than trying to find the perfect third-party boxes. That ended up being a huge relief—the costs were consistent, shipping was always completed within three days, and tracking was included.

To market her unusual baking business, Kat printed off a couple dozen paper tear-off sheets with her ad and website address. She hung them up on lightposts along her daily commute in New York City. It was an old-school marketing tactic, but it worked.

About a week later, Troll Cakes received its very first order. Kat was ecstatic—and a little terrified. She baked a cake, topped it with the rude comment that the buyer had sent along, found the troll's address with some clever online searching, and shipped it off. Despite mistyping the tracking number in an email to the customer, the first cake was a delicious success.

A couple of weeks passed by without many orders, but the next month was a turning point. After her Instagram profile began attracting a high

FUN FACT   Kat sometimes feels like she's at a giant party, and everyone wants to share their secrets with her. People she's never met will email her screenshots of online fights they're having, often with their own family members.

number of likes, Troll Cakes began getting featured in news outlets and on blogs. NPR told the story of Kat's home-baked cakes, and so did *Side Hustle School*.

By now, she was receiving at least several orders a week. In less than two months of business, Kat was nearing what she called "maximum baking capacity" in her tiny Brooklyn kitchen. Nearly every day her table was covered with hilarious troll cakes, with sayings that included these:

- "Oh no baby what is you doin'"
- "Short hair really doesn't suit you"
- "I don't like your dog"
- "I'm horrified by your disturbing post"

. . . and my personal favorite:

- "Britney Spears, you need Jesus"

And then the oven heated up even more. BuzzFeed, the mother lode of internet press, cast its charms upon Troll Cakes in the form of a featured article. Kat was flooded with *hundreds* of orders. She went to every baking store she could find in all five New York City boroughs to buy out their candy letters, and she still didn't have enough. She thought about ordering more online, but the lack of supplies was only half the problem. Even with unlimited candy letters, she simply didn't have the time to meet all of those orders.

Kat emailed all the customers, explaining that there was a waiting period of at least two months. Over half of those orders ended up being refunded, but a surprising amount of customers were more than happy to wait. As the saying goes, "Revenge is a dish best served cold."

Sales slowed down in the months after the big rush. Some months, she was baking several cakes a day. Other months, she had more free time.

Through it all, she's never considered Troll Cakes to be a business she wants to do full-time. She now sells at least one cake per day on average, and considers the income as "parking money," not something she counts on in her budget for regular living expenses.

Kat isn't sure how sustainable the flow of orders will be months or years from now, but she plans to keep enjoying the absurdity of it all while working her regular job.

ARCHITECT CHANGES COMMUTING,
ONE POCKET-SIZE BOOK AT A TIME

A Chicago-based architect makes access to classical literature easier for readers, raising $50,000 on Kickstarter along the way.

NAME
DAVID DEWANE

LOCATION
CHICAGO, ILLINOIS

STARTUP COSTS
$5,000

INCOME
$100,000 IN YEAR ONE

WEBSITE
MOUSEBOOKCLUB.COM

In a dual career of professional architect and journalist, David Dewane has always believed in the unique power of the written word. As a lifelong fan of books, it's little surprise that his passion for literature became his side hustle.

David spends his work days thinking about how to build ideas and bring them to life in design. But like many good ideas, the inspiration for David's side hustle came out of nowhere—or more specifically, the inspiration arrived on a bus.

His snowy, slow bus commute in South Side Chicago was the one place he could zone out during the day, at least for a few minutes. He takes this route at least five days a week, and a trip he took recently started out like all the rest. It changed when David noticed that everyone on the bus was looking down at their phone. Everyone, that is, except him.

Instead of looking at his phone, he was looking at a pocket-size book in his hand, with dog-eared corners and worn-out pages from regular reading. Breaking the ritual and joining the crowd, he took his phone out of his pocket to check a text from a friend. That's when he noticed that his phone and small book were pretty much the same size. They were both easy to travel with. Furthermore, they both held worlds of possibility.

The more David thought about it, the more he realized that everyone holding a phone was *reading*. Because they were already reading while commuting or waiting in line at the grocery store, it wouldn't be hard for them to read something else if it were within easy reach.

He looked around the bus again. Everyone had their eyes glued to their phone. If people had a real book in their pocket, something that gave them a richer and more engaging experience than scrolling through their feeds, David wondered if they'd be more likely to pick that up instead.

The idea to revolutionize classical literature and put a book in those commuters' hands didn't happen overnight. First of all, there was an eight-hour work day in the way. But David didn't push his idea aside.

CRITICAL FACTOR

Going against the grain can produce a powerful narrative and marketing strategy. In an age when everyone is constantly looking down at their phones, David challenges people to look down at a book instead.

During his lunch break, he pulled the text of a short story from the internet.

He couldn't take just any story, because most recent books are under copyright. But a lot of books that are older, especially those published before 1923, are in the public domain—meaning that anyone can use them however they'd like.

He took that story, pasted it into Adobe InDesign, made a few formatting changes, and hit print. He called his idea Mouse Books, and he now had a prototype.

David hustled quickly. The pocket-size book went from idea to prototype to launch in less than a month. After printing a limited run of one hundred copies for his friends for Christmas, he found the validation he was looking for. He also thought about how he could get his pocket-size books in the hands of more people.

That's when he took the leap and launched Mouse Book's first Kickstarter campaign. It was a big success, bringing in $50,000 of capital from over one thousand backers. David used $20,000 to print and ship the first run of Mouse Books.

He invested the rest of the money to help prepare for the next installment. He built a website, hired a book designer, and brought an editor on board to help curate the book selection. David couldn't keep using the printer at work to publish thousands of books, so he also used some of the Kickstarter money to put down a deposit and secure an ongoing relationship with a Chicago-based printer.

The campaign's success was a huge turning point for David. It showed him that people wanted easy access to quality literature and would spend time reading books if they had them. He makes sure that each book he prints doesn't take longer than ninety minutes to read. That means that even the busiest people can find time to read Jane Austin, Walt Whitman, or Franz Kafka, bringing a light dose of big ideas into their day.

David's ultimate goal is to continue publishing Mouse Books to be a gateway into more classical literature for readers, especially if a book can go wherever the reader does.

The plans for Mouse Books don't end with just putting more books on campaign backer's shelves. David is adding an online book club so members can come together to explore the ideas they've read about.

Whatever happens next, it's sure to be a real page-turner.

"During our first Kickstarter campaign, we ran a promo where backers were sent a copy of *The Dead* by James Joyce as a gift. My friend was helping me mail them, and we were stuffing a public mailbox in the dead of winter with about one hundred copies of this book. He turned to me and said, 'I think this is the greatest act of public service I've ever done.'" —David

FUN FACT Mouse Books relies on books that are within the public domain. David usually chooses his titles on Project Gutenberg (named for the inventor of the printing press), which digitizes cultural works so more people can access them.

FINANCE PROFESSIONALS GO GORILLAS
FOR BAMBOO FIBER SOCKS

Two New York City financial industry employees decide to make their own brand of socks while rescuing gorillas. Totally normal, right?

NAME
GIANLUCA DE STEFANO AND GAVIN KAMARA

LOCATION
NEW YORK, NEW YORK

STARTUP COSTS
$15,000

INCOME
$10,000 IN YEAR ONE

WEBSITE
GORILLA-SOCKS.COM

FUN FACT Gorilla Socks recently signed up with an additional charity. In addition to mountain gorillas, it now supports ten more endangered species.

Gianluca De Stefano's side hustle involves both socks and gorillas. You might be wondering how those two things are related, but to Gianluca and his business partner, Gavin Kamara, the connection is clear.

The idea came to them one day while they were riding bikes along the Hudson River. They'd known each other since they were roommates in college, and now they both had jobs in Manhattan, working in the financial sector. Starting a side hustle was something they'd talked about for years, but they didn't have a specific idea to launch them on their way.

During this bike ride, Gavin mentioned that he'd been reading about bamboo fibers. He was intrigued to learn that bamboo fibers are eco-friendly. Bamboo is the fastest-growing plant in the world, and it requires one-third the water needed to grow cotton. Beyond the environmental factors, bamboo fibers are ideal for thermoregulation—the antibacterial fabric keeps you warm in the winter and cool in the summer.

With all these great features, and their shared love of fashion, Gianluca and Gavin thought that bamboo fibers would be worth exploring in socks. But they didn't just want to own a clothing business. They both had good jobs in finance, so starting a side hustle wasn't only about earning extra money. They wanted to have fun *and* do good with their business. So, from the start, they planned to partner with a nonprofit organization and donate a percentage of profits.

Before they could give back, they needed something to give. Specifically, they needed a product. They had noticed that business attire in the corporate world, in both New York and London, had slowly become more relaxed. Fewer men were wearing ties, and more were using socks as a way to differentiate their style. They wanted to tap into that market in a more sustainable way.

The goal was to create socks with personalities. They designed a mix of plain colors and patterns that they'd be proud to sport to work. During this time, they were also tracking down a manufacturer in China. Once they had a few prototypes created, they sent off the files to their manufacturer to get some samples.

"Keep your day job and test your business idea on the side. Find something you really care about and build your business around it. At Gorilla Socks, we are even more motivated to do well knowing that ultimately we will help an endangered species to survive." —Gianluca

Gianluca and Gavin now had a product in process . . . but what about those gorillas? They had just watched a documentary that highlighted the precarious situation of gorillas in the wild. It got them thinking.

From there, they looked into organizations working on conservation, and learned about the Dian Fossey Gorilla Fund. The fund has been working for the protection of gorilla habitats in Africa for over fifty years. It seemed like the perfect choice, so they reached out and were excited when the fund agreed to partner with them.

From there, Gianluca and Gavin were ready to launch and market their Gorilla Socks—but they encountered a King Kong-size problem. They thought they would post on social media, get some shoutouts from other brands to quickly build their following, and be all set.

Not surprisingly, it didn't work out that way. Before they figured out their marketing strategy, they made some mistakes and missteps. One of those mistakes was paying for advertising in a renowned print magazine. They got virtually no traffic or sales from the ad, and it served no purpose other than paying the magazine.

After a couple of months of pitching their product to anyone on and off the internet, they realized they needed to get much more targeted. They started zeroing in on their ideal customer, and they used online ads to target those people more specifically. They also got better at telling their story and sharing their cause, which increased the effectiveness of their pitch.

One other mistake they made was starting out with a fulfillment center. Outsourcing seemed like a good idea, but the reality didn't match up to the hype. Fulfillment centers work on volume, and they were a small fish in a big pond. They quickly switched to taking care of their own shipments, so they were in control and didn't have the extra overhead.

Four months in, they had made more than $10,000 in profit and made multiple donations to the Gorilla Fund. Gianluca and Gavin aren't monkeying around—they're finally building the venture they'd long imagined.

CRITICAL FACTOR

Gianluca and Gavin knew that socks with bold designs were increasingly popular, but no one was making them with bamboo fibers—a material that was both high quality and eco-friendly.

HAPPY HAMMOCKS BRING JOY
TO THREE FRIENDS

After discovering the life-changing magic of colorful hammocks, a longtime humanitarian recruits two friends to import them from Cambodia to the United States.

NAME
**STEPHANIE ZITO,
TIANNA WEAVER, AND
LAURA DAVIS**

LOCATION
**PHNOM PENH, CAMBODIA,
AND ADDIS ABABA, ETHIOPIA**

STARTUP COSTS
$1,000

WEBSITE
COLORCLOUDHAMMOCKS.COM

It all started in Phnom Penh, Cambodia. Or was it Washington, DC?

In any case, this story begins fifteen years ago when Stephanie Zito was living in DC after moving back to the United States from several years in Africa. She had a bright yellow-and-orange hammock she'd bought while traveling overseas. Whenever she hung it up in front of her row house on Capitol Hill, she noticed something unusual. The neighborhood was often full of busy people dressed in black suits, rushing by and looking down at their phones—but on days that she'd sit in her hammock outside, people would look up, smile, and stop to chat.

After many interactions on the front stoop, Stephanie came to the realization that *hammocks were magic*.

She told one of her friends that they needed to make their own brightly colored travel hammocks and sell them in the weekend art market. They spent weeks searching for fabric and teaching themselves how to sew—but after finally making their first hammock, they realized they didn't have a business model that would allow them to cover their costs, let alone earn a profit. The bright idea was consigned to the department of "Well, that could have been nice . . ."

Nothing else happened in the hammock hustle for a while. Stephanie took a full-time job working for a humanitarian organization in Cambodia, and ended up staying nearly four years. Early in her new life there, she was walking through the market and found some brightly colored nylon. She

FUN FACT Color Cloud Hammocks launched on Stephanie's thirty-seventh birthday. The three friends created thirty-seven color-combination hammocks with fun names for a special launch price of $37. They promoted the sale across their personal social media accounts, and sold out within a couple of hours. This ended up being enough to cover all of their out-of-pocket startup expenses, including international shipping.

bought two colors and took them to the shop of a seamstress she'd recently met.

Stephanie drew the seamstress a picture of the hammock she had tried to make two years earlier. The very next day, she had an affordable, well-made prototype. She went back to the shop with fabric to make four more hammocks with some different features, including a phone pocket and different-style bags to store them. These prototypes also came out well, and she now had a way to start her long-desired hammock hustle.

Color Cloud Hammocks, as she called it, grew part-time with Stephanie and two friends, Tianna and Laura, for the next four years. The partners had complementary skills, which allowed each to focus on her strengths. Stephanie was in charge of product, Tianna did web design and creative direction, and Laura focused on business development.

They eventually ramped up to shipping one thousand hammocks a year to fans and hammock lovers worldwide. Ever since Stephanie first found the seamstress in the streets of Phnom Penh, they've sold about five thousand hammocks—through their own store, on Amazon, and now through a number of gift and garden shops. They also have the capacity to brand hammocks for corporations and events.

Midpoint in the journey, their hammock making also changed countries from Cambodia to Ethiopia, where Laura now lives. As part of the change, they're able to manufacture and ship an entire year's worth of inventory in one production run, lowering costs and reducing complexity—and they're still supporting local women who make the hammocks.

"Many businesses focus on the marketing of giving back, but from our humanitarian experience, we know that it has an even greater impact to invest at the source of our supply chain." —Stephanie

 CRITICAL FACTOR

Color Cloud Hammocks produced a unique partnership on at least two levels: first between the three friends who had complementary skills, and second between seamstresses in Cambodia and Ethiopia and customers around the world.

As magical as hammocks are, the three friends experienced challenges. It was hard to get a consistent supply of fabric in Cambodia, and for a long time they were paying $11 each to ship them to the United States. This had a big impact on profit margins, and meant they couldn't afford to sell to retail shops until they figured it out. They finally solved this problem when they switched production to Ethiopia.

Another obstacle was that after competing with only a handful of other hammock makers, something changed around year four of their business. "The world discovered hammocks" is how Stephanie puts it, and all of a sudden there were a lot of competitors.

Most of these new hammock sellers made their products at low-wage factories in China and Indonesia, which meant that Color Cloud couldn't compete on price while maintaining quality. To compensate, they knew they had to make an exceptional product, and they had to make sure people knew the Color Cloud story.

Life is better in a hammock . . . and the right cause keeps you in the swing of things.

Hobby or Side Hustle?

One of the things I like about most of the stories in this chapter is that they've found a way to build a "social good" component into their businesses. This is different than just operating as a charity, where the entire goal is to raise money or provide a service to people in need.

Similarly, a lot of side hustle stories involve someone who takes a hobby and finds a way to get paid for it. The key difference is that instead of just doing something they enjoy, the person focuses their effort on how it helps other people. There's nothing wrong with doing something just for fun—not everything in life has to make money—but if you're trying to make it a side hustle, *it needs to make money somehow*.

Be clear on what you want to accomplish. If you don't have a plan to profit from your idea, you don't have a hustle. You have a hobby.

For more, visit SideHustleSchool.com/hobby.

There's an App for That

Social media and the "sharing economy" aren't just about being neighborly. There's money to be made! These stories feature affiliate marketing, mobile applications, and more.

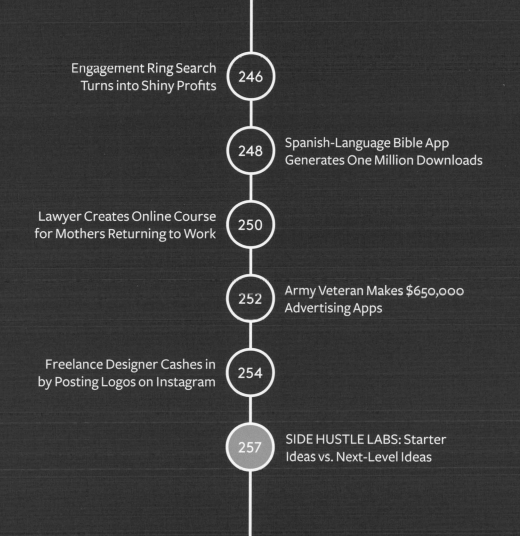

Engagement Ring Search
Turns into Shiny Profits — **246**

248 — Spanish-Language Bible App
Generates One Million Downloads

Lawyer Creates Online Course
for Mothers Returning to Work — **250**

252 — Army Veteran Makes $650,000
Advertising Apps

Freelance Designer Cashes in
by Posting Logos on Instagram — **254**

257 — SIDE HUSTLE LABS: Starter
Ideas vs. Next-Level Ideas

ENGAGEMENT RING SEARCH
TURNS INTO SHINY PROFITS

A search for the perfect engagement ring leads a software engineer on a quest to discover an algorithm for the ideal diamond. Along the way, he creates a business model with shining potential.

NAME
TONY FLORIDA

LOCATION
BALTIMORE, MARYLAND

STARTUP COSTS
LESS THAN $1,000

INCOME
$850/MONTH

WEBSITE
THEDIAMONDAPP.COM

FUN FACT Tony was able to earn a commission on himself, since he bought the diamond for his fiancée's engagement ring through his own affiliate link. Bonus!

* In other words, for every sale that Tony referred, he'd receive a 5 percent cut. Diamonds aren't cheap, so the potential for real money adds up quickly.

When Tony Florida knew it was time to propose to his girlfriend of nine years, he did what lots of guys do: he started researching engagement rings. His girlfriend, Jena, had hinted at what she wanted. The hint came in the form of very specific instructions. She wanted a 1.5 carat, round, solitaire, gold engagement ring. And she wanted it to be "super sparkly."

Meanwhile, Tony wanted to get the best bang for his buck, so with his shopping list in hand, he set to work learning all about diamonds. He quickly discovered that not all diamonds are created equal—and not all diamonds sparkle the same. He also learned that buying a loose diamond online was much cheaper than buying it in a physical store.

Tony didn't stop there. He learned all about the so-called 4Cs—*color*, *cut*, *clarity*, and *carat*—and also discovered that there are other factors that contribute to a diamond's appeal. Certain angles and ratios affect how "sparkly" a diamond is, as does polish and symmetry.

All this research led him to come up with an ideal range for the diamond to be as radiant, brilliant, and sparkly as possible.

As a software engineer, he saw an opportunity to write a program that analyzed a diamond's specifications to figure out if a particular diamond would be sparkly. He thought that other people might find it useful as well.

Around this time, he also learned about the world of affiliate marketing, where he'd get paid for referring customers to a business. One of the diamond websites that he was using paid a 5 percent commission on affiliate sales.*

Tony applied to be an affiliate and told the company he was building a website that would help people find the best diamond for their price point. They accepted his application, and he officially started on the path to earning commissions.

At this point, he still hadn't gotten around to picking out an engagement ring for Jena, which was the whole reason he got started on this project in the first place. With his program running the numbers, he finally picked

out the perfect diamond that featured the most sparkle he could get for the amount he wanted to spend. It was a big purchase—the most expensive purchase of his life, in fact. So before completing the checkout process, he thought about it for a couple of days.

Later that week, he checked on the diamond he wanted and saw that the price had dropped $633. This dip in price gave him the confidence to buy right away.

Tony and Jena went to St. Lucia, where he proposed with the diamond that he had set into an engagement ring. While they were on vacation, he kept thinking about how the price of that diamond had dropped so much in one night. Diamond prices weren't as fixed as he had thought—and with that new information, he saw yet another opportunity.

Not only could his program help people find the sparkliest diamond for their price range, it could also help them *track* diamond prices so they would be assured of getting the best deal. He wanted other diamond shoppers to gain the same confidence that he had acquired.

The day after they got home from their vacation, he did some quick research to make sure that something like this didn't already exist. He then bought a domain name for $10, and got to work building a price-tracking website for diamonds.

The site also included historical price data so users could know how the current price compared to the past. He kept this simple by naming the price categories bad, fair, good, great, and rock bottom, with rock bottom being the lowest price the diamond has ever been. He also added a feature where people can sign up for an account and track the price of a specific diamond. When the price changes, they get an email alert letting them know.

The world of diamond selling is an expensive business, which makes it an ideal industry in which to earn commissions. In the first few months his website was up, Tony made an average of just one referral a month—but that referral often resulted in a commission of $350 or more. He's since referred sales of more than $250,000 in total, for commission of at least $12,500.

Through the partnerships with the diamond retailers, Tony now has over one million diamonds on his website that people can search through. He's also finalizing the details of his affiliate relationship with three more retailers, which will add even more searchable diamonds to the database.

You never know when an idea will turn out to be a diamond in the rough.

"This website gives me more than just additional revenue—I feel ownership over it because I built it from scratch and invested so much time in it. Unlike the work I do for my job, I have complete control of the direction it goes." —Tony

CRITICAL FACTOR

The world of diamonds is shrouded in mystery—a fact that greatly benefits the companies that sell them. Tony's project helps buyers know more about what they're getting, and it also helps them save money.

SPANISH-LANGUAGE BIBLE APP
GENERATES ONE MILLION DOWNLOADS

Opportunity knocks for an underemployed accountant, leading to a fortuitous project that earns $70,000 in one year from a 99¢ app.

NAME
TREVOR MCKENDRICK

LOCATION
AUSTIN, TEXAS (ORIGINALLY SALT LAKE CITY, UTAH)

STARTUP COSTS
$1,000

INCOME
$70,000 IN LESS THAN ONE YEAR

WEBSITE
TREVORMCKENDRICK.COM

Trevor McKendrick teaches business finance for an online programming school. He began his career as an accountant, but quit his job to move to Utah when he got married. For a while, he found only part-time work and had extra time during the week to fill with something else.

It was during that time that he unexpectedly built his own software company. It happened when he discovered an opportunity to improve a low-tech and simple idea, and then get paid for bringing it to people's iPhones all over Latin America.

He found the opportunity by looking through the App Store, paying attention to the top-ranking apps. His goal was to find high-ranking apps that were poorly made or had a lot of bad reviews. The idea was that if an app was making money but failed to deliver a good user experience, there might be an opportunity to improve the idea and make *more* money.

When Trevor was twenty, he learned Spanish while living in Mexico for two years. That's why he paid particular attention to a handful of Spanish-language Bible apps with bad reviews that still ranked high in the book category. He didn't know how big the opportunity would really be, but he decided this was his best chance to test out the theory.

The project did well . . . *very* well, in fact. In his first twelve months, he made $70,000 in profit, selling the app to users for less than a dollar.

How did he do it? He didn't know how to make apps, so he hired a contract programmer to do it for him. To be fair, this part ended up being only a partial success. The guy he hired was from Romania and worked cheap, charging just $500 to make the app. However, in the end, Trevor got what he paid for because the contractor left some of the promised features unfinished.

FUN FACT Although Trevor had some experience in the tech field, he had never built an app before. His strength was in spotting the opportunity for the Bible app, and then figuring out how to get someone to make it.

Trevor decided to go for it anyway. He launched the app and it went straight to the top of the charts. Apparently, even a "mostly finished" Spanish-language Bible app was good enough to knock off the other ones.

A month later, he added an audiobook version for $5. In both launches, he did very little marketing, but because he had found this gap—poorly made apps but enough people who wanted them—he quickly surpassed the mediocre apps in the rankings. He began seeing dozens, sometimes hundreds, of downloads a day.

A few months after that, he experimented with making a free version of the app, then licensing content to sell materials direct to users. This ended up generating hundreds of thousands of downloads on its own, but because Apple took a larger commission on those sales, his profit margins were lower.

When net income was consistently around $8,000 a month, Trevor sold the app to a bigger company. The app had been downloaded more than one million times, he had made at least $70,000 from his experiment, and he's now hoping to replicate this success with another project.

"My tactic is simple: find high-ranking apps that are poorly made or have bad reviews. The idea is that if an app is making money but has bad reviews, there might be an opportunity for improvement lurking there." —Trevor

CRITICAL FACTOR

Trevor finds apps that are popular but poorly made. He then makes a better version of them, with the goals of replacing the chart-setters with his versions.

LAWYER CREATES ONLINE COURSE FOR MOTHERS RETURNING TO WORK

For her first side hustle, a Washington, DC, lawyer and new mom creates an online course for other new mothers returning to the world of work. She then gets creative and finds a way for employers to pay for it.

NAME
LORI MIHALICH-LEVIN

LOCATION
WASHINGTON, DC

STARTUP COSTS
$400

INCOME
$2,500/MONTH

WEBSITE
MINDFULRETURN.COM

Lori Mihalich-Levin lives in Washington, DC, where she's a partner in a major law firm focusing on Medicare reimbursement counseling. She represents academic medical centers, hospitals, and a broad array of other organizations. Lori is also the mother of two boys, ages three and a half and six, and it was the birth of her second child that inspired her first business, Mindful Return.

After returning to work full-time after maternity leave, she found that two children didn't feel like one-plus-one—it felt like all of a sudden, she had eighty-five children. This high-powered attorney says she was in tears on the kitchen floor more often than she'd like to admit. No one seemed to be talking about how hard it was to transition back after the typical three- to four-month American maternity leave.

She also realized that while there was seemingly a curriculum for pretty much everything baby related, from how to massage your baby to how to puree baby food, there was almost nothing on how to go back to work after maternity leave without losing your mind.

How could this be? Lori wasn't sure, but in any case, she decided to fill the gap.

The first step was to map out the curriculum. She had four themes she wanted new moms to be mindful of (self-care, logistics, leadership, and community), so she decided on a four-week format. She then broke up each week into five lessons and mapped out the topics that needed to be covered.

With the outline in hand, she got to work—both writing the lessons herself and recruiting experts in areas she wasn't an expert in. For a lesson on anxiety in new motherhood, she recruited a clinical psychologist. For the lesson on transitioning your baby to child care, she recruited one of her son's day care teachers.

ACTION PLAN

1. The best online courses have a clear target market and provide a solution to a problem. What problem can you solve?

2. Consider the best way to present your material. What do people need to learn to overcome their problem?

3. Recruit subject matter experts to fill in your gaps. If you're just starting out, ask if they'll contribute part of the teaching in exchange for a portion of the proceeds.

4. Write, record, or assemble your material into a set of modules or segments. Make it easy to go through, with actionable steps along the way.

5. Write and publish a clear offer for your course: Why should potential students sign up *now*, and how can they do so?

Once she had the entire curriculum written, she selected a hosting platform and set it up. She called the course "Mindful Return," pricing it at $99 and including an option for employers to cover the cost.

One week later, Lori was sitting in a meeting for her job. She checked her personal email during a break and discovered that someone had signed up. It was the first of five hundred customers who would eventually join in the first three years.

Mindful Return is currently averaging $2,500 a month in net income from course fees. She now has a course to help new working fathers navigate paternity leave, and is working on another one for parents of children with special needs.

 CRITICAL FACTOR

By encouraging employers to sponsor the course for their employees, she makes it easy for new mothers to sign up. More than thirty companies now offer it, and she markets to these companies directly.*

FUN FACT After the birth of her second child, Lori realized why nobody else had created this resource—new mothers are not blessed with an abundance of time, and more often than not, they're incredibly sleep deprived. She decided to break up the project into twenty- to thirty-minute bite-size pieces, tackling one at a time.

* A headline on her website reads "Offer Mindful Return as a Maternity Leave Benefit and Help Retain Your Top Talent."

ARMY VETERAN MAKES
$650,000 ADVERTISING APPS

A Wisconsin native hits the jackpot through his smart approach to blogging and mobile apps, bringing in multiple six figures with nearly zero overhead costs.

NAME
STEVE DELARWELLE

LOCATION
STURGEON BAY, WISCONSIN

STARTUP COSTS
$20/MONTH

INCOME
$650,000 IN ONE YEAR!

WEBSITE
REMOTEJOBR.COM

FUN FACT Steve struck it rich through mobile app advertising and acting as an affiliate for ad agencies. One example of how this works is when you're on your phone and are prompted with an ad to download another app. If you do, somebody makes money off of that action.

Steve Delarwelle was working at a paper company when he struck gold, earning an unexpected $650,000 from a new side hustle in one year.

Born and raised in the small town of Sturgeon Bay, Wisconsin, he had served three overseas tours for the army before returning to his home state, getting married, and studying computer programming at night.

Outside of his full-time job, Steve had been experimenting with repositioning mobile apps. The work involved buying source code, changing the graphics, and re-uploading them to the App Store.*

As part of this project, he signed up with an ad company, which meant he would make money off the impressions that his new app generated—sometimes up to $2 every time someone downloaded an app from the advertisement.

Steve decided to start a blog to document his attempt to make money from apps, along with his trials and tribulations. The blog cost him about $20 a month in hosting fees, but otherwise he had no setup or ongoing costs. He used the blog to publish revenue figures for all of his apps, separated out by publisher. From the ad revenue that his own apps brought in, Steve was generating a steady $600 to $900 per month.

Not bad, but it's not what this story is about.

What happened next ended up changing his life. Steve discovered that the ad company he was using was offering an affiliate program. With no further work from him, he'd have the chance to make more money.

This arrangement meant that if Steve got other people to sign up through his link, he would get a percentage of what the ad company ended up making off of them. He signed up and included the link on his blog, not expecting much.

Nothing happened for about a year. Then, suddenly, one day Steve woke up and discovered $13,000 sitting in his PayPal account. The money had come from that affiliate program he'd signed up for and then forgotten about.

* This is a bit technical. The point is that he was able to creatively reposition existing apps, modifying them a bit and calling them his own. This practice is allowed, especially if you modify the app in some significant way.

At first, he thought it had to be a mistake—but there was no mistake. Unbeknownst to him, it turned out he had referred a developer who ended up making a whopping $130,000 the previous month, which meant that Steve received $13,000 as his 10 percent commission.

After recovering from the shock, Steve celebrated by paying off his truck within days. He wanted to shed his debt in order to be free to start more projects.

And it didn't end there . . . the money kept rolling in! The next month, from the same source, his payout was $35,000, by far the most money he'd ever been paid in a month. Then it was $45,000 the next month, then $60,000, and so on. Before it ended, his highest month was over $100,000.*

When it was all said and done, Steve had brought in $650,000 for the year. There was no overhead or expense associated with these payments. *It was all profit*. And it all came from being an affiliate for an ad company he didn't work for, advertising an app he didn't own.

With the sudden windfall, Steve was able to pay cash for twenty acres of land and build his dream house. Even better, his wife now has the freedom to stay at home with their two young kids.

You could say this was a lucky break, and perhaps it was—but Steve notes that if he hadn't invested the time in consistently publishing his blog, or had the foresight to become an affiliate, it wouldn't have happened. In other words, he got lucky *and* he worked hard.

The Niagara Falls of money streams eventually ran dry. After about six months, the ad company changed the rules of their affiliate program—perhaps they got tired of paying him an average of $50,000 a month—and the cash slowed to a trickle, then stopped entirely.

But Steve's side hustling didn't stop. He soon launched a new business: an aggregate site for remote tech jobs. It takes data from different job-posting sites to find the best opportunities, and then posts them to his site.

This venture didn't cost Steve a cent, as he used his existing skills in computer programming to set it up. He spends about ten hours a week on the site, and it's getting about ten thousand visitors each month.

The new project makes $3,000 a month, usually through other affiliate links he displays. It's not a $100,000 payout, but it's real money and it continues to arrive.

And maybe one day, he'll hit upon another jackpot.

"I would advise anybody who wanted to start a side hustle to take a look at yourself, determine what skill you have, and leverage that to the max. Learn about anything you can—watch successful people and emulate them." —Steve

* With such big payouts, Steve learned the little-known fact that PayPal won't let you transfer more than $100,000 to your bank account. He had to make a transfer of $99,999.99, and then transfer the rest the next day.

CRITICAL FACTOR

Steve was fortunate in signing up for a program that paid him an enormous commission for a referral, but if he hadn't taken the step to blog about his experience in the beginning, it never would have happened.

FREELANCE DESIGNER CASHES IN BY POSTING LOGOS ON INSTAGRAM

After first rejecting Instagram as being "only for selfies," an Australian designer starts a popular account that earns steady affiliate commissions.

NAME
JONATHAN RUDOLPH

LOCATION
MELBOURNE, AUSTRALIA

STARTUP COSTS
$4,000

INCOME
$30,000/YEAR

WEBSITE
LOGOINSPIRATIONS.COM

Twenty-nine-year-old Jonathan Rudolph was born in Sri Lanka, but grew up in Melbourne, Australia. As a child, he loved sketching cartoon characters from comics like Batman and X-Men. His love for design was cultivated further as he watched his grandfather make beautiful handmade cards. That experience would inspire him to create and design beautiful things as he grew up.

When a teenage friend gave him a copy of Adobe Photoshop, Jonathan was hooked. He would spend his time after school on his computer designing cars, changing their colors, and adding new rims. He knew he wanted to work in this field for the rest of his life.

A year after graduating from university, Jonathan started freelancing, offering services in logo design and brand identity. He named his freelancing business The Graphic Illusionist and began looking for side jobs. Some amount of work came in every week and he was making a decent income, all while holding down a day job at a publishing house.

Jonathan first thought he could become a full-time freelancer and leave his job. But the freelance work quickly dried up as he faced increasingly stiff competition. Online freelancing sites had attracted more and more designers, increasing the pool of professionals who competed for a limited number of projects. The lowest point came when he was offered $175 for a logo project, and he accepted. That low-budget project would take him *three weeks* to complete.

"For a long time, it felt unfathomable to wake up every morning to see the page grow by a couple of hundred followers. I also remember seeing the first time one of my posts got one thousand likes." —Jonathan

Fortunately, he got a much better break that led to a much more profitable project. His wife had created an Instagram account using his business name (The Graphic Illusionist), and posted some of his designs. He was initially skeptical, believing that the social network was mostly for selfies. However, the account got his attention when it started to gain more likes and followers than either of them had expected.

After exploring the platform further, Jonathan found that there were a number of accounts curated by designers with huge followings—but there weren't any dedicated to finding the best logos on the Web. Having collected stamps and paper clippings of exotic cars as a child, Jonathan saw an opportunity. He decided to "collect" the best logos by walking the streets and taking photos of them.

Posting consistently helped to grow his Instagram account. Every day, Jonathan would post a couple of logos that he saw, and he'd maximize the reach of each post by using the appropriate hashtags. He had done his homework and discovered that even in the popular design space, there were some hashtags that simply had a wider reach than others. Within the first year, Jonathan gained *one hundred thousand followers*.

With this substantial growth in followers, Jonathan attempted to monetize his newfound platform. He offered to post the logos of companies and charge them for advertising, but that turned out to be the wrong approach. His only sale came from a single design agency, which paid him $200 for including a link in his caption. He continued to proactively send out advertising pitches to companies, but got no reply.

ACTION PLAN

1. Want to get paid for posting photos? Assuming you're not a celebrity, you'll need an angle. Jonathan chose logos because no one else was doing it.
2. Choose a topic that is specific on its own but still connects to a broader community. In this story, the study of logos connects closely to the design community, which has high engagement on a social network known for sharing images.
3. Post consistently and make your images recognizable. Use popular hashtags that relate to the broader community you're trying to reach.
4. Engage with followers, "liking" their posts and responding to comments.
5. When you have a strong base of initial followers, apply for affiliate programs that are a natural fit for your topic.
6. Once in a while, post something promotional—but not too often! Focus mostly on sticking to your topic and giving your followers something to enjoy.

It was only when he changed tactics that Jonathan found a way to get paid *over and over*. He was contacted by a company named LogoCore, which offered affiliate commissions for promoting their logo design program. At that point, the Logo Inspirations account had grown to 250,000 followers. Within a few days of making a single post that mentioned LogoCore, Jonathan made $250.

This experience opened his mind. By using affiliate marketing, he didn't have to pitch companies at all. This was the revenue model he would pursue.

With a working model in place, he began to look more seriously at the project. He scheduled more posts on his Instagram account as well as on his blog. He joined affiliate programs from other companies. The income he makes from affiliate marketing sometimes reaches $1,000 a week, and shows no sign of stopping as Jonathan continues to grow his platform.*

Startup costs for Jonathan's side hustle were next to nothing. Even today, he spends only about $300 a month for web hosting, email marketing, music licenses, and video-recording software.

For those interested in growing their Instagram accounts, Jonathan has a couple of tips. It might seem obvious, but the most important thing is to make sure you post daily and be consistent, while taking care to only share high-quality images.

If you're trying to grow an account that focuses on a specific topic, stay on topic. Do your homework and make sure you use relevant hashtags for your niche, and don't be tempted to use too many third-party apps because the service may penalize you for it.

Jonathan is now exploring the possibility of creating his own products, such as e-books and courses for designers. He's also started a YouTube channel, which has already surpassed ten thousand subscribers. The ultimate aim for him is to turn his side hustle into a full-time job.

This designer was pleased to learn that Instagram was more than just selfies. When he put in the real work, he received real money.

Starter Ideas vs. Next-Level Ideas

A lot of people use the phrase "side hustle" to refer to any kind of work they do apart from their main job. But I try to make a distinction: not all "extracurricular" work is created equal. If you leave your office or worksite and then head off to a part-time job, you're not doing much more than just tiring yourself out

Participating in the so-called "gig economy" isn't going to get you very far. If you're dependent on some other company's platform, you're bound by their rules and their limits.

Thus, the distinction: A starter idea is one where you experiment, learn the ropes, and hopefully make some extra money. Nothing wrong with that! But if you want to truly create a new source of income—preferably one that is passive or at least sustainable—you need a *next-level* idea.

Here are a few examples of each:

- STARTER IDEA: Sell some of your unused or unwanted items.
  NEXT-LEVEL IDEA: Learn to sell *someone else's* unused or unwanted items, and then do it over and over.

- STARTER IDEA: Drive for a rideshare company.
  NEXT-LEVEL IDEA: Coach rideshare drivers (see pages 310–11).

- STARTER IDEA: Sell handmade jewelry.
  NEXT-LEVEL IDEA: Sell handmade jewelry *while building a values-based brand* (see pages 161–63).

For more, visit SideHustleSchool.com/starter.

XIII

Keep It in the Family

Some side hustlers start young, and some parents involve the whole family in their entrepreneurial adventures. These stories feature kids, families, or partnerships.

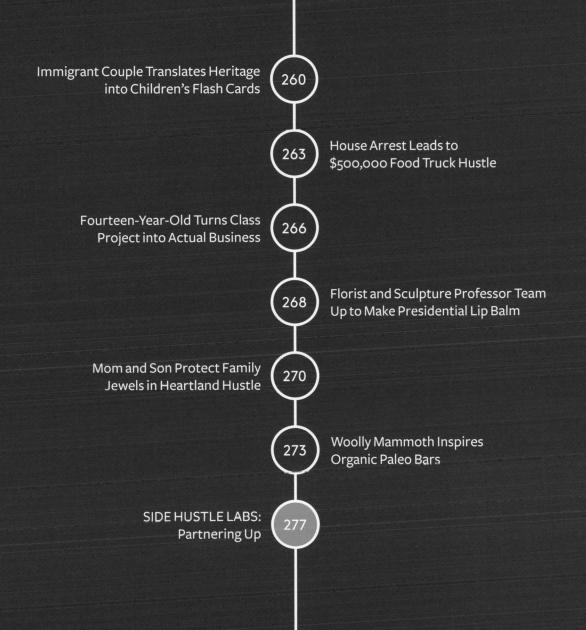

Immigrant Couple Translates Heritage into Children's Flash Cards — 260

House Arrest Leads to $500,000 Food Truck Hustle — 263

Fourteen-Year-Old Turns Class Project into Actual Business — 266

Florist and Sculpture Professor Team Up to Make Presidential Lip Balm — 268

Mom and Son Protect Family Jewels in Heartland Hustle — 270

Woolly Mammoth Inspires Organic Paleo Bars — 273

SIDE HUSTLE LABS: Partnering Up — 277

IMMIGRANT COUPLE TRANSLATES HERITAGE INTO CHILDREN'S FLASH CARDS

Two children of immigrants from Laos meet the needs of an underserved community in a $50,000 per year hustle.

NAME
MYKOU AND TOUGER THAO

LOCATION
SAINT PAUL, MINNESOTA

STARTUP COSTS
$1,500

INCOME
$50,000+/YEAR

WEBSITE
HMONGBABY.COM

When the Communist Party took over Laos in 1975, the small country in South Asia became hostile toward the Hmong ethnic group. As allies of the United States in the Vietnam War, the Hmong people (pronounced "Mong") were considered risks to Communism, and a violent wave of persecution began.

Thousands fled the country and relocated in America, including the parents of young Mykou and Touger Thao. After settling in Minnesota and getting married, Mykou and Touger had their first child. They enjoyed reading to her, but were disappointed by the lack of language-learning

KUV UA TAU
I CAN DO IT

White Hmong

By Mykou Thao
HMONGBABY BOOKS

tools for the Hmong language. There were no children's books, no magazines or primers—almost no resources at all.

The couple wanted their daughter to be bilingual in English and their heritage language, so they began looking into creating their own Hmong flash cards. A month later, they hired a freelance designer to create twenty-six images for their animal flash cards, printing them out in their home office.

The cards looked great! But in terms of a side hustle, they didn't do anything with them immediately. They questioned whether anyone else would want them and put the project on pause.

After more time went by, Mykou and Touger realized they were sitting on an idea that could help thousands of displaced families in the country. They agreed to set aside their hesitations and test it out. The couple made a short video of Mykou teaching their one-year-old daughter the names of the animals and uploaded it to YouTube. They then posted it on Facebook with a link to purchase, but the video only received one thousand views—a small number, at least in their minds.

"It was an amazing feeling to create something that people actually wanted enough that they would pay us for it. We were blown away!" —Touger

Despite the relatively low number of views, the couple sold 125 flash-card sets at $20 each, bringing in more than $2,500 over a two-week period. Mykou and Touger fulfilled everything manually using PayPal invoices, self-printed shipping labels, and a spreadsheet. When it was all said and done, the couple had profited $1,000 from this initial set of cards.

That first launch wasn't a particularly large success in terms of sales, but the extremely high conversion rate was encouraging. One in ten viewers had ordered the cards!

As the new year rolled around, Mykou and Touger began brainstorming ways to expand. They hired another freelance designer and created three new sets of flash cards. In addition to animals, they now had numbers, food, and objects. After setting up a website, the couple made another video. This time they thought that they might have better luck if they uploaded the video straight to Facebook, skipping YouTube.

FUN FACT Mykou and Touger increased their video's views by 1,500 percent by uploading the file directly to Facebook, rather than publishing it on YouTube and then sharing it.

Their hunch was right. In less than three days, the new video displaying four new sets of flash cards had been viewed 150,000 times. Over the next thirty days, Hmong Baby received $10,000 worth of orders. Shopify actually put a hold on the store's revenue because the system tagged the dramatic spike in sales as a possible scam. After they made a couple of anxious phone calls, the site was able to function again.

Thankfully, fulfilling these orders was much more efficient than it was with the first flash-card set launch. Shopify handled the payments, shipping, and inventory with ease.

On fire with the thrill of sales, Mykou began working on a new project: a Hmong children's book. Over the next few months, she wrote the story, rehired the designer for illustrations, and began exploring printing options.

Compared to the flash cards, the logistics of printing a book were far more complicated. The flash cards were printed locally, which made communicating with the printer fairly simple. The books, however, would be printed in China, which was stressful since they couldn't communicate with the printer in person. They also had to do a lot of Googling to figure out how freight forwarding and customs worked.

Once they had their sample book and were satisfied with it, they began crafting a crowdfunding page on their website. Many of their customers had expressed interest in a children's book, but Mykou and Touger wanted to validate that interest by asking those customers to support the production costs.

Once again, they made a video. This one was viewed over 125,000 times in under seven days, prompting more than enough preorders to fund the project. A couple of months later, hundreds of Mykou's books were being read to kids across the country.

In their first year of business, Mykou and Touger generated just over $50,000 in sales through Hmong Baby. Not only have they created a way to teach their daughter the language of their heritage, but their business has enabled them both to become self-employed so that they can spend more time at home.

Next, they want to create more products and streamline their method to be more effective and efficient. They've also received inquiries from people in other immigrant communities who want to replicate their success.

Most of all, they're glad they overcame their initial hesitation and took a chance on making that first video.

HOUSE ARREST LEADS TO
$500,000 FOOD TRUCK HUSTLE

Unable to leave home after a run-in with the law, two cousins get creative in the kitchen. It grows into a food truck and catering business in rural Pennsylvania.

Zach Ellsworth had just heard some bad news. His cousin, Teddy Smith, was under house arrest for a DUI. Zach and Teddy had grown up playing together in southwest Pennsylvania. By that point, however, they were leading very different lives. Teddy, at age thirty-three, was having run-ins with the law, while Zach was married with four kids, and held down a steady sales job.

During the long idle months while under house arrest, Teddy grew restless, and Zach started keeping him company. Before his unfortunate encounters with law enforcement, Teddy was a talented chef who had worked in several French restaurants.

To pass the time, Teddy started hosting a Tuesday supper club for his girlfriend, Zach, and Zach's wife. It was over these weekly, house-confined gourmet dinners that Zach and Teddy started to voice discontent with their careers—as well as talking of starting a business together.

The cousins live in an economically depressed region in rural Pennsylvania, where 20 percent of the people live below the poverty line. You have to drive over an hour to Pittsburgh to seek out good restaurants. With all these data points in mind, Zach and Teddy hit on a mission: to bring reasonably priced, "city-quality" cuisine to their county.

This idea remained all talk and no action, at least until an opportunity fell in their laps. One day, a friend approached Zach with a conundrum. Her sister was getting married in six weeks, and the Mediterranean restaurant that was supposed to provide the catering had canceled without warning. She wondered if he knew of any other options.

Right there and then, Zach decided to launch the side hustle. He told his friend that he would cater the wedding himself, and then called Teddy to say that they had a job.

What they *didn't* have was a kitchen. But after pleading with local businesses, they ended up paying just $25 to use a church kitchen. Then they successfully catered an eighty-five-person Mediterranean wedding— right in the middle of a field.

NAME
ZACH ELLSWORTH AND TEDDY SMITH

LOCATION
FAIRCHANCE, PENNSYLVANIA

STARTUP COSTS
$10,000

INCOME
$50,000 IN YEAR THREE

WEBSITE
FOUNDRYLEBANON.COM

FUN FACT For a while, the sous chef for Teddy was someone who used to compete in eating competitions. He was featured on *The Colbert Report* for his unusual skills and appetite.

With one event under their belts, the cousins went into high gear. They continued to do occasional gigs that first year, bringing in $20,000. The following year, they launched the first food truck in their area—a long-time dream for both of them. They served lunch specialties like peanut butter and pepper jelly burgers and crab cake sandwiches, totaling up $125,000 in sales between the truck and the catering.

In year three, the cousins expanded once again—opening a restaurant serving modern American food, and generating $235,000 in sales from all three arms of the company. But the food business isn't easy, and this third expansion proved to be a challenge. At the outset, local restaurants tried to have the food truck shut down because of the threat it represented, and the cousins had to figure out how to weather the down months when few wedding gigs presented themselves.

There were also a lot of unexpected costs. The cousins had to invest about $120,000 up front to open the restaurant, which was only possible after asking their fathers for a loan. The truck itself cost $83,000, but then there was insurance, equipment, gas, electricity, water, registration, tax, and parking expenses to contend with—which totaled about $2,000 in one-off costs and $8,500 yearly. This excluded business registration, website, branding, and payment-processing expenses.

All along, the pair invested almost every dime they made into growing the company. Teddy focused on the kitchen, while Zach managed the marketing, systems, and sales. Zach put in about twenty to thirty hours per week in addition to his day job, and Teddy, who began to work on the business full time, invested forty to fifty hours.

Their best marketing came through the food truck, which provided built-in visibility for the company on a daily basis. Outreach on Facebook was also successful, but with a twist. Instead of buying ads, they offered a free meal to a random follower each time they post about something important, such as a new menu or service. They say those posts ended up with five times the visibility, and at far less cost.

In year four, Zach and Teddy exceeded $500,000 in sales and $50,000 in profit, and begin planning their way to $1 million. Unfortunately, at that point they realized they'd made a mistake. The catering side of their business produced the bulk of profits, while their restaurant dreams ended up being more of a drain. Customers liked the food truck, but didn't flock to the restaurant the way they'd hoped.

They decided to regroup, going back to the drawing board to see what lessons they could learn and what they'd do next.

FOURTEEN-YEAR-OLD TURNS CLASS PROJECT INTO ACTUAL BUSINESS

When this eighth grader was given a school project, she didn't just want a passing grade—she wanted to create a real business.

NAME
EMILY RUDNICK

LOCATION
DENVER, COLORADO

STARTUP COSTS
$1,500

INCOME
$250/MONTH

WEBSITE
RUDSPICE.COM

When most eighth graders are handed a school project, they hope to come out with a good grade and enough time left over to hang out with their friends. But Emily Rudnick in Denver, Colorado, wasn't like most eighth graders. When she was handed her school project, she came out with a full-blown business—and an extra $250 a month in her pocket.

Despite being just fourteen years old, Emily had spent hundreds of hours locked away in her kitchen laboratory with her father, David, creating spice blends. They would play around with ingredients trying to come up with a hot new seasoning that could blow the competition out of the water (or at least off the table).

For her class project turned business, Emily wanted to officially make and bottle her own spice. This challenge required multiple attempts. Upon cooking one of her initial recipes, the entire family had to vacate the house for a day, leaving all the doors and windows opened.

After "spicegate," Emily and David went to talk with experts at another local business, the Savory Spice Shop. This is where she gave her project a name: RudSpice.

After receiving the class assignment, she went back to the staff of the Savory Spice Shop once more to enlist their help in turning her hobby into something more. It was there she learned her first real lessons in business. The shop's co-owner, Janet, offered a beneficial exchange. If Emily could make the product more accessible to people, and reduce the amount of money she spent on making each vial of the spice, the shop would put it on the shelves for sale.

Going back to the drawing board, Emily managed both to find a similar blend of spices that more people could eat

FUN FACT When Emily went to Spain, she visited Arzak, a wildly popular restaurant that holds three Michelin stars. The head chef tried RudSpice and encouraged her to continue.

without their eyes watering, and to bring the manufacturing cost of each mixture down to $2.74. That same recipe now stands on the shelves of the shop, retailing at $6 a bottle.

Safe in the knowledge that she'd passed her class assignment, it was now time to take RudSpice to a wider market. But to do that, she was going to need more money—and she didn't want to take it from her current investor, her dad. So she decided to crowdfund her project through Kickstarter.

David and Emily wrote a campaign description, made a video, and set about raising $1,500 to cover expenses. After just a few weeks of word-of-mouth marketing and getting her story featured in a local newspaper, the project raised more than $2,760.

The school project is long since over, but Emily is still heating up. RudSpice now offers three products: the original five-spice product from her project, a slightly hotter ten-spice blend, and a cooking rub.

Of the $250 a month she made during the first year, Emily is yet to spend any of it personally. She's investing it back into the business and into her college fund, resisting the urge to buy the hot tub she's always wanted.

Spice-wise, she's focusing on getting the product in local restaurants, reaching out to farmers' markets, and creating more bottles to put on the retail shelves. It's a business model with a real *kick*!

"I want to take RudSpice to a larger level and see it in restaurants and grocery stores. My ultimate goal is to have it replace salt and pepper at the dinner table." —Emily

CRITICAL FACTOR

Emily upgraded her school project to a fiery-hot side hustle. By telling her story in a crowdfunding campaign, she was able to cover 100 percent of the expenses.

FLORIST AND SCULPTURE PROFESSOR TEAM UP TO MAKE PRESIDENTIAL LIP BALM

A gift idea for family and friends blossoms into a full-fledged lip balm biz.

NAME
MEGAN LUCKEY AND KHARA KOFFEL

LOCATION
SPRINGFIELD, ILLINOIS

STARTUP COSTS
$50

INCOME
$55,000/YEAR

WEBSITE
SERIOUSLIPBALM.COM

Megan Luckey is a freelance sign-language interpreter and florist living in Springfield, Illinois. Her side hustle is making all-natural lip balm. She runs it with her business partner and former teacher, Khara Koffel, a sculpture professor at a nearby college.

The business started by accident, when Khara wanted to make lip balm as Christmas gifts. On the way back from visiting her parents, she looked on Pinterest for recipes. Then she ordered small amounts of each ingredient.

Khara convinced Megan to help her, and they began playing around with the ingredients. They found that it wasn't that hard to make a decent balm. Before long, they were making batches in Khara's kitchen, giving them away to people they knew. Their friends and family asked for more, so they ordered additional tubes and ingredients, and decided to charge to cover their costs.

Next, Khara heard about a coffee shop in town that was changing locations and looking for items to sell. They sent a message to the owner, who agreed to let them give it a try. After creating labels for what they called Serious Lip Balms, they started selling wholesale and at vendor fairs.

At one of those fairs, they met the woman who manages the gift shop for the Abraham Lincoln Presidential Library and Museum, located right there in Springfield. She liked the balms and wanted to sell them in the shop, but there needed to be some connection to the president.

Abe Lincoln wrote down a lot of notes, but unfortunately he'd never said much about his favorite lip balm. So instead, Megan and Khara took home some recipes of his favorite desserts, and they matched their scents to

FUN FACT Early on in the business, Megan and Khara were going to order cheap shirts online, but decided at the last minute to order from a local shop. That small T-shirt order turned into a strong friendship. Now, whenever they need a service or product, they try to look locally first in order to support their community.

those. The next time you're at the presidential museum, you can pick up one of their balms in your choice of Mr. Lincoln's Lemon Pie, Mrs. Lincoln's White Cake, and Honest Abe's gingerbread.

The first order was 150 balms, which they delivered on a Thursday. By Monday, the museum was reordering and placing orders for Gettysburg and Ford's Theatre, two other Lincoln-themed shops.

As they've been making balms for Honest Abe and other customers, they continued to work their day jobs. In year two, they made 3,789 balms. In year three, they made 42,496. When they first bought lip balm tubes, they bought 25. They now buy them 10,000 at a time.

Megan has a fourteen-year-old son, and Khara's son is three. Recently, a bunch of custom orders needed to be made on the weekend, and the kids jumped in to help out. "It absolutely must be leaving some sort of impression on these boys to see their mothers making a business out of nothing, and hustling their hearts out to make it happen," Megan said.

Surely America's first president would approve . . . at least as long as they saved him some lemon pie.

"Everything that we did in the beginning, and even now, we did ourselves. It's never really been about spending money, it's been about investing our time." —Megan

 CRITICAL FACTOR

A product like lip balm is widely available, and therefore needs good branding to stand out. As they grew, Megan and Khara improved their labeling and began making custom blends, including the ones commissioned by the Abraham Lincoln Presidential Library and Museum.

MOM AND SON PROTECT FAMILY
JEWELS IN HEARTLAND HUSTLE

A Kansas City–area mom and her young son invent an essential product for young male athletes.

NAME
BRANDI AND KYLER RUSSELL

LOCATION
KANSAS CITY, MISSOURI

STARTUP COSTS
$20,000

INCOME
$10,000/MONTH

WEBSITE
THECOMFYCUP.COM

Brandi Russell knows a lot about kids, both professionally and personally. By day, she's a pediatric occupational therapist. By day and night, she's a mother of two. Three summers ago, Brandi teamed up with her eleven-year-old son Kyler, becoming his business partner for a concept he had first imagined while playing Little League in a suburb of Kansas City, Missouri.

The idea? A protective, yet comfortable, athletic cup for young male athletes, aptly named the Comfy Cup.

Kyler loved baseball, but didn't love the bulky equipment that boys are required to wear when playing sports. From the shelves of their local sporting goods stores to the depths of online retailers, Brandi bought him every different athletic cup available on the market . . . but they were all a pain in the crotch.

After weeks of protest, Brandi finally told Kyler, "If you don't like something, quit complaining about it and come up with a solution!" Cue the Comfy Cup.

Kyler came to his mom the very next day with the idea to invent an athletic cup that's soft, lightweight, and moves with your body. The mother-and-son team then crafted a one-of-a-kind, hand-sewn cup right in their living room, using foam, fabric, and Brandi's trusty sewing machine. Product testing was held right there in that same room, with both Kyler and his dad serving as models. (Brandi assures us that no family members were harmed in the making of this product.)

This self-described "battle-tested, kid-approved" arts-and-crafts project has come a long way since then. The Comfy Cup is now available from various online retailers as well as their own e-commerce website.

CRITICAL FACTOR

Lots of boys and young men play sports that require protection. Since so many of them were uncomfortable with the existing options, there had to be a better way—and it seems like Brandi and Kyler have found it.

FUN FACT   The Comfy Cup was featured in the Grommet, an online website with 2.5 million subscribers. Only 3 percent of products submitted to the popular retailer are approved, and fewer are featured.

THE COMFY CUP

- protects vs 40mph ball
- washable
- fits in compression shorts

- revolutionary
- unique
- solution
- protection
- youth athletics

soft

comfy

air gets through

Kyler=CEO inventor

mom president

dad C.F.O.

Elle V.P.

The entire Russell family now has a part-time job in the business of protecting the family jewels. Kyler and his ten-year-old sister, Ellison, work to fill orders before and after school. Throughout the day, Brandi weaves in conference calls and meetings between her scheduled therapy sessions with her clients. She also runs the brand's social media campaigns. This work ethic and entrepreneurial spirit seems to come naturally to her—she's also written two children's books as what she calls her "side side hustle."

The Russells work out of their home office and use their basement as a warehouse. The Comfy Cup retails for $12.99. They pay $2.79 per product, which is now manufactured in Hong Kong, plus $0.60 per product for shipping. After miscellaneous seller and shipping fees, it comes out to a profit of $6.92 per product.[*]

They reached a big milestone one year after starting, when the business broke even. Sales are now consistently over $10,000 per month!

Brandi says that the best part of the whole project is seeing her son's idea become a reality. She remembers when they produced their first one thousand cups and she thought, *How in the world are we going to sell all these?* But then they were gone in just a few months.

The Comfy Cup brand is now growing as a retailer *and* wholesaler. They've applied to *Shark Tank*, and they have a proposal in with Walmart. The Russells also want to expand the product line to include sizing for tweens, teens, and even grown-ups.

They're also thinking about venturing into other athletic equipment like shin guards—because while you're protecting one part of the body, you might as well protect them all.

[*] Another expense is an annual charge of $1,200 for liability insurance. Given what the cup is protecting, it seemed like a good idea to get insured.

WOOLLY MAMMOTH INSPIRES ORGANIC PALEO BARS

Frustrated by the lack of snack bars devoid of added sugar and weird ingredients they couldn't pronounce, two hungry fitness enthusiasts create their own tasty paleo bar—and hustle their way to multiple six figures.

Michael Winchell and Anthony Ostland weren't trying to start a food business. They were just *hungry*.

Michael, a financial analyst, and Anthony, a CrossFit instructor, both follow a paleo diet. Eager to eat well on the go, they were looking for a nutrition bar that was made out of real food. Their ideal bar wouldn't have any added sugar or "weird stuff," and would still taste good. But despite the plethora of snack bars and supplements on the market, they couldn't find one that met their requirements.

They began prototyping bars in their kitchen at home, using organic ingredients like sprouted nuts, coconut, dates, and egg-white protein. Their friends and family loved what they were making, and they had to borrow more and more Cuisinart mixers as they continued to experiment. By the time they got to five Cuisinarts in their home kitchen, they realized that maybe they should consider renting space in a commercial kitchen. Their hobby was becoming an obsession.

Renting space allowed them to produce the bars more easily and keep up with the demand from friends and family. But before they started selling the bars to strangers, they set up a blind taste test with the kind of people they hoped to sell to. They compared their recipe to ten other bars that were similar, using a simple rating system that took several factors into consideration: taste, texture, and the all-important question, "Would you pay money for what's in your mouth?"

FUN FACT One particularly late-night session, Michael and Anthony had just finished making five hundred bars. As they headed to the car with boxes of neatly packaged bars and one last tray of unwrapped bars, Anthony tripped on the curb—and every single unwrapped bar went flying into the street. After a second of shock, they both burst out laughing at the ridiculousness of the moment.

NAME
MICHAEL WINCHELL AND ANTHONY OSTLAND

LOCATION
SAN FRANCISCO, CALIFORNIA

STARTUP COSTS
$30,000

INCOME
$25,000/MONTH

WEBSITE
MAMMOTHBAR.COM

"When you start a side hustle, there are going to be times when nothing goes right and it would just be easier to give up and say 'Fine, you win . . . I'm done.' And I don't think there's anything unique about our story other than the fact that we never did that." —Michael

Based on feedback from their blind taste testers, they went through close to one hundred iterations across four different flavors, until they got their recipes dialed in. As Michael explains, "This is a process that I think very few food startups actually go through, because they just assume that people will like what they make. We didn't assume anything; we tested it until we knew we had a winning hand."

As it turned out, their target market preferred bars with less sugar and more real food. With their recipes set, Michael and Anthony were ready to scale up and introduce their paleo Mammoth Bars to the masses.

The name refers to the legendary woolly mammoth. "We doubt that he did much surrendering back in the day," Michael said, "and we like that attitude when it comes to health and nutrition."

So with that liberation in mind, they introduced the Mammoth Bars in a clear wrapper with a simple white label. They kept this packaging for over two years as they continued to grow their supply to meet increasing demand.

During those years, they had to grapple with a lot of decisions—some of which they had anticipated and some they hadn't. They knew they were going to write their own content, design their website using Shopify, and do their own accounting. Those parts were straightforward enough.

But as a food business, there were some additional puzzle pieces that had to be configured. They had to find organic suppliers, figure out what licenses they needed, and make sure they got all the proper inspections.

And because they were set on being certified organic, they had to jump through even more hoops.

As Michael and Anthony scaled up, they encountered a temptation to add preservatives or tweak their recipe to make it easier to create in a larger kitchen and extend the shelf life of the product. This is what many nutrition bar producers do, so it wouldn't be terribly unusual.

But they made a decision early on that they would figure out a way to scale up without sacrificing quality, and to continue handling production themselves instead of outsourcing it. This meant that they were in the kitchen every weekend and many weeknights grinding out the bars.

While they did almost everything themselves, their startup costs still added up. All told, they invested about $30,000 of their own money the first two years. Most of this investment, $20,000, went to ingredients and packaging materials. The remaining $10,000 was spent on leasing the kitchen space, website hosting, consultants for specialized topics like food science and manufacturing, and paying to rent space at events.

As their audience continued to grow, they knew they needed a brand overhaul—something more than their initial clear packaging with a white label. For phase two, they launched their product to a larger audience via Kickstarter.

They set their goal at $10,000 and offered pledge levels from $5 to $1,000. In the very first day, they surpassed their goal and went on to raise over $50,000. This strong endorsement meant they could fully move forward with their rebranding.

But at the same time, they now had to make *a lot* more bars than they'd ever made in such a short period of time. Prior to the Kickstarter campaign, their average monthly revenue was $6,000. To fulfill $50,000 worth of bars, they put in even more long weekends and all-nighters.

Beyond just running a successful Kickstarter campaign, it also boosted their monthly revenue up to an average of $10,000. Even more significantly, they were approached by Peet's Coffee about carrying their bars in stores. Peet's tested their bars in twelve Sacramento area stores, to great response at the end of the year. Early the next quarter, they began to roll out the bars to their stores nationwide.

ACTION PLAN

1. Everything begins with the right recipe. Get in the kitchen and start experimenting!
2. Find your target audience wherever they are: yoga studios, offices, gyms, or wherever is best suited to your product.
3. Resist the temptation to assume that you know what your target audience prefers. Instead, follow Michael and Anthony's lead by conducting blind taste tests, comparing your product to those of competitors, and making adjustments after each round. This is a lot of work, but worth it in the end.
4. Consider a crowdfunding campaign as a means of fund-raising *and* getting more people involved.
5. Improve the packaging as you go. Product comes first, but good branding will help you stand out.

More recently, their monthly revenue has been hovering around $25,000, split evenly among Peet's Coffee sales, direct online sales, and sales at all other independent retailers.

As big as those numbers sound, Michael and Anthony still both have their day jobs. They finally hired a couple of people to make the bars for them in their shared kitchen, but they say there's always something that needs to be tweaked.

From improving a production process, finding backup suppliers, getting into a new retailer, or thinking about launching new flavors, they have their work cut out for them.

And they wouldn't have it any other way. As Michael said, "Once things stop being a challenge, I think I'd probably hang it up and move on to the next project. But I'm guessing we'll never get to that point."

Partnering Up

Thinking of partnering up? Think again . . . or at least, think carefully.

For every partner story we feature on *Side Hustle School*, we have at least one that starts as a partnership before dissolving into a one-man or one-woman show. Why? Simply because when it comes to side hustles, almost inevitably one partner will be more committed to it than the other. And if this isn't the case at the outset, it often changes as time goes by.

All things being equal, if you have the choice between "owning" your idea completely or sharing it with a friend, it's better to own it yourself. This doesn't mean that you don't get help from others—everyone needs help! It just means that going into partnership can add complexity to a process that should be simple.

Clearly, there are occasions where partnering up makes good sense. Just keep these principles in mind:

- It's usually best to partner with someone who has different skills and strengths than you do.

- Have a clear, written agreement for what happens if one partner needs to move on.

Following these principles will help you focus on the things that matter—and perhaps avoid unnecessary conflict down the road.

For more, visit SideHustleSchool.com/partnership.

XIV

Start Your Own Factory

If you build it, will they come? Maybe, but first you have to build it. The people in these stories learned about sourcing, manufacturing, or both. Even complex projects (a boat in a backpack?) can be done part-time, without quitting your job.

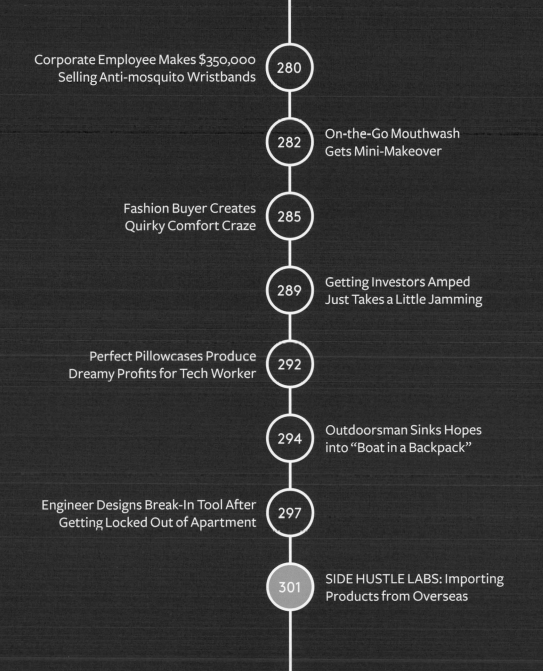

Corporate Employee Makes $350,000
Selling Anti-mosquito Wristbands

280

282

On-the-Go Mouthwash
Gets Mini-Makeover

Fashion Buyer Creates
Quirky Comfort Craze

285

289

Getting Investors Amped
Just Takes a Little Jamming

Perfect Pillowcases Produce
Dreamy Profits for Tech Worker

292

294

Outdoorsman Sinks Hopes
into "Boat in a Backpack"

Engineer Designs Break-In Tool After
Getting Locked Out of Apartment

297

301

SIDE HUSTLE LABS: Importing
Products from Overseas

CORPORATE EMPLOYEE MAKES $350,000 SELLING ANTI-MOSQUITO WRISTBANDS

When mosquitoes attack, this marketing manager creates a wristband to ward them off. The project is a swarming success!

NAME
MATTHEW KONSTANECKI

LOCATION
TORONTO, CANADA

STARTUP COSTS
$200

INCOME
$350,000 PROFIT IN YEAR ONE

WEBSITE
INVISABAND.COM

Matthew Konstanecki has always had a knack for knowing what would sell. As a marketing manager at a software company, his responsibilities involve seeking out small businesses that would benefit from having a better inventory management system. In his previous job, Matt was responsible for sourcing medical supplies and equipment from China. These experiences gave him the exposure and knowledge he needed for running his own business.

He'd had several side hustles, but each of them ran their course and didn't produce a ton of money. He kept thinking that surely he could launch something more substantial . . . he just had to figure out what it was.

The two problems Matt had to figure out were what to sell and how to sell it. The answer, at least in this case, was both strange and sensible.

In his extensive travels, especially in the Caribbean and other humid places like Thailand, he found himself struggling with mosquitoes. With the airplane restrictions on liquids and aerosols, he kept looking for an anti-mosquito product that would be easy to travel with, yet still powerful and effective. He couldn't find such a product, so after much research, he decided to create a mosquito bracelet that would release geraniol oil, a substance that was proven to repel mosquitoes.

He didn't invent the wristband idea—he simply branded it. Matt contacted potential suppliers through Alibaba, and hunted for one that was willing and able to produce what he wanted. He then purchased generic wristbands, slapping a brand name on them to differentiate the product from the rest. Invisaband was his name of choice.

The second challenge was figuring out how he would move his products from supplier to consumer. Searching for a distribution company, he

> "The best part of this side hustle is the 'safety' of knowing that even though I still work in my full-time job, I don't need to if I don't want to. There's something super empowering when you're in control of your life." —Matt

FUN FACT One customer bought one hundred Invisibands to keep mosquitoes away from their horses. They chained the bracelets together and put them around the horses' necks.

stumbled upon Fulfillment by Amazon, a service that helps sellers store, pack, and ship their products. It even handled customer service and served as the perfect solution for Matt's needs.

None of this would have mattered if Matt wasn't able to generate some sort of demand for his product. As a marketer, he understood this, so he listed his new wristbands on Indiegogo before he even sold them. His hunch that Invisaband would sell was quickly validated, as he raised $12,315.

Being successful with crowdfunding can be an art by itself, but the gist of what Matt did just came down to hard work. He says that the most common mistake people make is simply publishing their creation and hoping for an audience to come. Unfortunately, this isn't usually how it goes.

Among other strategies, Matt was successful in searching for journalists and writers who had covered similar products, and then reaching out to them with a special angle. For him, that angle was underpromising and overdelivering. Backers of Invisaband could expect to receive a batch of five bracelets within two weeks of making a pledge of just $19. He had committed to manufacturing two thousand wristbands before launching to ensure that they would be instantly ready to ship when backers placed their order.*

*"Delivering what you promise" may not sound like a radical strategy, but the world of crowdfunding products is filled with skepticism after too many campaigns have let down their backers.

How did it go? Well, apparently a lot of people are annoyed by mosquitoes, because the business grossed $647,244 in the first year. With profit margins of around 50 percent, *Matt made over $350,000.*

For such a huge profit, startup costs were minimal. His first batch of product cost just $200 to manufacture, and he only scaled up production when demand for Invisaband was validated.

Matt's worst experience was having a $10,000 shipment seized at the border because of documentation issues, which almost crippled the business at that point in time. He had to fly down to the United States from Toronto and negotiate with border agents for them to release his goods. It worked out in the end, but it made for a stressful few days.

True to the spirit of side hustling, Matt has now gone on to create two more brands in completely different niches. Both have since generated enough profit to replace an entire full-time income. In addition, he's expanded to consulting and helping other clients with product launches.

His new winning streak has taken the sting out of those previous misses.

 CRITICAL FACTOR

Anti-mosquito wristbands have been around for a while, but Matt branded his and created a strong marketing campaign combined with "above and beyond" customer service.

ON-THE-GO MOUTHWASH
GETS MINI-MAKEOVER

Two Florida State grads create a mini-mouthwash empire, selling thirty-five hundred bottles in less than a year.

NAME
MIKE BRACCIALE AND NICK TELFORD

LOCATION
TALLAHASSEE, FLORIDA

STARTUP COSTS
$20,000

INCOME
$35,000 IN THE FIRST SIX MONTHS

WEBSITE
FLYMOUTHWASH.COM

FUN FACT Before mouthwash was invented, people chewed on peppermint, eucalyptus, or vanilla beans. The original manufacturers had a hard time getting their product to stick. It was only when they invested in marketing that people began to buy it.

Until two college students decided to rinse, swish, and repeat, the world of mouthwash hadn't seen a major innovation in the past one hundred years. And it all started with a potentially embarrassing moment.

Mike Bracciale found himself in the starring role of this moment while cramming at the library for an organic chemistry test. As most college students do, he was pulling an all-nighter, which involved copious amounts of coffee and food that should only be consumed with caution after age twenty-five.

He could have braved the storm. But as fate would have it, in walked his sophomore-year crush. Since tables are in short supply around midterms and finals, she opted to share his. At any other time, Mike would have welcomed such an opportunity, but with the lack of a breath mint at hand, things were just a little too close for comfort.

Feigning a desperate need to visit the restroom, Mike dashed home to freshen up before heading back to the library.

We're not sure how Mike did on that chemistry test, and he didn't end up getting the girl—that's a story for another book—but he did walk away with a big idea.

Around this time, students all over campus were walking around with small bottles of a concentrated flavored liquid that they used to spruce up water. While the bottle contained only about 1.62 fluid ounces, that was enough concentrated flavor to add to twenty-four 8-ounce servings of water. With the struggles of bad breath fresh in his mind, Mike couldn't help but wonder why no one had thought to do the same with mouthwash.

Being on a premed track with several terms of chemistry under his belt, he knew that the average bottle of mouthwash was mostly just water. If he could find a way to take the water out of mouthwash, he could create a product that didn't yet exist.

He'd also be able to save a ton of money on shipping, reduce the amount of plastic needed per unit, and target a group of people who might be thrilled to take advantage of a mouthwash that was capable of being on the go as much as they were.

Despite his excitement about the idea, Mike didn't end up acting on it right away. Instead, he spent the next two years getting as much feedback as possible from friends, family, and fellow students on campus. After he graduated, he moved to south Florida for graduate school, and then quickly realized that he wanted something different. That's when he started looking at his fresh breath idea with fresh eyes.

Just as Rome wasn't built in a day, neither is an innovative mouthwash empire. Enter Nick Telford—Mike's fraternity brother and fellow mouthwash enthusiast. Nick was one of the people Mike had approached for feedback back in his fraternity days. He loved the idea of advancing the cause of fresh breath. They divided responsibilities, with Nick working on financing and brand development, while Mike focused on the product itself.

"Your product can be great in theory, but if you can't produce it at scale, you'll never be able to bring it to the mainstream market." —Mike

The goal was daunting: it needed to taste at least as good as most mouthwash in the market, it had to have a major cleaning effect on your mouth, and it also had to be capable of being produced in a concentrated form. With each test run, they were able to get feedback, take it back to the lab, and pump out a new and improved version for testing. Swish, rinse, repeat!

After months of testing, tasting, and revising, Mike and Nick ended up with a concentrated formula that actively fought bacteria, plaque, and tartar for up to eight hours, and would be able to pack sixty uses into a single 1.62 ounce bottle. And, of course, it tasted fantastic.

Since they were transforming oral care by making it accessible on the fly, they decided to call their product Fly Mouthwash. The name is also a nod to the fact that it's a TSA-approved product and perfect for those who fly often.

Once they finally found the winning compound, it was time to locate a manufacturer. This seemed like it would be the easiest part of the process, since they had a clear vision for packaging—a small bottle similar to the one that inspired the product, along with a narrow opening at the top.

The search turned out to be harder than expected. They couldn't afford to purchase orders in the large numbers the manufacturers were asking for. Eventually, they found a company in Ohio that would let them start with seven thousand units—still a big commitment for them, but one that was manageable.

All in all, $20,000 of their hard-earned cash went toward getting Fly Mouthwash to the masses. It wasn't pocket change, but when they had the physical product in their pocket, they knew it was worth it. As for the pricing, they figured that since each of their mini-bottles contained sixty uses, it made sense to price them around $10 each, or $0.16 per use.

Within the first six weeks, they'd already sold fourteen hundred bottles— all with spending only a few hundred dollars on ads.

They got started by selling on Amazon, which was a fantastic way to prove their concept—but it also came with challenges. Crucially, there was no way for them to collect any data on the people who were purchasing their product, making it virtually impossible for them to narrow down who their ideal customer was. And for the few ads they did pay for, there was no real way of telling whether a click-through led to a sale, or which of the ads did better than any other.

The second and third months of operation were dedicated to building a website and e-commerce platform. By the time we featured them on *Side Hustle School* a few months later, they'd sold more than half of their stock of Fly Mouthwash . . . all within their first six months.

Next, they tried shifting to a subscription model, offering a club where frequent buyers get a new shipment each month in exchange for a small fee. To their surprise, fifty people signed up over the first weekend they offered it. Mike says that for every individual sale, they're now bringing in five new monthly subscribers to their "Fresh Breath Club."

They've also been able to give back. Fly Mouthwash has partnered with Water.org to provide safe water for people in the developing world. For every bottle sold, they make a donation that allows local nonprofits to provide safe water to one person for one month.

These days, the mouthwash mavens are looking to move away from marketing their product as merely a "portable" option and are instead looking to replace traditional mouthwash entirely. With funding recently secured from an outside investor who was interested in their product, mouthwash greatness seems to be inevitable. They're restoring confidence and freshening up the world, one mouth at a time.

FASHION BUYER CREATES QUIRKY COMFORT CRAZE

He always had a unique and edgy taste in fashion. Thanks to a BuzzFeed article forwarded by a friend, he's been able to create a brand that appeals to other people like him.

Kyle Bergman never anticipated that reading BuzzFeed on his office computer would have an impact on his life beyond passing the time. But, thanks to the recommendation of a friend, it gave him the idea for a most unusual side hustle.

Around the Bloomingdale's offices where he worked as a men's fashion buyer, Kyle wasn't afraid to take risks. He was the guy who would turn up on casual Fridays in a Hawaiian shirt, when everyone else wore button-downs and jeans. Because of this quirkiness, one of his colleagues forwarded him a BuzzFeed article she thought he would appreciate.

The article was all about a new fashion craze that combined sweatpants and overalls—and Kyle was sold on the concept as soon as he saw it. But he was also disappointed. The entire article featured *women's* sweatpant overalls, and he wanted a pair for himself.

When he got home from work, he spent the entire evening scouring the internet trying to find a pair of these overalls for men. But to his dismay, there were none.

As a last-ditch effort, he decided to look on Alibaba, where he found a single factory drawing of male sweatpant overalls. But because the factory was targeted at retailers, he'd have to order at least three hundred units. It seemed he was out of luck.

Over the next eight months, Kyle kept the unconventional overalls at the back of his mind, but never did anything about them. It was only when he started studying for an MBA at NYU that he decided to take action.

FUN FACT Early in the project, Kyle attended the Comedy Cellar in New York and took a pair of his Swoveralls with him, on the off chance he bumped into a celebrity. He ended up giving a pair to Amy Schumer, who posted a photo to her online followers. Not bad for his first piece of big exposure!

NAME
KYLE BERGMAN

LOCATION
NEW YORK, NEW YORK

STARTUP COSTS
$25,000

INCOME
$24,000 IN YEAR ONE

WEBSITE
THEGREATFANTASTIC.CO

He logged back into Alibaba and sent a message to Mandy, the Chinese supplier who first told him he'd need to order three hundred units. He asked about ordering a sample, and when she quoted him $150 for a single pair, he felt disappointed yet again.

It would be another six months before Kyle finally responded to that quote and bought a sample from her. He managed to negotiate her down to a lower price of $111, merely by jumping on the phone and asking for it. He put in an order . . . and a few weeks later, he received his prototype.

That prototype exceeded his expectations. The fit was good, and it looked like a premium product. Altogether, the experience gave him the resolve to move forward with his business idea.

He called up Mandy the supplier again, asking for some changes to make the product look "more manly" with thicker straps, a more masculine bib, and a jogging-pants cuff. He also gave her a sizing guide based on his measurements, because he was the typical "large" size for a male. She made these alterations for free, and six weeks later he received a finished product that met the requirements.

Then came the biggest step of all: putting in an order of five hundred units at a per-unit cost of $16.40. Combining this with his other expenses brought his total startup costs to around $25,000—not cheap, but he believed in the product.

Kyle began looking at different ways he could sell his new all-in-one apparel item, and settled on the Fulfillment by Amazon program. By choosing this option, he could send his product to one of Amazon's warehouses directly, where they'd store it and deal with orders, shipping, and any returns. He'd pay a 15 percent commission and a $5 flat fee on each unit he sold from the warehouse. It seemed like the most viable option for Kyle to keep his potentially high up-front investment down.

In order to use this system, he had to be an official business, not just a sole proprietor. He discovered that registering his business as an LLC (limited liability company) was as simple as contacting his state's small business registry, giving his company a name, and paying a fee of $250. Kyle called it The Great Fantastic, after a phrase his mother had used. He chose an equally hipster-esque name for his product, calling them Swoveralls.

He set the price for a pair of Swoveralls at $85. In making this decision, he factored in the costs of making the product and storing it with Amazon,

"Having an idea, and then a few months later being able send an order to someone in Whitehorse, Yukon, is special sauce that fuels my entrepreneurial spirit. Yes, I like sweatpant overalls, but the real driver for me is the ability to produce ideas and concepts and get sh*t done." — Kyle

which came to $37.15, and looked at the competitive market for other on-trend products. This meant he was selling at a competitive retail price, but still making a 56 percent profit margin on his product.

To get to market, Kyle created a tongue-in-cheek style of branding that he modeled on the Chubbies swim shorts brand. It's playful and funny, adding to the quirky nature of the Swoveralls themselves.

He applied this style to his online communication to try to bring in new customers to his business. He also reached out to people in his network, including friends who played lacrosse and their extended network, to find models who would pose wearing his product.

The major portion of Kyle's first sales came from his mailing list. However, this wasn't a mailing list in the traditional sense. Instead, he manually compiled a list of over seven hundred people he had personally met who he felt might be interested in his new product.

He reached out to them (*all of them, one at a time*) on the day that he launched the product. This intensive outreach effort was met with a strong response, bringing in a few thousand dollars in orders before the day ended.

However, Kyle's biggest break was when one of his friends got the product featured in an article in Thrillist, another popular news site. The article about his overalls went viral and began getting picked up by local media and blogs all over the world. Luckily, by then he had set up a website using Shopify to refer all of these people to.

This combination of networking, branding, and reaching out to his old contacts helped Kyle to make over $65,000 in year one, ending up with $24,000 of profit. Who said men's sweatpant overalls were a risky proposition?

GETTING INVESTORS AMPED
JUST TAKES A LITTLE JAMMING

A Toronto science teacher and musician creates an attachable guitar amplifier that pairs with a smartphone for improvised jam sessions wherever you are.

Anyone who teaches kids how to make LEGO robots and plays in a band called Death Valley Yacht Club is going to be an interesting and curious person. So it's not surprising that Toronto science teacher Chris Prendergast created the JamStack, a lightweight, easily attached guitar amplifier that works with a smartphone. The JamStack gives musicians a simple way to practice while incorporating custom sounds and tracks from smartphone apps into the mix.

Chris had grown increasingly frustrated with the effort and hassle of setting up amps and other equipment whenever he wanted to play electric guitar. And because of his teaching duties, where he helps kids with those LEGO robotics, he was comfortable tinkering with electronics.

The tinkering led to a side hustle worthy of the greatest hair bands: Chris created a modular amp that fits on the bottom of guitars. The amp includes a mount for a smartphone and all the necessary cables. At less than two pounds, the setup is nothing like carting a bulky amp around, and it allows for playing along with other tracks, loops, and effects through a smartphone app. When you're finished jamming, you can also share the tunes online.

But wait, there's more! The JamStack is portable enough to fit in a guitar case (for all your busking needs), it runs up to eight hours on a charge, and it works with all major smartphones. At 10 watts, the speaker has plenty of power and fidelity to sound great at high and low volumes. It can even double as a portable Bluetooth speaker.

In short, the JamStack is the Ginsu knife of portable amps.*

FUN FACT Chris installed a plug-in on his site that tells visitors whenever another customer makes a purchase, along with their first name and location. This simple tool is powerful: "watching" other people buy can help you feel more confident in making a purchase of your own.

NAME
CHRIS PRENDERGAST

LOCATION
TORONTO, CANADA

STARTUP COSTS
SUBSTANTIAL

INCOME
$250,000 IN PREORDERS

WEBSITE
JAMSTACK.IO

* The only question is, can you turn it up to 11? Perhaps Chris will add this feature in a future version.

Because the phone is mounted right on the guitar, players can set up loops and perform samples on the fly, whether they're jamming by themselves, practicing with other band members, or performing in a small setting. Using the right apps, the device can re-create virtually any guitar sound without the need for bulky and expensive computer gear. The JamStack can also be used just as a small amplifier without a smartphone—though it won't play that perfect "Stairway to Heaven" solo for you.

Less than a year after developing the concept, Chris built a prototype and launched crowdfunding projects on Kickstarter and Indiegogo. The Indiegogo campaign surpassed $250,000 in preorders, and the device is now being shipped to backers after being manufactured in China.

Just before Indiegogo, he won $10,000 in the Canadian Music Week Startup Launch Pad pitch competition, granting him one-on-one access to lawyers and record company officials who work with licensing. Finally, he pitched JamStack on *Dragons' Den*, the original *Shark Tank*. Although he didn't end up taking the offer they made, he says he learned a good deal about how investors think.

As for what's next, his future seems harmonious. Even though he's busy with robots and rehearsals for Death Valley Yacht Club, he's also twanging out ideas for new hardware and software.

Keep your ears open for the next big thing.

"If you've got a great idea you can really defend, people will believe in you and want to help you. I started touring innovation hubs, visiting design firms, and entering pitch contests. I found partners that supported my dream." —Chris

CRITICAL FACTOR

The JamStack comes ready to rock, allowing musicians to jam, practice, and even perform without the need to cart a bulky amplifier everywhere they go. It also brings new meaning to the phrase "plug and play."

PERFECT PILLOWCASES PRODUCE DREAMY PROFITS FOR TECH WORKER

Tired of battling split ends and hair breakage, an exhausted tech employee switches to satin pillowcases. She then learns to make and sell her own, earning six figures annually.

NAME
DALE JANÉE

LOCATION
DALLAS, TEXAS (ORIGINALLY SAN FRANCISCO, CALIFORNIA)

STARTUP COSTS
$11,000

INCOME
$100,000+/YEAR

WEBSITE
SAVVYSLEEPERS.COM

For nearly a decade, Dale Janée worked for a commercial real estate company in San Francisco. It wasn't a dream job, but it met her basic needs.

To pursue other interests, Dale started a fashion and lifestyle blog featuring clothing reviews, tips on getting legs like JLo's, and lessons in making classic Italian cocktails. This project was fun and somewhat profitable—she got paid for occasional sponsored posts—but she mostly considered it a form of mental escape.

The long days and stressful city life, along with some dating drama, led to her feeling frazzled . . . and her hair was frazzled too.

Dale's aunt was a hairdresser. During a visit, she noticed a lot of split ends and breakage, and recommended sleeping on a hand-sewn, satin pillowcase. After just a single night on the new pillowcase, Dale noticed a difference in her hair and skin. Satin really was the miracle fabric.

But it was hard to find a high-quality satin pillowcase—so, as one does, she set out to make her own.

She called her idea Savvy Sleepers. Through a friend, she met a woman from Shanghai with multiple connections to factories producing high-end bedding brands, including Pottery Barn.

A month later, she flew to China with her sister and best friend, who was fluent in Mandarin. They went to factory towns and tested over two hundred satin blends to find the best quality and shades of color. They then designed the pillowcase, complete with a secret pocket embroidered with her new Savvy Sleepers logo.

FUN FACT Dale chooses playful, pun-worthy names for her pillowcases, like *Nappuccino, White Russian,* and *Pinot Greige*—more fun and memorable than calling them brown, white, and gray.

Initial startup costs, including ordering inventory, building an online store, and that in-person scouting trip, were around $11,000.

Dale expected sales and orders to roll in like a flock of sheep ready to be counted. Unfortunately, some of those sheep must have taken a detour on the way to dreamland. Within the first six months, she'd had just under $10,000 in sales. In a lot of our stories, those results would be stellar. But for Dale, they were discouraging.

Yet she persevered, and things began to turn around in the second and third years. Savvy Sleepers was featured in a beauty subscription box, which brought more attention. In turn, that feature led to more press coverage, causing additional spikes in sales. Sales continued to grow over the next eighteen months, and in year three, she hit six figures—a baseline she's stayed at ever since.

As this side business continued to grow, Dale considered making a big change. Her employer was bought by a competitor, and a number of her coworkers were leaving. She had enough savings to last up to a year even if Savvy Sleepers failed, so she made a careful plan to transition.

That was three years ago, and she hasn't looked back. Dale's satin pillowcases are now available in the world's largest blow-dry bar chain, and also in hair salons and spas nationwide. Her next step involves international expansion, and her long-term goal is to make $1 million in annual sales.

Was it all just a dream? No, this six-figure income is a reality that exists long after Dale wakes up from her savvy satin sleep.

"I knew I had enough savings to last me at least six months to a year if my business failed. I would never recommend quitting your day job until you have a full plan of how you will support yourself, and pay for health insurance and living expenses." —Dale

CRITICAL FACTOR

It works! Many people who try sleeping on a satin pillow notice an immediate difference in healthy hair and sometimes even their quality of sleep.

OUTDOORSMAN SINKS HOPES INTO "BOAT-IN-A-BACKPACK"

A passion for the great outdoors leads a project manager to design and manufacture highly portable kayaks.

NAME
PETE FLOOD

LOCATION
HOLLY SPRINGS, NORTH CAROLINA

STARTUP COSTS
SUBSTANTIAL

INCOME
SUBSTANTIAL (EVENTUALLY)

WEBSITE
FOLDINGBOATCO.COM

Pete Flood has always enjoyed traveling, especially when it involves nature. Getting away from the crowds and up to the mountains, lakes, and rivers is his refuge from everyday life. He's spent many a trip camping, fishing, and scuba diving—from the Bahamas to Alaska— and he wanted a boat that could make exploring these hard-to-reach places a little easier.

For years, he would wake up in the middle of the night, thinking of a slightly different way to design this boat. It would have to be light, versatile, and easy to assemble. And it would help if he could carry it *like a backpack*. Unfortunately, this boat of his dreams existed only in those dreams.

After years of living with an active imagination, Pete took a trip to the hardware store. He purchased PVC pipe, glue, and some fittings. Then, he began what turned into a long process filled with trial and error. Fortunately, he was patient.

Since Pete has a full-time job as a senior project manager for a software company, he spent his nights and weekends, off and on for a couple of years, building over twenty prototypes until he was happy. Before he showed it to anyone other than his wife, he made sure to get it patented.

With his patent filed and a prototype in hand, Pete headed to the Outdoor Retailer Market in Salt Lake City. While at the event, he landed an important meeting with someone who helped him see that, even after all those revisions, his design was problematic and needed more work.

Another inventor might have given up, but Pete ditched the design he brought to the show and started over. Completing another twenty-plus revisions, he invented an even better design for what he calls his K-Pak folding boat. This new design allowed the boat to go from completely packed to ready for the water in four minutes.

After patenting this new design, Pete needed to find a manufacturer who could bring the prototype to retail reality. This led him on a three-year quest around the country, from New York to California to Virginia. Pete eventually made three trips to China, trying to find a manufacturer that would work with him.

Ultimately, he ended up going with a Chinese manufacturer. After more than five years of dreaming, the first round of K-Pak boats was shipped to Pete back home in North Carolina.

FUN FACT One time, when Pete was out paddling around with the camouflage covers on his boat, a beaver swam right up to it and was about to climb on board. The beaver realized just in time that it wasn't a log.

The end of one successful chapter meant the beginning of another. Now that he had a product in hand, it was time to market it and get these boats into the hands of adventurers. Pete started by creating a website that included lots of photos and videos demonstrating just how easy the boat was to set up. He set up the usual social media channels and a way to process payments.

He also approached some outdoor stores about stocking his boats, but soon realized that it wasn't a good fit. Unlike other boats, Pete's boat-in-a-backpack requires a bit of explanation. The average consumer in a store would see a black backpack—and then an assembled boat—and have to make a mental leap to connect the two. And since it sells for just under $900, it's not exactly an impulse buy.

Not only that, but Pete's boats don't require anything other than a paddle and a life jacket. Any other boat usually requires a variety of other products, including a bailer pump, a skirt, a cart, and a lift system to help store it. Outdoor stores would miss out on these additional sales with Pete's boat, so they were resistant.

With this knowledge in hand, he focused on selling direct. Pete hired a marketing manager to help him beef up his online presence. They also started to narrow down their potential markets by doing some focus groups. One of their first target markets came as a surprise to Pete: urban women who head to the outdoors on the weekend became some of his most active buyers.

When it comes to finances, this hasn't been a $100 startup or cheap side hustle. Getting it going required more than $200,000, spread out across many years. About $100,000 went toward the first production run, and the rest went toward the patent process, materials for his dozens of prototypes, sourcing all the different materials required, traveling around the country to find a manufacturer, and creating a setup for outdoor shows.

Here's the key point: by keeping his day job throughout the ten-year startup process, Pete was able to invest in his boat dream without stressing over how he'd pay the bills. The job *enabled* the side hustle to get started—and eventually became profitable.

Pete is a perpetual inventor and tinkerer. He's already come up with a new butterfly design that will shave minutes off the already quick setup. He's recently been hitting the outdoor shows again, trying to find partners so that he can sell his boat in as many channels as possible.

But first, he has another adventure trip booked. When we last spoke with him, he was heading off to Norway with his wife to celebrate thirty years of marriage. Naturally, the boat-in-a-backpack was going with them.

CRITICAL FACTOR

This wasn't a quick, cheap, or easy success. But by remaining at his job, Pete was able to build his invention and see it to market without the pressure of depending on the income

ENGINEER DESIGNS BREAK-IN TOOL AFTER GETTING LOCKED OUT OF APARTMENT

After being locked out of his home one too many times, this curious engineer develops a tool to carry in a wallet. In year one, he sells fifty thousand units.

Nate Barr's hustle began after he locked himself out of his apartment. Again. He had just run out to pick up something at the corner store when he realized he'd brought his wallet but forgotten the keys.

As he was waiting in the cold for someone to come let him in, an idea came to him. If he only had some sort of metal shim, he thought, he might be able to get the door latch open.

He also thought how convenient it would be if he had a bottle opener on him at all times—because a man never knows when he might be called upon to open a bottle. And of course, having such a tool available at all times meant that it would have to fit in his wallet.

Once he got back in his house, he immediately started thinking about what this tool might look like, and what other things he could fit in there. He wanted it to be super thin and feel like a credit card, so that he would carry it with him by default.

With the general idea in place, Nate made a list of all the things that would be cool or useful to have on this tool. He knew it wouldn't necessarily be a replacement for a pocket knife, but he wanted it to be super functional.

He used free, open-source software to work on the design during evenings and weekends. A couple of weeks and about one hundred iterations later, Nate came up with a design that packed as many tools as possible into one tiny metal card. It had that metal shim and bottle opener he'd thought about the night he was stranded in the cold, a pair of screwdrivers, a hex wrench, a phone kickstand, a headphone wrap . . . and about a half dozen other features.

At the last minute, he'd added a stenciled monkey into the design, which served a couple of purposes. First, it looked pretty cool. Second, it made the product protectable under trademark law. He called his new tool the PocketMonkey.

NAME
NATE BARR

LOCATION
PORTLAND, MAINE

STARTUP COSTS
$27,550*

INCOME
MULTIPLE SIX FIGURES/YEAR

WEBSITE
ZOOTILITY.COM

*Amount raised through Kickstarter campaign

> "By controlling our entire supply chain, we can tell the difference between something that is actually hard to do versus someone trying to create hype to justify a high price. Since we've done it all ourselves, we've learned about each step along the way." —Nate

With a functional yet aesthetically pleasing design completed, he was ready to test it out. For the first trial, he just cut the design out of cardboard and made sure that it felt right in his hands while doing each function. From there, he sent the design to a group that does laser cutting in metal so that he could test it on a material slightly closer to the end product. Once he'd refined the metal prototype to the point that he was confident it would work, it was time for a Kickstarter campaign.

Nate decided to try crowdfunding the product for a couple of reasons. First, it would give him some capital to create the product in larger quantity. But just as important, he wanted to make sure there was really a market for his idea. Asking people to put down their money in the form of advance commitments seemed like the best way to test this question.

Since the end of the year was drawing near, Nate hurried and launched his Kickstarter before he felt completely ready, knowing that the PocketMonkey would be perfect for holiday presents. The campaign launched on November 30, and by December 14, it had over nineteen hundred backers. Nate raised over $27,000 on Kickstarter and an additional $20,000 on his own newly created website.

Nate was encouraged by the enthusiasm for the campaign. His enthusiasm slowed, however, when he realized he had been overconfident in the time it would take to produce the tool in bulk. He'd promised that the finished product would be in customers' hands by Christmas—a promise that proved impossible to keep.

As he called factory after factory, he heard the same story. Each manager would politely hear him out, and then tell him that it wasn't the right fit for the type of metalwork they do. Almost everyone gave him a referral to another manufacturer that might be able to help him out—so he kept calling around.

The project continued to stall even when he thought he'd found the right partner. Whenever someone was willing to work with him, he'd get them the design files and then spend more time going back and forth about various details. But then he wouldn't hear anything for a while.

Finally, they'd admit that they had hit a roadblock and wouldn't be able to deliver. This happened multiple times, where he spent hours modifying his design thinking that he'd found his manufacturer, only to learn that his new partner couldn't handle the job.

It took him five months after launching the crowdfunding campaign to find a partner who would actually produce his PocketMonkey. This meant his promised Christmas delivery turned into the next year, with PocketMonkeys going out in batches as he received them from his manufacturer, extending all the way into June. He still delivered the goods, but the timing wasn't ideal.

The experience got Nate thinking about two things: first, how he could control more of the manufacturing process himself, and second, what other products he could make that would fit into this brand. He knew that making just one product and launching it in a campaign wouldn't change his life overnight, so he wanted to keep expanding the brand. But before he could do that, he needed a steady stream of revenue.

Nate took his remaining revenue from the Kickstarter campaign and spent it all on getting himself to a trade show in New York City. Including the rental and staging of a pricey booth at the show, the trip cost more than $10,000. It was a risk, but the decision turned out to be a wise investment. At that one show, retailers from all across the country placed orders.

With some predictable income in place, Nate was able to hire a couple of employees to run the business while he was still working his 9-to-5 job as a software engineer. It wasn't until two years later that he felt comfortable enough to quit his day job and devote all his energy to growing further. Part of this was because he did everything he could to control his own manufacturing process.

As he described it, "We slowly started swimming upstream in our supply chain and began acquiring more and more machines: first the polisher, then the laser engraver, and on up until we had everything we needed to make the products in-house."

Having the ability to do almost everything himself made it much easier to launch new products, because he could do the bulk of the work himself.

* No good deed goes unpunished: after all that, the good Samaritan's WildCard got confiscated by the TSA on his way home.

This innovation helped Zootility, the name of his new company, begin making real money. Nate was able to continue to bring on more people while sticking to his ideals: manufacturing and creating jobs in the United States while creating a high-quality, functional product at a competitive price point.

And he's managed to keep doing this. He's now up to eighteen employees and dozens of products. To date, Nate has sold over *five hundred thousand* PocketMonkeys alone, and he has no plans to slow down. He recently launched a line of tool jewelry called Tülry, and has more ideas in the prototyping and percolating stages.

Looking back, he's glad he didn't take his keys with him that cold November day in Maine. He's also glad he followed up on his crazy idea.

FUN FACT   Nate's inventions may have saved at least one person's life. A customer was hiking in Moab, Utah, when they stopped to watch a rock climber as she was rappelling down an arch. When she was 30 feet from the ground, her hair got stuck in the belay device. She didn't have a knife on her, and her hair was getting more stuck the longer she tried to fix it. The customer happened to have a WildCard in his wallet, which has a small knife built into it. He managed to throw the card up to her so she could cut herself free.*

Importing Products from Overseas

If you're ready to take the plunge—or just dip your toe in the Pacific Ocean of reselling—you might want to take a look at the behemoth of factory listings, Alibaba.com. Upon visiting Alibaba, you'll encounter thousands of product listings, complete with prices, terms of purchase, and reviews of the manufacturer from other customers.

The simple and easiest way to get started is to select some kind of product line to experiment with. Yoga mats? Remote-controlled tractors? Adjustable cat furniture? It's all there on Alibaba—just be aware that browsing the site is an easy way to lose an entire afternoon.

You'll likely be more successful if you find some way to "brand" the items you buy. Matthew Konstanecki's anti-mosquito wristbands were made to include the name *Invisiband* on them. Another popular *Side Hustle School* story featured a guy who made $300,000 reselling manual coffee grinders on Amazon. The *only* physical difference between his product and other, generic ones was a line of text that included his business name. (The real value came in the way he interacted with his customers.)

Finally, you can also hire a manufacturer to custom build a product for you, just like several of the stories featured here. Download a list of questions to ask potential partners at the site below.

For more, visit SideHustleSchool.com/factory.

Ramp Up: Million-Dollar Side Hustles

Side hustles are great for earning extra cash—and sometimes they earn a *lot* of it. These stories represent people with hustles that produce high six figures or seven figures in annual income.

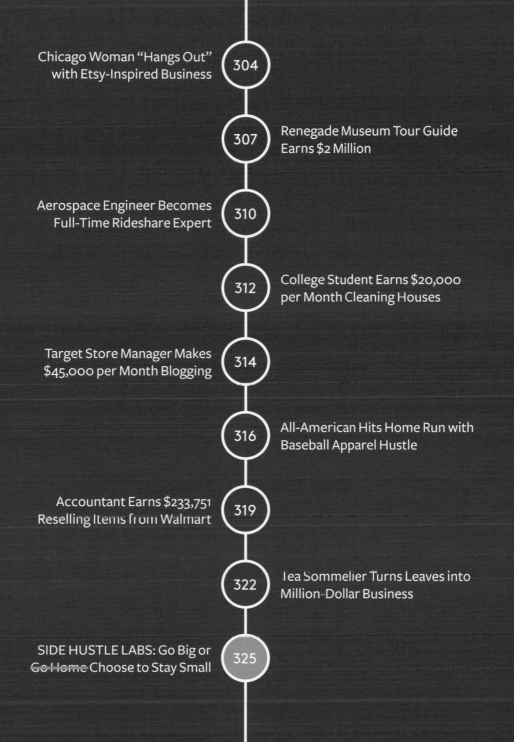

Chicago Woman "Hangs Out" with Etsy-Inspired Business — 304

Renegade Museum Tour Guide Earns $2 Million — 307

Aerospace Engineer Becomes Full-Time Rideshare Expert — 310

College Student Earns $20,000 per Month Cleaning Houses — 312

Target Store Manager Makes $45,000 per Month Blogging — 314

All-American Hits Home Run with Baseball Apparel Hustle — 316

Accountant Earns $233,751 Reselling Items from Walmart — 319

Tea Sommelier Turns Leaves into Million-Dollar Business — 322

SIDE HUSTLE LABS: Go Big or Go Home Choose to Stay Small — 325

CHICAGO WOMAN "HANGS OUT" WITH ETSY-INSPIRED BUSINESS

A Chicago-based plastic recycling sales rep transforms her love for DIY lamp shades into a multimillion dollar business.

NAME
JENNIFER BROWN

LOCATION
CHICAGO, ILLINOIS

STARTUP COSTS
MINIMAL

INCOME
MULTIPLE SIX FIGURES/YEAR

WEBSITE
HANGOUTLIGHTING.COM

Jennifer Brown has been starting projects since she was ten years old, beginning with selling Beanie Babies on eBay and dog sitting for $30 per day. In high school, she tried repainting abandoned furniture from an alleyway. Then, in college, she found her stride and took her creativity to the next level.

At a local craft show, Jen saw a liquor bottle with lights inside of it. Always looking for her next DIY project, she decided to make one for herself. Once she'd placed Christmas lights inside a painted liquor bottle, her friends kept asking her to sell them one—so like any resourceful artist, she followed through on their requests.

Then, one day, she tried something else: Jen covered a balloon in Elmer's glue and wrapped it with yarn to create a lamp shade. She had never seen anything like it. That very same day, a good friend told her about the online marketplace called Etsy.

Within a week, Jen had listed her creation and made her first sale for $60. She sold a second lamp shade a few days later for another $40. With a $300 rent payment looming, $100 was a significant amount of money.

What excited her most was that she was just getting started. What would happen if she invested more of her time and efforts in making more fixtures?

She began looking around for other things on Etsy that she could create. She saw some wooden chandeliers and, much like the lighted liquor bottles, thought, *Hey, I can make those too!*

Not only did her bedroom transform into her production studio, but sometimes she couldn't use her shower because she had hung so many yarn spheres in there to dry. Every time she received a customer request

"Make sure you have high enough margins, and keep improving as you go. Learn from each sale about what people want—then do more of that." —Jen

FUN FACT Jen may have turned her side hustle into her main business, but she still likes to dabble in new projects from time to time. And occasionally, whenever she sees rare Beanie Babies for sale, she can't resist picking them up for old times' sake.

for a new color, she would make it for them, take a picture, and add it as another item in her store. This organic growth was wonderful, but one can only make so many yarn lamp shades.

As she was quickly outgrowing the limited production capacity of her bathroom, Jan decided it was time to charge more. In a story as old as time, the more she raised her prices, the more she sold. Years later, she still recalls the moment she realized she could turn $10 in supplies into a $300 light fixture.

For years, her DIY lighting hustle was just a side gig as she worked her day job as a sales rep at a recycling company. In fact, it was the job that had made selling on Etsy so easy. Her background in sales, marketing, graphic design, and search engine optimization (SEO) put her leaps and bounds above other home-crafters selling their wares at the time.

Since Jen could work from home a few days per week, everybody told her not to quit her day job. For years, she dutifully maintained the status quo, working full-time and selling her wares on the side. That is, until one day, when a friend asked her to question the opportunity cost of continuing to keep both jobs.[*]

With that change in perspective, Hangout Lighting became more of a priority. Jen knew that she couldn't continue to grow the business if she was building lights all day long, so she began to consider hiring employees to help out.

Going all-in allowed Jen to brighten up Hangout Lighting's sales to multiple six figures. What started as a side hustle now gives Jen total financial and schedule freedom. The Etsy side of Hangout Lighting grew to $1 million in sales in just three years. Between her various online channels, she now brings in up to $70,000 per month.

While she could be taking home large profits per month, Jen reinvests much of it back into the business to, as she puts it, "continue growing my dreams." By pursuing those dreams, her bright ideas have brightened up thousands of homes.

* Jen also mentioned that she never understood the "risk" that everyone said she was taking in walking away from her job. As she saw it, remaining at the job would have been a much bigger risk.

RENEGADE MUSEUM TOUR GUIDE
EARNS $2 MILLION

A New York City man goes on a forgettable date, but falls in love with the idea of creating his own museum tour company.

Several years ago, on a Saturday night in December, Nick Gray was on what was supposed to be a romantic date. He and his companion were taking a private tour of the Metropolitan Museum of Art. As snow fell outside over New York City, they traveled through the Met's dimly lit hallways and cavernous rooms, filled with sculptures, paintings, and Egyptian artifacts.

According to Nick, that night something magical happened: he fell in love . . . with the museum.

As for the date, that relationship didn't work out. In fact, he barely remembers her. Instead, he remembers being entranced by the artworks all around him, documenting more than five thousand years of human history.

These observations quickly turned into an obsession. While Nick spent his working weeks selling avionics equipment—a job he was happy with—he started spending every weekend at the Met.

He began offering free tours of the museum to his friends and family, which mainly consisted of showing them his favorite things. He says he was having so much fun doing the tours that the first time someone tried to offer him $20 at the end, he turned it down.

As word spread of his skill, the off-hours tours began consuming more and more of his time. Given his newfound love for museums and desire to share it, he decided to set up a side business.

His idea was to offer nontraditional, "renegade" tours at the world's best museums. By this point, he had increased the quality of his tours, using library research as well as turning to the trusted friend of every student who's written a paper in the past fifteen years, Wikipedia.

His friends started telling their friends, and the word continued to spread. At one point, a blog wrote about his tours, and the next day Nick received

NAME
NICK GRAY

LOCATION
WORLDWIDE

STARTUP COSTS
MINIMAL

INCOME
MULTIPLE SEVEN FIGURES/YEAR

WEBSITE
MUSEUMHACK.COM

FUN FACT   In one recent year, twenty-six guests got engaged on marriage proposal tours. And yes, they operate tours designed specifically for popping the question.

hundreds of requests to sign up. He officially launched his company, Museum Hack, a few months later, offering public tours for $59 a person and private tours for $99 a person.

The setup was simple: Nick financed almost all of his startup costs, including a website, by charging for the tours. And he attracted most of his customers simply through word of mouth. After guests went on the tours, they would post about them online, creating additional interest.

He also started hiring part-time guides, who now include Broadway actors, stand-up comedians, and scientists. These guides design their own routes, based on what they're most passionate about. The museum benefits too. Museum Hack pays them an admission fee for each guest.

The goal is to tap into a whole new market of museum goers: essentially people who think they hate museums—a group which, Nick admits, used to include him. His tours are two to three times faster than traditional ones, incorporate games throughout, and reveal the juicy gossip behind the paintings and other exhibits. One of the taglines he uses is "This isn't your grandma's museum tour."*

It's safe to say all of this touring has been a huge success. In its first year, Museum Hack made about $40,000. In the following year, *income increased twelvefold*, to just under $500,000. About two years after launching the tours, Nick's side hustle officially became his full-time gig. He still liked his day job, but running a part-time project of this size was like painting the Sistine Chapel at night while working as a bank teller during the day.

At last count, Museum Hack has led over twenty-one thousand people on semiprivate tours in five cities. The business has sixty-plus employees, as well as contractors and associates who regularly do tours and events, along with a leadership team that keeps everything running smoothly.

As the team expanded, Nick made another big change, promoting his chief of staff to take over his job as CEO. He continues to be highly involved, but he felt like someone more focused on process and organization would be better suited at the helm. Accordingly, he's shifting his focus to an advisory role, and looking for more creative ways to expand the business even further.

A side hustler at heart, Nick is already busy with a new hobby—this time, hosting a pioneering style of cocktail parties. Naturally, he's testing it out on his friends first.

"Do it for your friends first! I spent hundreds of hours giving my friends free museum tours so I could create an entirely new product. This feedback from them, in combination with their word-of-mouth referrals, is what helped me launch my business." —Nick

* One of the most popular tours that Museum Hack offers is the consistently sold-out "badass bitches" tour—a feminist celebration of women in the Met.

CRITICAL FACTOR

"Museum tours for people who hate museums" proved to be a powerful selling point. Then, as Nick branched out and began to hire guides, he made sure that visitors would have a stellar experience by choosing people with outgoing, engaging personalities.

AEROSPACE ENGINEER BECOMES
FULL-TIME RIDESHARE EXPERT

A Boeing employee earns $34,000 in one weekend referring drivers to Lyft, and then sets out to become an industry expert. His website now brings in multiple six figures annually and receives hundreds of thousands of visitors each month.

NAME
HARRY CAMPBELL

LOCATION
LOS ANGELES, CALIFORNIA

STARTUP COSTS
MINIMAL

INCOME
MULTIPLE SIX FIGURES/YEAR

WEBSITE
THERIDESHAREGUY.COM

Like several of our featured stories, Harry Campbell's extracurricular activities began at an early age. In his case, it started in the high school lunchroom. His mom made the best lunches, and the other kids would offer him money for them.

Eager to capitalize on this opportunity, Harry started asking his mom for two bags of chips, two iced teas, and sometimes even two sandwiches—reselling the extra items to his classmates for a 100 percent profit. He still remembers his best customer: a girl in English class who bought a bag of chips every day.

Many sandwich sales later, he became an aerospace engineer for Boeing. The job paid well, and when Harry started driving for Uber and Lyft on the side, some of his friends and coworkers made fun of him. Why did he need to ferry people around after he'd already worked a full day?

Well, for Harry, it wasn't so much about the money he earned for each ride as it was the idea and the opportunity. He'd started driving in the early days of ridesharing, when the companies were desperate to sign up drivers and began awarding a lot of incentives for referrals.

In fact, the incentives were much more lucrative than the actual driving. He first signed up for Lyft, but then earned $500 for joining Uber and completing a single, ten-minute ride.

"I think finding the right side hustle is all about trying lots of different things. It's important to do your due diligence and research ideas without jumping right in, but at a certain point, you need to just start experimenting." —Harry

He struck the mother lode of incentives when Lyft ran a promotion offering new drivers $1,000 for doing one ride, and paid the referring driver $1,000 as well. Harry spent three days trying to convince everyone he knew to sign up.

FUN FACT   I first met Harry when he attended a book event of mine in Orange County, California. He gave me a ride back to the hotel that night—and I didn't even have to pay!

People told him it sounded like a scam, but it wasn't—he ended up referring thirty-four drivers and earning a $34,000 bonus.*

When he first started driving, Harry noticed a lot of people were asking the same questions over and over in Facebook groups for drivers, but no one had the definitive answers. It seemed to him that if he could create a resource that answered those questions, it could get people off Facebook and onto his website, granting him the authority in this new industry.

At first, the site was just another part-time project. Harry made around $25,000 from it that first year, a lot more than he was expecting. But traffic was growing, he was starting to get more media attention, and he figured that if he went full-time, the numbers would only get better.

So once his new site, The Rideshare Guy, was getting around one hundred thousand page views per month, he quit his day job. He was pretty sure that he was going to eclipse his engineering salary within a year, and just in case it didn't work, he had a good emergency fund saved up.

He didn't need the emergency fund. In his first year going all-in, the business made over $100,000 in profit. He's now expanded into advising and advertising. A team of two full-time employees handle content management, and around ten freelancers do everything from writing and making videos to virtual assistance and editing. It's a rideshare empire!

Year after year, Harry continued to grow the business. He wrote a book and began consulting with auto manufacturers and public policy experts. He even planned to host the first-ever rideshare conference.

In the midst of all the rideshare projects, his wife gave birth to their first child. Because of the flexibility that his new work provides, he was able to take several weeks for full-time child care, and then work half-time for a couple of months. From the lunchroom where he hustled chips and iced teas to leaving his engineering job to become an expert in a new industry, Harry's willingness to follow his curiosity and to experiment has led him to a life where he's fully in control.

If you find yourself in need of a ride in Los Angeles, pay attention to who your driver is. Once in a while, he still turns on his Uber or Lyft app to pick up passengers. He says that it keeps him on his game.

CRITICAL FACTOR

It's estimated that more than three million people have signed up to drive for rideshare companies. Until Harry created his website, however, there was no central gathering point for them to share information.

*In other words, the company was paying $2,000 to acquire a driver who might only work for them once. It's no surprise that this promotion was short-lived.

COLLEGE STUDENT EARNS $20,000 PER MONTH CLEANING HOUSES

A Washington, DC, student identifies problems in the cleaning industry, then takes his insights to the bank—all without ever scrubbing a floor of his own.

NAME
CHRISTOPHER SCHWAB

LOCATION
WASHINGTON, DC

STARTUP COSTS
MINIMAL

INCOME
$20,000+/MONTH

WEBSITE
THINKMAIDS.COM

Christopher Schwab's side hustle turned into his main gig in a very short period of time. The business is called Think Maids, a residential cleaning service in the Potomac area of Washington, DC, Maryland, and Northern Virginia.

He started Think Maids during his last semester of college. Even as a student, he spotted a demand for transparent, high-quality cleaning services. Every city has a ton of cleaning companies, but many are unreliable and have hidden costs.

Christopher believed he could fix many of the complaints people had about cleaning companies. He also thought the cleaning industry was a safe option for a side hustle, because there's no shortage of people who need their homes cleaned. The way he saw it, it was simply a matter of learning how to effectively reach those people.

After researching the competition and mapping out how he'd deal with the common problems in the industry, Christopher started by putting up a website with instant online booking. He then added his business profile to Yelp, Thumbtack, and other forums where customers actively look for cleaning services. He made sure his online presence was impeccable, unlike most maid company sites that are outdated and don't accept online bookings.

Next, he worked to find reliable, quality cleaning teams. He posted recruitment ads on Craigslist, set up interviews, and had people clean his own apartment so he could see how skilled they were.[*]

FUN FACT Christopher was able to travel to Japan for ten days, and his hustle didn't slow down. This was only possible because he had built systems in his business that weren't dependent on him.

ACTION PLAN

1. This kind of business isn't really about cleaning—it's about systems. Instead of going out to clean houses (or whatever you decide), think first about how to construct the project in a way that doesn't rely on you to do much of anything once it's going.
2. Follow Christopher's model of radical customer service. Be reliable, honest, and quick to reply to inquiries.
3. For every customer interaction, devise a script or protocol that others can follow. If a customer is unhappy, how should your team respond?
4. After going above and beyond, ask for referrals.

[*] He pays the people who clean his house, even if he doesn't end up hiring them.

He learned to trust *and* verify. When he hires someone, he gives them a few jobs their first week to battle-test them before deploying them to a dozen houses or more in a few days. Several prospective cleaners said they had a lot of experience, so he didn't interview them . . . but none of those people worked out. Lesson learned: Always do the interview.

In launching Think Maids, Christopher discovered that the three biggest problems with the industry were reliability (cleaners being late or just not showing up), the hassle involved with booking (since many services didn't accept online bookings), and the lack of honesty or integrity.

To address these problems, he makes sure he works with cleaners that are easy to contact, punctual, and personable. Think Maids offers simple online booking, easy schedule changes, and the ability for clients to share special instructions. The company is easy to contact by phone, email, or text, and has a goal of trying to respond within five minutes.

When a customer schedules a clean, they get a reminder email three days before, one day before, and then on the day of their clean. They also get text messages when the cleaner is on their way. After each booking, customers get an email asking for a rating.

Customers receive a phone call the day after a cleaning to see how things went and if they want to sign up for a regular service. If there's a problem, Think Maids will call the customer as soon as they find out about it, and work to make it right for them that same day or as soon as possible.[*]

In a short period of time, Christopher had ten people who cleaned for him on a regular basis, as well as two assistants who helped with booking, scheduling, feedback calls, and other tasks.

He was also earning up to $20,000 a month. A big portion of revenue comes from gently pushing clients to sign up for recurring services so that he can count on their business month after month. Additionally, he focuses on move-in or move-out cleans on the last week of each month, where weekly income is twice that of the other weeks. Other maid services are typically booked up then, but Think Maids makes sure to have availability.

The best part of the experience is having enough time to do what he wants. Christopher has worked hard on automating and delegating as much as he can.

His goal is to grow Think Maids to $50,000 a month while only working three to four hours a day. He's also putting thought into a second side hustle that complements this one.

Meanwhile, he's *cleaning up*.

> "I was working on the cleaning company during my final semester at college. I grew it enough that once I graduated it shifted effortlessly to my main work now."
> —Christopher

*Does all of this sound like a lot of work? Well, it is! And that's the point. Think Maids stands out in large part because it emphasizes so much customer contact.

CRITICAL FACTOR

How is it possible that such a common industry could be plagued with such consistent problems? Christopher didn't understand why either, and he set out to address those problems from the outset. The proof is in his many positive reviews—and, of course, his $20,000 a month in billings.

TARGET STORE MANAGER MAKES
$45,000 PER MONTH BLOGGING

He'd been interested in personal finance since he was thirteen, but he had no idea this passion would go on to transform his life, earning a huge profit even as he continued working his first job at Target.

NAME
ROBERT FARRINGTON

LOCATION
SAN DIEGO, CALIFORNIA

STARTUP COSTS
MINIMAL

INCOME
MULTIPLE SIX FIGURES/YEAR

WEBSITE
THECOLLEGEINVESTOR.COM

Investing has been a lifelong obsession for Robert Farrington. From when he first sat down to help his dad with his taxes at the wise old age of thirteen, to a few years later when he received $1,000 from his grandfather to buy his first stocks, he was hooked.

When he got to college, Robert was hoping to find some of his peers and share his ideas by joining their investment club. But when he turned up at the club's meeting, he was disappointed to learn that all of the advice they were giving was centered on penny stocks and day trading. This was advice he not only disagreed with, but also felt was outright bad for students to follow.

He started a blog, *The College Investor*, to be a transparent voice and share the strategies he felt were more honest and viable for students.

Using a free website template and spending only minimal amounts of cash, Robert published his first post that first year of college. He committed to post three times per week, and spent most of his first year as a blogger to learn the trade.

He didn't know anything about marketing or writing or creating headlines—but, as he put it, "nobody was really reading the site anyway," so he could afford to make mistakes. Gradually, he learned what the people who did read the site responded to.

Then, almost a year and a half of writing later, *The College Investor* finally made its first $25 of income through an affiliate product sale. He'd spent fifteen months working for that $25, but Robert couldn't have been prouder. He knew his site was no longer just a passion, but a *business*.

FUN FACT   Over the years, most of Robert's coworkers at Target didn't know about his "other job," but once in a while someone would approach him and say something like "I saw an article in *Forbes* . . . and it was written by you!"

All this time, Robert was going to school and working at Target. He started as a team member and then became a supervisor. After graduation, he became an assistant manager, and finally a full store manager in his hometown of San Diego.

And as he rose through the ranks at Target, the income on his blog began to rise as well.

The main source of income came through affiliate commissions. In posts and guides on the site, Robert will recommend a product or service—like an online broker, a real estate investment, or student loan refinancing—and if a customer chooses to buy through his link, he receives either a flat fee or a percentage of the sale.

This requires Robert to consistently create good content so that people trust and believe his recommendations. Relationships with readers can take months or years to build, but once you get the right content with the right recommendation in front of the right reader, the commissions can start to roll in over and over.

The site has come a long way since that first $25. When we profiled Robert for *Side Hustle School*, it was pulling in as much as $45,000 a month. That's not a typo, and there aren't many expenses. It's simply a lot of money, all built on a lot of commissions from a lot of customers.

After seven years in both roles, Robert finally quit his job at Target to transition himself into being the full-time CEO of his site. He hopes the change will allow him to give his business an extra push to become the go-to site for student investing in America.

"Your first year of blogging is about learning, and you have to remember to put in that practice if you want to be successful." —Robert

CRITICAL FACTOR

Robert chose a profitable topic to write on, and then he just kept writing, day after day. The eventual reward was well worth the effort!

ALL-AMERICAN HITS HOME RUN WITH BASEBALL APPAREL HUSTLE

After first learning to use design software to forge his report card, a Hawaiian baseball enthusiast creates a clothing line that goes on to earn millions of dollars.

NAME
TRAVIS CHOCK

LOCATION
PORTLAND, OREGON

STARTUP COSTS
$3,500

INCOME
MULTIPLE SEVEN FIGURES/YEAR

WEBSITE
BASEBALLISM.COM

A native of Hawaii, Travis Chock has always loved baseball. He started playing when he was five and hasn't stopped since. He would go on to make the club baseball team at the University of Oregon and transform himself into a two-time All-American. Baseball wasn't just a sport—it was his life.

So it comes as no surprise that Travis's first job would be related to his favorite pastime. Drawing on his sports experience, he sought out a job as a junior varsity coach at a nearby high school, but discovered there just wasn't a strong baseball culture in Eugene, Oregon. For someone whose identity was centered around the sport, Travis was shocked. As an Asian American from Hawaii, he didn't feel like he fit into any social groups in school, and baseball was where he found people he could relate to.

Since the baseball community in Oregon was in need of some cheerleading, he decided that he'd try to fill the void himself. He got together with some former teammates from his club baseball days, and they worked to put together a series of youth baseball camps.

For each week that summer, Travis and the gang taught twenty-four kids between the ages of seven and twelve everything they knew about the sport they loved. They called the camp—and eventually their growing business—Baseballism.

Most camps give out free T-shirts to participants, but they don't put much effort into design or print quality. Travis wanted his shirts to look good. He used Adobe Photoshop and Illustrator, which he had experience using in school.* When his knowledge was insufficient, he would watch online videos for the information he needed.

* Travis's high school experience with design software was creative: he recalls using the programs to change his grades and show his parents a doctored report card.

FUN FACT As a nod to their history with baseball and passion for the sport, each of the partners for Baseballism has a picture of himself from Little League on his business card.

The summer camp ran successfully for two years, but eventually the four friends went their separate ways and got "real jobs." Travis ended up scoring employment as a physical education teacher, assuming that his side hustle had run its course. But little did he know, Baseballism wasn't going to sit on the bench for long.

Travis continued to wear his camp T-shirts around town. Once in a while, people would stop him on the street and ask him where he purchased his shirt. He casually brought it up one day with his old partners, and discovered that this wasn't an isolated trend—people were asking them where they got their shirts too. It seemed like an opportunity was calling from the bleachers. The infield team began to consider how they could transition Baseballism into an apparel company.

Travis took a chance and used $3,500 from a credit card to get their new side hustle off the ground. They used the money to launch a fund-raising campaign, featuring a preliminary batch of Baseballism-branded shirts, baseball caps, stickers, and computer backgrounds for their supporters.

> "You'll never know if something will work unless you dive in headfirst." —Travis

After fifty-five days, they exceeded their campaign goal of $13,000 and got to work. Travis hit up a local screen-print shop, which recommended several blank T-shirt manufacturers. His team decided among them by taking a look at the samples they provided.

It helped that the other three teammates had specialized skill sets as well. One had become a lawyer, another worked in finance, and the last had experience in sales and operations. Their skills complemented one another, and they operated with a philosophy found in baseball: "Know your role, trust your teammates, and don't get in their way."

Travis's garage became Baseballism HQ for all incoming and outgoing orders, and they focused their attention on building a strong audience through social media. They used quotes like "You'll never know until you dive" and "Live life like a 3-1 count"—none of which would make much sense if you didn't play baseball, but that was the point.

The posts kept going, to the point where Travis maxed out his limit for posting on Twitter in the first few days. This proved crucial to the success of Baseballism as they attracted only the right people who would buy their product. It also created an exclusive community of baseball fans that deeply supported them, and their business exploded.

Sales of the new apparel line grew so much during the holidays that it was no longer feasible to run the business out of Travis's garage. It was one thing when Travis started experiencing issues maneuvering around all of the merchandise, but it became more pressing when his neighbors began to complain about the trucks that were taking up all available road space when they were collecting shipments from his house. It was a good problem to have, but it also meant that they needed to look into a more permanent solution.

They eventually rented a small storefront—but, like the garage, it was quickly outgrown as they brought in over $300,000 in revenue their first year. Travis became the full-time CEO of Baseballism, Inc. in year two. The business would go on to do $1.3 million in revenue that year, $2.7 million in year three, just under $7 million in year four, and *more than $10 million* in year five. They now have four brick-and-mortar stores, with plans for several more. What had once started out as a passion project has taken off and turned into a thriving business.

The road to the playoffs has sometimes gone into extra innings. Travis remembers packing orders till 3 a.m. while holding on to his day job and other commitments. Still, there's nothing else he'd rather do, as he says that "it is the closest thing to being in the big leagues."

Clearly, Travis and his friends have knocked it out of the park.

ACCOUNTANT EARNS $233,751
RESELLING ITEMS FROM WALMART

A young accountant masters the art of reselling, purchasing textbooks, dental floss, and Cheerios from retail stores in bulk—then earns hundreds of thousands of dollars in profit by selling it online.

As an accountant at a large firm in downtown Minneapolis, Ryan Grant's main responsibility was working on financial statement audits for a variety of clients. At night—or whenever he had the time—he transitioned to a very different role as an online reseller.

Ryan had grown up on a small farm in southeast Minnesota. His family grew pumpkins and strawberries to sell, and raised a variety of animals.

The projects on the hobby farm weren't highly profitable, but they helped him learn the values of hard work and delayed gratification from an early age. With pumpkins, for example, you have to plant the seeds in the spring, take care of them all summer, and you don't get to harvest them until October. Understanding this lesson was a very valuable experience for what came later.

In college, he began to experiment with the art of side hustling, buying and reselling textbooks. We could call this episode of his life "Ryan vs. the university bookstore." At the close of his first semester of freshman year, he went to the college bookstore to sell back his books. They offered a low price compared to what he had paid for them, so he turned around and sold them online for significantly more. And the next semester, he started selling books for friends in return for a percentage of the sale. The pumpkin patch mentality was blossoming.

After that, Ryan started buying textbooks directly from students on campus. He and a friend set up a table in the student union right next to the college bookstore, at the same time the bookstore was buying books back at the end of the semester.

FUN FACT Ryan has sold products in just about every category you can imagine. His strangest success? A particular flavor of Cheerios that he sold over and over for $19.99 a box.

NAME
RYAN GRANT

LOCATION
MINNEAPOLIS, MINNESOTA

STARTUP COSTS
MINIMAL

INCOME
MULTIPLE SIX FIGURES/YEAR

WEBSITE
ONLINESELLINGEXPERIMENT.COM

They put a sign on the table that said "cash for books." They would also stop students as they were walking by to say that they were buying textbooks and paying more than the bookstore.

They said they could make those students an offer on the spot, or the students could get a quote from the bookstore and they would beat it by at least 10 percent.

At first, the bookstore didn't mind them being there, and they actually sold them some books. The store had a program where they would pay at least $1 for every book, no matter how many it already had in stock. This led to them buying books they didn't need, so Ryan was able to buy them direct from the bookstore for a fraction of the current selling price. After he bought all of the books, he would then resell them online.

Eventually, however, the bookstore wised up and realized they were losing a lot of business to these ambitious students.

Ryan and his hustling friend were summoned to a meeting with the university's legal department. They were told that they needed to shut down the website or start paying the school a fee. They responded with a logical argument: "We're already paying the school a lot of money. It's called tuition."

For some reason, this argument was unpersuasive. They weren't able to work out a deal, and ended up shuttering their textbook hustle.

With the college textbook hustle behind him, Ryan was eager to experiment further. He graduated from college and began work for an accounting firm, but his focus was elsewhere.

Then, like a few other people you've read about in this book, he started selling online using the Fulfillment by Amazon program. With this program, you're able to ship your inventory to Amazon's warehouses, and they take care of the rest—you just have to respond to messages and handle any issues that come up.

At first, he sold textbooks, since that's what he knew, and then he began to buy items at local stores to sell online. He discovered that with enough research, he could sell items online for more than what he paid for them in person. By working about ten hours a week, he quickly found a way to make an extra $1,000 a month. That was a good start . . . but what would it look like if he could spend more time—and also get smarter about the process?

In short, it looked like a lot more money.

CRITICAL FACTOR

Specific products were irrelevant to Ryan. He focused entirely on pricing arbitrage: buying at one price, and selling for a higher one. He improved his skill in the art of reselling, not in the mastery of any particular item or category.

Ryan learned to purchase products from big-box stores like Walmart, Target, and Home Depot, and then resell them online for a higher price. He also learned to find wholesale sources, typically manufacturers and distributors of existing brands that are looking to have their products distributed online.

He focused on improving his skill in the art of reselling itself, not what kind of products he should specialize in. In fact, he didn't specialize in any kind of product at all. He sold items in just about every category you can imagine, everything from dental floss picks to maximum strength Ex-Lax to silverware sets to video game consoles. If he could find a way to profit from the difference in price between buying and selling, he'd do it.

For the first twenty-one months that Ryan worked on this project, he earned more than $230,000. He paid himself a salary of $60,000 a year, and invested the rest of the profits back into the project. This was a few years back, and the growth hasn't stopped. The not-so-small project has crossed the million-dollar point in sales and continues to produce hundreds of thousands of dollars in annual profits.

Ryan quit his job at the accounting firm to focus full-time on reselling. He says the greatest benefit is freedom of schedule. When he started, his number one goal was to feel more in control of his life and not have anyone telling him how to spend his time. It's safe to say he's achieved this goal in full.

From his early days in the pumpkin patch, to the brawl with the university bookstore, to clearing out the shelves of Walmart while looking for products to resell, Ryan has created a tremendous source of security—and an all-new life for himself.

This is the way of the side hustle.

"I quit my job as an accountant to pursue selling online full-time. I walked out of the office on that day with a big smile on my face, and I've never looked back." —Ryan

TEA SOMMELIER TURNS LEAVES INTO MILLION-DOLLAR BUSINESS

A Canadian tea lover uses her formal training and entrepreneurial spirit to turn a new product line into a steeping success.

NAME
SHEENA BRADY

LOCATION
OTTAWA, CANADA

STARTUP COSTS
$500

INCOME
$60,000 TO $80,000/MONTH

WEBSITE
TEASETEA.COM

Sheena Brady had worked in the hospitality industry for many years, both in her native Canada and abroad. When a new luxury hotel in Toronto invited her to launch the most extensive tea program in the city, she looked forward to a new challenge.

Sheena was familiar with tea as a consumer, but she knew she needed more formal training. She took courses and tests, eventually earning the title of tea sommelier from the Tea and Herbal Association of Canada.

Running such an impressive tea program was rewarding, but it had its drawbacks. The required wardrobe had no room for interpretation: she had to show up in a suit, pantyhose, red lipstick, heels, hair in a bun, and beige or clear nail polish. For some people, a limited wardrobe and routine can help create focus and clarity—but for Sheena, it was constricting.

She needed more room to express herself, so she started creating her own tea blends after work. The entrepreneurial spirit kicked in. Before she knew it, she had developed an entire brand from the ground up. She got in touch with her tea leaf connections from the hotel, sent them her packaging design, and placed her first order. After a $500 investment, she was ready to launch Tease Tea.

The business was slow going at first. Sheena had an idea to make tea "sexy" with flirty names and descriptions, but it didn't go over well. Lesson learned: Nobody wants sexy tea. They want tea that will make them feel good and will fit into their lifestyle.

FUN FACT One time Sheena flew to California to open the tea program at the Four Seasons Hotel in Silicon Valley. Her checked baggage full of tea was detained by customs, and in her words, "The tea lady showed up without any tea." After repeated phone calls and begging, she finally received her bags two hours before the event.

"The secret to getting ahead is getting started. Too often we bog ourselves down with the granular details and problems that might not even exist or matter yet. Get messy, dive in, and tweak later, if necessary." —Sheena

She adjusted her marketing to focus on "prescribing tea for your every desire and goal." Instead of trying to make tea bring sexy back, she was now recommending teas based on how the customer was feeling. For example, her Turmeric Tonic anti-inflammatory blend promised to boost a customer's mood, while relaxing the mind and body. This customer-centric model was almost instantly more successful.

Still, there were challenges. A big portion of her expenses, especially in the beginning, was devoted to shipping. After nearly giving up because of high shipping costs, she realized she had two options to continue.

One, she could focus more on international orders. Because of some weird economics and tax issues, shipping across Canada could cost as much as $14, but shipping to any other country in the world could be done as cheaply as $8. It made financial sense to sell elsewhere.

Alternatively, she could try to raise the average order size. Shipping 50 grams of tea was just as expensive as 2 kilograms, so it made sense to encourage customers to order more.

One way she increased order size was by offering free shipping on orders of $50. Though Tease Tea takes a small hit by absorbing the cost, customers are far more likely to make larger orders, making that hit worthwhile.

She also began offering a larger portion of tea in a collectible tin at a slight discount, which gave people even more reason to add something else to their shopping cart. Customers who want a reusable and more attractive container are likely to purchase this option.

Sales grew as the months went by, and Sheena began to long for more time to work on Tease Tea. Though it felt scary, she decided to leave her job at the luxury hotel and accepted a different, part-time job that only takes two days out of her week. The job was with Shopify, the same company that was hosting her site. She credits them with providing support and mentorship that allowed her to take the business to another level.

Two years in, Sheena made Tease Tea available to consumers on Amazon. Growth has been extra-caffeinated ever since. Sales continue to climb, with average monthly revenue of between $60,000 and $80,000.

The Four Seasons Hotel chain began buying her teas exclusively. She was constantly invited to talk about tea on television and radio shows. She began donating a portion of sales to organizations around the world that empower women with skills and education.

Then it was time to take it another step further: a tea café in New York City. A landlord in Manhattan had an opening that was perfect for a small tea shop. Sheena signed a lease, and began the sprint to get the shop ready. She had only six weeks to open or the landlord would give the space to someone else.

Naturally, she hit the deadline. The main goal with the shop was not to sell directly, but to attract area tourists who would then go home and order online. And it worked. A few months later, Sheena launched a second pop-up shop in Manhattan.

Tease Tea recently crossed the $1 million all-time sales mark. Back when she started, it was hard to imagine that her side project would turn into such a thriving business, but that's exactly what happened.

Keep an eye out at your local supermarket or gourmet grocery store. If it's not there already, Tease Tea may show up on the shelves before too long.

Go Big or ~~Go Home~~ Choose to Stay Small

A side hustle can grow far beyond what the person who starts it ever imagines. In addition to the stories in this chapter, I regularly hear from many other people with multiple six-figure and seven-figure businesses that they started while working a regular job, and without spending a lot of money. Yes, it's possible!

But it's also just as interesting to choose *not* to scale. In addition to the people who "go big," I hear from many others who are perfectly happy with their side gig being something they look forward to working on an hour or two each day, without stress or pressure. I also hear from people who speak of their side hustle as their creative outlet from a job that doesn't utilize all their skills.

In other words, there is joy in staying small or in growing. Embrace this way of life, and make it your own.

For more, visit SideHustleSchool.com/grow.

UNEMPLOYED AUTHOR PUBLISHES
BOOK WITH HELP OF GOOD FRIENDS

No one was really sure what Chris Guillebeau did for a living. Sure, he was a writer and world traveler, but who gets paid for such things? On airplanes, he'd taken to telling his seatmate that he was in refrigerator sales. No one asked any questions after that.

Through a life that ranged from aspirational car thief (age fourteen) to bestselling author (age thirty . . . and counting), Chris had managed to cobble together a career where he worked all the time, but reported to no one. For ten years, he pursued a quest to visit every country in the world. Midpoint in the journey, he started writing about it—thus leading to a series of books, events, and other activities that allowed him to continue deferring any real employment.

One day, Chris decided that he would start a podcast. He had always liked speaking into a microphone on a desk. And, like Gandhi said, you should be the podcast you wish to see in the world.

So he got to work, but he also started getting help.

His most able-bodied and consistent help in this effort came from **Whitney Korenek**, a professional cat herder (also known as "content manager"). Through nearly one thousand episodes and counting, Whitney has wrangled details from busy side hustlers, coordinated a gaggle of writers—more on them in a bit—and otherwise made the whole project much better than it would have been otherwise.

The podcast is brought to life each day by a competent and good-looking team, always eager to fix Chris's mistakes. Senior producer **A. C. Valdez** corrects the pronunciation of sixth-grade-level words, tells Chris to speak slower, and encourages him to drink fewer cups of coffee before recording. Assistant producer **Sarah Barrett** has dutifully mixed more than two hundred episodes. Side Hustle sidekick **Jedd Chang** is in charge of email, customer service, and anything related to trucker hats.

Then, one day, Chris had another bold idea: *he wanted to write a book.* This book would be different from any other. It would have words *and* pictures. It would show *and* tell. It would be available online *and* at local bookstores.

He called up his longtime friend and literary agent, **David Fugate**. David shopped the book around the publishing world, and was met with a range of responses. One publisher asked if we could do the full-color, photographic book in black and white, and without any photos. Another one asked, "Isn't Chris a refrigerator salesman?"

But then David spoke to **Lisa Westmoreland** at Ten Speed Press, who loved the idea. She led the process of shepherding the manuscript through the publishing trifecta of writing, editing, and production. Although she may regret it now, creative director **Emma Campion** was willing to say yes to the idea of crowdsourcing images from more than eighty different people. A whole team at Ten Speed pitched in to help, many of whom are unnamed here but appreciated nonetheless.[*]

With a team in place, all Chris had to do was write the book. But though he'd done such a thing before, this book was different from all the rest.

He needed help from the gaggle of writers that works on *Side Hustle School* stories, interviewing the featured case studies, researching their businesses, and crafting an initial narrative. At press time, the group included no fewer than eighteen people: **Tom Bentley, Jan Black, Joanna Mayhew Brewster, Sean Brison, Yolanda Enoch, Yael Grauer, Brendan Hufford, Louis Chew Chong Jin, James Johnson, Whitney Korenek, Eleanor McCrary, Elizabeth McIntyre, Garrett Oden, Becca Warner, Tami Weiss, Chris Wheary, Carlee Wright**, and **Dean Yeong.**

While Chris is responsible for any errors, the story drafts from the writers, as well as many of the puns and other contributions, made the book much better.

Last but not least, research shows that a photographic book usually looks better with photographs. Chris's favorite photographer of all time, **Tera Wages**, traveled to six cities, even bunking down as a temporary refugee in the O'Hare Airport after a late-night flight cancellation. Other photographers, credited in the book on page 330, also chipped in.

Fact-checking was another challenge of Olympian proportions. In this responsibility and many others, **Tina Hart** deserves a gold medal. She spent several weeks emailing and calling dozens of people over and over to confirm important details in our featured stories about chicken saddles, bounce houses, and more.

It really does take a village to produce a podcast and publish a book, just like Abraham Lincoln explained in his popular "Nine Ways to Get More Followers on Social Media" national address.

Further challenges appeared on the hero's journey to publication date, including the case of the disappearing manuscript file, the frivolous

[*] The author would like to thank the person in charge of setting these footnotes, as well as anyone who actually ends up reading them.

lawsuit of a disgruntled blogger, the onset of mortality signified by the author's fortieth birthday, Russians hacking the election, and so on.

Nevertheless, he persisted. Somehow, he managed.

After the first attempt at delegation failed ("Alexa, write this book"), he buckled down and got to work.

When publication day arrived, he looked around and knew that he was lucky. He felt fortunate, relieved, and grateful.

He was grateful, most of all, to the person reading this book. He hoped it would inspire something in them. He hoped they would know they could do something just like the people in the book. He wanted to encourage dreamers to rise above the negativity they encountered—especially the criticism they applied to themselves.

And most of all, he was glad he never had to sell any refrigerators.

About the Author

Chris Guillebeau is a bestselling author, entrepreneur, and traveler. During a lifetime of self-employment that included a four-year commitment as a volunteer executive in West Africa, he visited every country in the world (193 in total) before his thirty-fifth birthday.

His daily podcast, *Side Hustle School*, is downloaded more than two million times a month. He is also the founder of the World Domination Summit, an event for cultural creatives that attracts thousands of attendees to Portland, Oregon, every summer.

Subscribe to his popular newsletter or say hello at ChrisGuillebeau.com.

🔲 @193countries

🐦 @chrisguillebeau

📘 /ChrisGuillebeau

ALSO BY CHRIS GUILLEBEAU

Side Hustle
Born for This
The Happiness of Pursuit
The $100 Startup
The Art of Non-Conformity

Image Credits

Image on **page 11** copyright © Rachel Williams; image on **page 12** copyright © Rachel Williams; image on **page 14** copyright © Adrian D. Greenway; images on **page 19** copyright © David Marszalec; image on **page 21** copyright © Shaelan Donovan; images on **page 23** copyright © Habit Nest; images on **page 29** (top) copyright © Stu Smith and (bottom) copyright © Brian Thompson; image on **page 31** copyright © Tera Wages; images on **page 35** copyright © Tera Wages; image on **page 37** copyright © Jeremy Enns; image on **page 38** copyright © Jeremy Enns; images on **page 41** copyright © Marco Billmaier; image on **page 42** copyright © Sara Randolph; image on **page 47** copyright © Ryan Rose; images on **page 52** (top) copyright © Lisa Holtby and (bottom) copyright © Strazzanti Photography; images on **page 55** (top left) copyright © Trent Veazy, (top right) copyright © Kerrisa Treanor, and (bottom) copyright © Sam Franklin; image on **page 58** copyright © Liron Erel/Superr; image on **page 61** copyright © Kirti M Rawat; image on **page 63** copyright © Adam Shafi; image on **page 65** copyright © Lisa Dowty: Lisa Turner Photography; image on **page 67** copyright © Patrina Anthony; images on **page 70** copyright © Alana Clark; image on **page 73** copyright © Tera Wages; image on **page 78** copyright © Lisa S. Chin; image on **page 82** copyright © Amy Anaiz Photography; image on **page 87** copyright © Alana Clark; image on **page 89** copyright © Jennifer Neal; image on **page 90** copyright © Anna Schmitz: Anna Lee Photography; images on **page 93** copyright © Anna Schmitz: Anna Lee Photography; image on **page 101** copyright © George Mihaly; image on **page 104** copyright © Alana Clark; image on **page 109** copyright © Oliver Asis; image on **page 111** copyright © Lucas Brown: Kickstand Studios; image on **page 114** copyright © Tera Wages; image on **page 115** copyright © Tera Wages; image on **page 117** copyright © Tera Wages; image on **page 123** copyright © Tera Wages; images on **page 127** copyright © Alexandra Kenin and Urban Hiker SF; image on **page 128** copyright © Alexandra Kenin and Urban Hiker SF; image on **page 130** copyright © James Hookway; image on **page 132** copyright © Tera Wages; image on **page 135** copyright © Becca Lemire; images on **page 136** copyright © Becca Lemire; images on **page 139** copyright © Sarah Crowder; image on **page 149** copyright © Alex Moore: @goldpanpete; image on **page 150** copyright © Maury McCoy; images on **page 153** copyright © Phil Kalas; image on **page 156** copyright © Khachik Simonian; image on **page 157** copyright © Nick Karvounis; image on **page 159** copyright © Joseph DiGiovann; images on **page 162** copyright © Katie Childs; images on **page 164** copyright © Jason Huot; image on **page 171** copyright © Gerald Lau; images on **page 173** (left) copyright © Emma Fried-Cassorla: Philly Love Notes and (right) copyright © Heidi's Bridge; image on **page 174** copyright © Emma Fried-Cassorla: Philly Love Notes; image on **page 180** copyright © Scott Laverty; image on **page 182** copyright © Marc Johns; images on **page 183** copyright © Marc Johns; images on **page 189** copyright © Tan Kurttekin; images on **page 191** copyright © Niclas Ericsson; images on **page 195** copyright © Michael Sindicich; image on **page 197** copyright © Charlotte McGhee; image on **page 203** copyright © Foodist Films; image on **page 204** copyright © Elise Hines; images on **page 206** copyright © Jeff Slaughter; image on **page 208** copyright © Emilie Simmons; image on **page 209** copyright © Sheldon Steere; images on **page 213** copyright © Julia O Test Photography; image on **page 217** copyright © Tera Wages; image on **page 218** copyright © Tera Wages; image on **page 223** copyright © Leslie Baum; image on **page 225** copyright © Jenny LeJeune, LeJeune Photography; image on **page 227** copyright © Emily Berger-Crawford; images on **page 228** copyright © Rebel Nell; image on **page 231** copyright © Sidney Hamm; images on **page 232** copyright © Tera Wages; image on **page 235** copyright © Tera Wages; image on **page 239** copyright © Tera Wages; images on **page 241** copyright © Stephanie Zito; image on **page 242** copyright © Kevin Kosub; image on **page 247** copyright © Tera Wages; image on **page 251** copyright © Tera Wages; image on **page 260** copyright © Mykou Thao; image on **page 261** copyright © Touger Thao; images on **page 265** (top left) copyright © All Heart Photo & Video and (top right and bottom) copyright © Caitlin's Living Photography; image on **page 266** copyright © Emily Rudnick; image on **page 269** copyright © Khara Koffel and Darren Iozia; images on **page 271** (top) copyright © Julie Gorby, (bottom left) copyright © Brandi Russell, and (bottom right) copyright © Becca Pento; images on **page 274** (left) copyright © Kelsey Bell and (right) copyright © Tera Wages; image on **page 281** copyright © Tera Wages; image on **page 283** copyright © Enrique Morgan; image on **page 286** copyright © Tera Wages; images on **page 290** copyright © Ingrid Forster Photography; image on **page 294** copyright © Adam Mowery; image on **page 295** copyright © Adam Mowery; image on **page 297** copyright © Kaitlin Callender; images on **page 305** copyright © Hangout Lighting; image on **page 308** copyright © Tera Wages; images on **page 311** copyright © Harry Campbell; image on **page 313** copyright © Yuki Sugama; image on **page 315** copyright © Oliver Asis; images on **page 317** copyright © Sara Atkinson: Sea Photography; image on **page 322** copyright © Paige Cody: Mauve Brand Designs; images on **page 323** (top and middle) copyright © Laura Ben: Gooseberry Studios and (bottom) copyright © Paige Cody: Mauve Brand Designs.

Index

Copyright © 2019 by Chris Guillebeau

All rights reserved.
Published in the United States by Ten Speed Press,
an imprint of the Crown Publishing Group,
a division of Penguin Random House LLC, New York.
www.crownpublishing.com
www.tenspeed.com

Ten Speed Press and the Ten Speed Press colophon are registered
trademarks of Penguin Random House LLC.

Library of Congress Cataloging-in-Publication Data is on
file with the publisher.

Hardcover ISBN: 978-0-399-58257-8
eBook ISBN: 978-0-399-58258-5

Printed in China

Interior design by Emma Campion
Cover design by Zak Tebbal and Emma Campion

10 9 8 7 6 5 4 3 2 1

First Edition